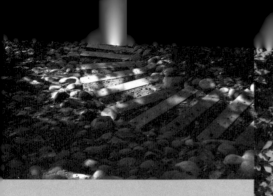

What else lurks in this mysterious garden?

I decide to plant oregano and thyme between the flagstones to provide a fragrant landing pad for the butterflies.

The delicious odor of mud and soggy leaves floats to my nostrils.

The pagoda is the perfect balance of light and dark.

This new city could be home, too.

The cord presses into my back, imprinting the memory of the moment.

Unearthed

Unearthed

Love, Acceptance, and Other Lessons from an Abandoned Garden

ALEXANDRA RISEN

Houghton Mifflin Harcourt

BOSTON   NEW YORK

2016

Library of Congress Cataloging-in-Publication Data
Names: Risen, Alexandra, author.
Title: Unearthed : how an abandoned garden taught me to accept and love my parents
/ Alexandra Risen.
Other titles: How an abandoned garden taught me to accept and love my parents
Description: Boston : Houghton Mifflin Harcourt, 2016. |
Includes bibliographical references.
Identifiers: LCCN 2015043038 (print) | LCCN 2015046581 (ebook) |
ISBN 9780544633360 (hardcover) | ISBN 9780544636477 (ebook)
Subjects: LCSH: Gardening—Philosophy. | Gardening—Therapeutic use. |
Gardening—Anecdotes.
Classification: LCC SB454.3.P45 R57 2016 (print) | LCC SB454.3.P45 (ebook) |
DDC 635—dc23
LC record available at http://lccn.loc.gov/2015043038

Book design by Chrissy Kurpeski
Illustrations by Heidi Berton

Printed in the United States of America
DOC 10 9 8 7 6 5 4 3 2 1

In loving memory of my parents,
their fellow emigrants who became family,
and their enduring legacy.

"Sometimes a tree tells you
more than can be read in books."

— *C. G. Jung*

Contents

Author's Note

This book is a collection of reminiscences molded into my story. They are as accurate as my consciousness allows, and narrated through the lens of my personal experiences, tempered by the passage of time. Others' interpretations may vary, but it is my intention to be accurate, and always from a place of love and acceptance. Some of the names are changed to respect privacy. Individuals and companies hired for the garden restoration are identified with pseudonyms. I've included one minor composite character, and some people and events were omitted. Time, events, and conversations have been edited, condensed, or reordered for narrative purposes, with an attempt to remain faithful to the overall story's integrity. The garden restoration took place over approximately ten years. Finally, most of the recipes were adapted from sources I've gratefully included in the bibliography. Please note the foraging guidelines on page 267.

NEVER TASTE OR EAT ANY PART OF A WILD PLANT UNLESS YOU ARE CERTAIN OF ITS IDENTIFICATION AND SAFETY. THE PUBLISHER AND THE AUTHOR DISCLAIM RESPONSIBILITY FOR ANY ADVERSE EFFECTS RESULTING DIRECTLY OR INDIRECTLY FROM INFORMATION CONTAINED IN THIS BOOK.

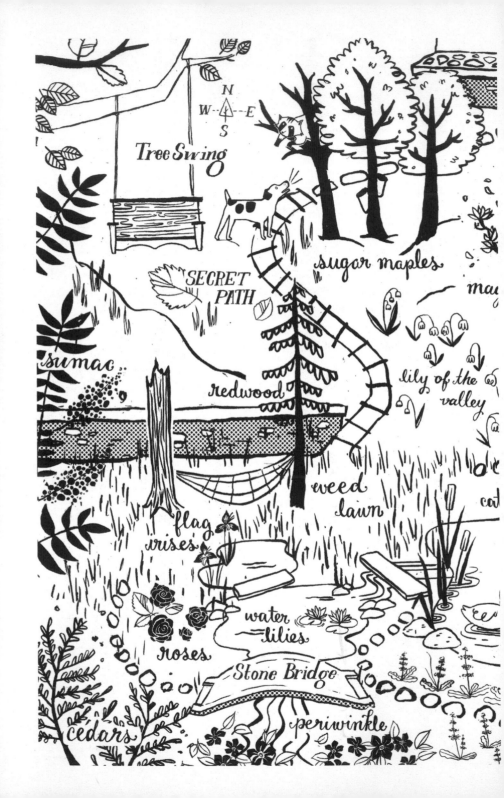

Unearthed

Roots

THE ISOLATION OF INTENSIVE CARE suits my father. His coma asks nothing of him but silence. My insomnia dragged me here, but it's an excuse. Something else, something unrecognizable made me drive in the amber streetlight glow, through the darkness, asking me if I'm still willing to try after all these years.

The night nurse decides to break the rules. "Okay, don't tell anyone. Follow me," she whispers.

Her voice merges into the fluorescent lights' hum. No day and night here—only the nonstop drone of the machines that we let take over at the end, because that's what Mom decided.

The nurse leads me to Father's bedside and pulls up a chair between two monitors. An electric jungle of wires starts and ends under the thin sheet that covers him up to his neck. I close my eyes, take a deep breath, exhale, and swallow. Open your eyes, I tell myself, and as I do, I notice that Father's hands and feet are encased in pale blue Styrofoam blocks, like the plant protectors I use to shield my roses from winter frost. Only his fingertips protrude, long and brown with perfectly trimmed, ridged yellowed nails.

"What are those?" I whisper, pointing at a block, avoiding the important questions I'm afraid to ask.

"We need to manage his body temperature."

"Temperature?"

"We try to keep the body cool and the extremities warm for circulation."

It's a body then. A gray-skinned cadaver heaving with artificial air. Nausea roils my stomach.

"Talk to him if you want. Say what you came to say," the nurse says.

"I didn't come to say anything." What is there to say? This isn't the place to express years of resentment. I examine his tidy nails, because I don't know where else to look.

"Maybe you did," she says. "They can hear, you know."

"No, he can't. The doctor said his brain is dead." *Completely unresponsive*, he'd said, *so sorry*.

She looks up from her clipboard.

"Why do you work here?" I ask.

"So people can die better than my parents did."

"I'm sorry," I say. "Thank you."

"Talk to him, he can hear. Been doin' this long enough. Doctors don't know nothin'." She looks toward the hall. "Say your piece, dear, and then you better be off, or I'll lose my job."

I watch her walk away. Her pale green bouffant cap and hospital scrubs fade into the wall color. I'm alone. I look around, behind me, and above to the suspended machines, ignoring Father's sheet-covered figure. Definitely alone. Time is at a standstill, and yet it's speeding by. Nothing to do but begin.

"Funny, huh?" I say to the blue sheet. "Even if you want to speak to me now you can't." I wait and watch. His chest rises and falls. "I don't know what to say."

The machines beep consistently as if to offset my racing heart. The room's air circulates around me, bathing me in memories and disinfectant. I swallow my queasiness and continue.

"All those years of complete silence, and now we're here. So you fell out of the apple tree. Figures—for pies probably." The fragrance of childhood Sunday morning wafts into my memory—cinnamon and burnt sugar. No fairytale smiling mother in an apron, though. Just a silent man, eating pie alone at the table. I *hate* apple pie.

"I thought about it, you know. In the twenty years I lived at home, you said maybe twenty words to me. One a year, on average. No one would believe it if I told them."

I catch myself, my heart pounding. I didn't come here to be angry. Or maybe I did.

"Did you forget Megan is getting married, and I'm supposed to stand up for her in ten days?" I continue. "She wants to cancel the wedding. I even offered to make the wedding cake. Now all we have is rotten apples on the ground, and you're here."

I babble, on and on, and my words shift to the everyday. "The garden is in full bloom, but too small. Over-planted and overgrown. Cam's ready to move again for privacy and a bigger garden. He's crazy. I just finished renovating, and Max loves his big-boy bedroom."

After half an hour of small talk, I stand, feeling stupid. What am I doing, trying to reconcile with my father's brain-dead body. I'm terrified to experience death for the first time, a hollow death of a man who never came out of the shell he is about to go back into. Sweat rolls down my chest under my T-shirt. I'm used to his silence, but this is different. This silence is pure and deep and driven by the end. It's unfair of me to take advantage of it, to fill it with my indignation. I need to leave, and never tell Mom or Sonia that I came— they'd want to know *why*, and I have no answer, except that a root, a weak root that barely anchored me to this world, is withering away, and suddenly I realize I need it.

"Goodbye," I whisper, and squeeze his fingertips. "Maybe you'll find peace where you're going."

I glance at his face, and, incredibly, a tear escapes the corner of his closed eye. It follows a crease in the wrinkled skin. I check more closely, beyond the crinkled ventilator tube and white surgical tape. Another tear follows, and then another.

Tears?

I run. I run through the slippery hallway, through the parking lot, to the car before I take a breath. What the hell? He can hear. We talked about *pulling the plug*.

He can hear. But, like always, he will not, cannot, talk to me.

CHAPTER 1

Sour Cherries

THE PATTERNED LINOLEUM of Father's tiny bathroom is curled back under the cabinet, the glue dried up long ago. Everything dries up: glue, skin, love. The cabinet's bottom is sticky and stained with age, crowded with half-empty bottles of aftershave, shampoo, and other toiletries. Mom and Sonia didn't have the courage to clean out the bathroom, so I volunteered. I've decided to stay for a few weeks, now that the funeral is over, to help Mom with whatever needs doing. I'm okay with the worst tasks, perhaps to relieve my guilt for not living nearby and for letting Sonia, the dutiful daughter, carry the weight.

All garbage, I decide. I pour as many liquids down the avocado-green sink as I can; they swirl around the rusty drain stopper and soon I am floating in a stink of Resdan hair tonic and Listerine.

The sharp fumes burn my nostrils. I hold my breath as I wash away a life; it all comes down to some pill bottles, checkered work shirts in the closet, and a few boxes. My arms are heavy as I work, and my hands shaky from lack of sleep. Strange dreams and chest pains now punctuate my ongoing insomnia. Stress, Sonia says. I wonder what a heart attack feels like, and whether Father shouted as he tumbled off that ladder. My dreams are a slide show of the past few days, images I hope to soon erase: Max, heavy with sleep on the pew, thankfully unaware of the terrifying open-casket, incense-filled Mass that no toddler should witness; the line of tombstones

near Father's, because our parents and their friends, a group of displaced immigrants, prepurchased a row of plots together when they
all turned fifty; Mom's tombstone, waiting, her name, and below it
1924–, as they lower Father's oak coffin into the adjacent plot.

I was transfixed by the blank space, waiting for its inevitable date,
on the dusty tombstone. My parents did us a favor by preplanning,
but more importantly, they wanted to be together at the end. A
symbolic gesture that recognized that they understood each other in
ways their children never would. They were right.

We didn't talk about anything much after the funeral except for
the one demand Mom made from the hearse's back seat.

"If I'm sick, no machines, no feeding tubes. That's an order. If I
can't live on my own, you girls must let me go."

"What if you can still hear us?" I asked. I never did tell her that
Father heard me from the depths of his coma. Too much had been
said, and not said, and then it didn't matter.

"If I can't live without machines, it's not real life," Mom answered.

I promised, ignoring the sickening dread in my stomach. Sonia
escaped into the hazy view through the dust-covered window. I understand Mom's point — she, Sonia, and I watched the doctors remove Father's machines when his organs gave out. Still, my heart's
conflicted, and my head's too heavy to think about what I would
want if it were me.

Since the funeral, Mom has been in the garden. August is a busy
time. She prepares vegetables and fruit for winter during the day,
and spends the evenings with Max in front of the television. Mom
doesn't understand *SpongeBob SquarePants,* and Max doesn't understand *The Price is Right,* but *The Nature of Things* seems to bridge their
seventy-year divide.

I've been cleaning out house cupboards, and I'm surprised by
the things I've long forgotten and the sentimental memories they
arouse. My first rock collection fascinates Max, especially the smelly

yellow sulfur chunks that I picked up from the rocky railroad beds of the tracks that ran directly behind our first house. I twirl a sharp granite rock between my fingers, and I'm suddenly playing on the tracks, creosote in my nostrils, as the trumpet of an oncoming train's horn shoos me away from my rock search. I was never afraid.

I snap back into the present. Mom's canned goods from twenty years ago, in neat dust-covered rows, however, terrify me. I ruthlessly trash them — someone has to save her from botulism.

"What about the garage?" I walk past Mom to the old-fashioned metal garbage cans at the driveway's end.

"Not now." She shakes the dirt from an onion. "Your sister and I can sort through it during the winter. I'll have to sell the car, though."

My chest tightens. I've always hated that car.

"Okay, I'll keep to the closets for now," I say. She doesn't hear me because she's already moved to the shrubs along the south-facing stucco wall: red currants, gooseberries, and chokecherries. Jellies to be made.

Sonia arrives when I'm sorting through the basement closet.

"Look at all this camera stuff. Do you want it?" I ask.

"My basement's full. Why don't you take it?"

"No, I'm flying." Father had amassed a sophisticated camera and lens collection, all in their original boxes. "Did he ever use this stuff? It looks brand new."

"Perhaps Max will want it someday? He's already showing his technical side," she says.

She's right. Max is crouched on the floor, his expression intense as he joins plastic LEGO action figure pieces. He's working on *For Ages 8+,* beyond his years, Sonia observes proudly.

We find a shoebox filled with old crinkled-edged photos.

"These are mostly their friends at parties in the basement," I tell her, flipping through the box. "Want them?" Father didn't have to talk to people if he was behind the camera.

"No thanks," Sonia answers. "You?"

What's the point? They're photos of local Ukrainian friends we know as little about as we do our parents. None of them are family, or maybe they are, because we don't even know if we have aunts and uncles somewhere in the Ukraine. It's not that we don't care; we've become used to not knowing what we're missing. When our curiosity occasionally surfaced, we were too afraid to break the silence, and then it slowly, simply ceased to matter.

"Nope. Although Cam likes to save stuff like this for Max. I'll take it for him."

We fill Sonia's car with "things Max might want in the future." She doesn't have her own children, and I'm moved by her thoughtfulness. She's also a pack rat.

"Where's Mom?" she asks.

"Garden."

"Have you discussed the wedding yet? How's Megan?"

"Megan still thinks we should cancel. It's up to Mom." I can't believe I'm going to indirectly prevent my best friend's wedding.

We walk up the stairs to the kitchen. Mom, in her dirt-covered T-shirt, is stirring instant coffee. Her fingernails are filthy, but she doesn't seem to notice or care. A bowl of lime-green berries, hairy and translucent with thin white stripes, sits on the table.

"For you," she says to my sister. For a moment I sense the closeness between them and I fight the insecure feelings that surface. Mom grows those berries especially for Sonia. And peas, and corn, and they trade flower seeds. I hate gooseberries, and I don't fit in here.

"Why do you like those things?" I ask Sonia. "They look like they come from an alien berry farm."

"Dennis likes the jam," she says. Edmonton is the world's preserving capital. The summers are so short that gardeners grow what they can for two months and store it for the other ten.

"Mom, about Megan's wedding," I start.

"I thought about it." She puts down her cup. "Your dad was happy she's finally getting married. So am I. And Peter is such a handsome man. Ukrainian, too. The wedding must go on."

What? I look at Sonia's expressionless face. Since when did marrying into our culture matter? I wonder if Sonia is mentally justifying her marriage to a Brit while I defend mine to an Italian. I thought we were good if we simply stayed away from Russian Communists. And Father happy, for God's sake? Impossible. He was silent, angry, or nothing at all, but definitely not *happy*.

"Your friends won't criticize?" I ask Mom. Suppose not, they're all Ukrainian.

"Marriage comes first," Mom says as she heads toward the door. "Besides, life is for the living. I'm going back outside if you girls don't need me."

Some things never change. Maybe we *do* need you. Maybe, just once, just this time, we need you.

Sonia picks up her bowl of berries. "I'm off, then."

Once Mom makes a decision, it's solid. I call Megan. "Good to go, we all agree. It gives us something to look forward to." I secretly hope this bad timing doesn't doom her marriage.

"So stuff like this doesn't only happen in movies," Megan says. "Although Peter's way taller than Hugh Grant."

"Did you know my parents were thrilled you decided to marry a Ukrainian?"

"Wow," Megan says.

"That's what I thought. I better start baking. Lucky that Mom planted carrots this year."

The cake is mildly crooked. I blame the old stove—it's worn out from baking hundreds of apple pies. Mom's plentiful dark red roses allow me to disguise the slope with petals strewn across the cream cheese frosting. Megan is touched that the cake's ingredients come from the garden—Mom's bounty fed much of our neighborhood over the years. The wedding is a subdued success; Mom gets her fair share of attention from Megan's family, and I decide a burgundy-and-beige wedding is an excellent remedy for a funeral.

"Don't forget your Nintendo," I say to Max a few days later. I cram clothes into the suitcase. It's time to go home.

Thump!

I run down the stairs to find Mom sitting on the stoop that leads to the kitchen, her back against the wall.

"Are you okay? What happened?"

Her skin is pale, the color of the yellowed white wall paint behind her.

"I lost my balance. It's nothing," she says. But she's not standing up. She touches her head.

"You bumped your head. I'll get ice." I shouldn't be going home.

A bruise starts to form near her eye. "I'm fine," she insists. "I don't know what happened. My head was buzzing, and I felt dizzy."

"Mom, this is a big house for you—," I start.

"I'm not moving," she says. "I'm not so old yet. I'm just tired and hungry."

Sonia arrives a few hours later. "Mom should sell the house," I tell her.

"She's not ready. It's too soon after the funeral."

"It's dangerous. She fell. She'll be rambling around alone in here."

"I'm close," Sonia says. "I'll check in, don't worry."

"I'm not selling the house." Mom walks into the room. "You girls forget that I've been alone since I went to Germany. I was seventeen, and I survived the war. I think I'll be fine here."

That old line we've heard before. We know she was a farm laborer, but not much beyond that. She's never talked about the war.

Mom's upper arm sports a bright red mark to match her cheek. She looks like she's been beaten. She brings a bowl of cherries to the sink, washes and pits them, letting them drop into the enormous Mason jar that sits on the counter. It's the same jar that sat there every summer, right under the window beside the tin breadbox. A bottle of Stolichnaya, the next ingredient, is nearby. I want to ask why she uses Russian vodka when she despises most things Russian, but I bite my tongue. We don't ask questions in this family, at least ones that include the word *why*.

"Who still drinks your liqueur?" I ask instead.

"John next door. He helps with the snow. I'm sure he won't mind doing a bit more now that your father is gone. He can help me sell the car."

This discussion is over. She isn't moving. She pours enough vodka into the jar to cover the cherries and stirs with a stained wooden spoon.

"Besides, I need to take care of the old lady, and bring her food and all that. She's in a wheelchair and no family left."

"Who?" I look at Sonia.

"She's eighty-seven," Sonia says. Ten years older than Mom. "From the village."

"Well, then, I guess that's decided," I say. *What village?*

"Our turn will come," Sonia says, as I walk her to the car. "Let's let her have her garden for as long as she can. We all need to hang on to something."

My sister is right, as usual. Although she didn't see Mom's face after the fall.

"She keeps locking herself out, forgetting her keys. What if she leaves the stove on?"

"I'll get her checked out, don't worry."

I head back to Max and our packing. Mom needs her sense of purpose—her garden and some mysterious old lady. And Sonia's berries. I may as well go home.

That night, I dream of Mom as a seventeen-year-old girl, in one of the only stories she shared. The recurring dream is my sole marker of her youth, embellished over the years, and cherished by my subconscious in an otherwise barren family history.

Mom holds a woven twig basket in a tiny orchard near a farmhouse. She carefully cuts sour cherries from their stems and lets them drop into the basket. She knows better than to pull at them like she did as a child, breaking the stalks and making her mother angry. Fresh air from the distant mountains whips at her hair, and in my troubled sleep I feel it blow across my face. She whispers, as if she is having an argument with herself. Across the lane, another farmhouse has boarded-up windows. She walks into her home when her basket is full, taking a last look at the dying plants across the way. Her eyes are sorrowful; her lips are turned down in angry hatred.

"The Germans are coming," whispers her eldest sister at dinner. "They're looking for workers. I heard so in the town. Posters everywhere!" She chews anxiously on a small pork rind.

"I know. Better them than the damn Communists," says Mom, and her mother rises from the rickety wooden table and smacks her face. Her sister jumps from the table and draws the curtains over the small kitchen window.

"Be quiet," she whispers. "Our friends are dead for such words."

"Be quiet? What's the point of living, then?" Mom asks. "Our people lost the chance to be a nation in the last war — what's left?" No one responds, as her parents sip homemade cherry liqueur from tiny glasses.

"He has no future," Mom says, pointing to her little brother, whose tears stream down his face as he tries to silence his sobs.

I wake suddenly. *Only the dream*, I tell myself, falling back into fitful sleep, visions floating in and out.

German soldiers marching, a sea of greenish-gray wool tunics and caps. Black boots kicking up dry soil as they search for young "volunteers."

My young mother gripping her little brother's hand, saying, "I don't want to die here. I promise to come back and help you."

Sun rising over the golden wheat fields. My mother picking a few cherries from her family's trees, laying them beside her brother's pillow while he sleeps, putting a few dark serrated leaves into her pocket.

My mother heading for the village meeting point without looking back.

"Mommy, Mommy, wake up." Max pushes my arm.

"Wha-what?" I open my eyes to see him fearfully examining my face. "Are you sad?" he asks.

I touch the wet skin under my eyes. I need a few seconds to recognize the familiar bedroom walls.

"I was having a bad dream. It's okay now, snuggle up," I tell him. He curls into me, and I breathe in his body's warmth and hold his flannel pajamas as we fall back asleep.

"Sonia's driving us to the airport," I tell Cam on the phone the next morning. "I can't wait to get home, but I feel guilty. What will she do?"

"She'll manage. She's tougher than you guys think. Give her some time. By the way, Wesley called. He sent you a gorgeous sunflower bouquet."

"That's kind."

"Believe it or not, he said something about showing us a house."

SOUR CHERRY LIQUEUR

Ingredients:

1 pound fresh sour cherries, stems and pits removed

3 cups vodka or grain alcohol (80-proof)

1½ cups sugar

- Clean and pit cherries and add to a 2-quart Mason jar or other glass or ceramic container.
- Add vodka and mix thoroughly. Cover.
- Let macerate for 4 weeks at room temperature. Stir daily for the first week, weekly afterward, with a wooden or nonmetal spoon.
- After 4 weeks, add sugar, stir thoroughly, and cover. Let macerate for another 4 weeks.
- Strain the vodka mixture through a stainless steel strainer into a large bowl.
- Gather the remaining cherry pulp into cheesecloth and squeeze out liquid into same bowl.
- Pour liquid back into Mason jar, close, and age in a cool place for 3 to 4 months.
- Siphon off the clear liqueur, leaving sludge behind in jar, or filter liquid through paper towels and then coffee filters (twice each) to clarify. Store in clean sterilized bottles.

See page 267 for information on safety and sourcing of plants.

CHAPTER 2

❧

Knotweed

THE ANONYMOUS HIDDEN HOUSE with inconspicuous owners is in our neighborhood: right across the street, in fact. Although we've seen their car coming out of the long lane, we've never met. I've pictured them living in a tiny converted garage—there can't be much space back there. I'm curious because I love hidden places, like the secret houses that I built out of shoeboxes as a child. This can't possibly be the house that Wesley found for us?

It's been on the market for a year without a "for sale" sign. Wesley walks us across the street and down the long, narrow lane that runs about fifty yards between and behind two neighboring houses.

"Privacy *and* a garden." He grins, his white teeth sparkling from his handsome tanned face.

The driveway opens to an asphalt courtyard in front of a rectangular one-story ranch-style building with a flat roof.

"The brickwork looks like what they used for schools in the sixties," Cam says.

"Maybe," Wesley agrees, "but wait until you see the back. An acre of garden."

Impossible, I think.

I stare at the twelve-foot-high brick facade. It *is* like a shoebox house.

"Where's the doorstep? This is another reno," Cam whispers to me.

We stare at a gaping hole at the base of the door. Its perimeter sprouts weeds and jagged dandelion leaves; instead of a welcome mat, the yellow flower heads serve as a greeting committee.

"Sorry about the weeds," Wesley says. "Uh, the place might need a little work."

"Fairy clocks. Not weeds," I say.

"Excuse me?" Wesley asks.

"She loves dandelions," Cam says. "Don't apologize. Believe it or not, those are working in your favor. Definitely not in mine."

"Dandelion flowers close at dusk and open in the morning light," I explain.

Wesley struggles with the door lock, which appears to be broken. No agent worth his salt is going to question the idiosyncrasies of his clients.

Dandelions. Mom introduced me to my first flower when I was a toddler. It was not a noxious weed on our dry prairie lawn, but one of my first toys.

"Look for the longest stems," Mom would say. And I did, because the garden was the only place I got her attention.

I picked as many as possible, the milky sap sticking to my fingers. She braided yellow chains into crowns and bracelets that I would wear for days. Mom stored them in the refrigerator at night to keep them fresh. They made me feel important.

It was the beginning of a lifelong love affair.

"It was being renovated." Wesley's voice brings me back. "They never finished."

"Great," says Cam. He gives me his *I told you so* look.

We jump across a wooden plank into the interior.

"Oh!" I hate it.

The first room is painted red, and another has ornate ceiling trim and numerous wall niches. I really hate it.

Sensing my dismay, Wesley points out an impressive skylight directly above us. I look up to see towering oak branches. I'm in

a tree house! The previous owners found an ideal way to capture
the natural light and usher it inside. Seeing my approval, he hurries
us through a large living area to glass doors that open to a cantile-
vered balcony. We have our first view of the garden. The forest. The
jungle.

"God!" someone says. Me.

A flower unfurls in my heart. A cliff of bedrock slopes sharply
downward for at least a city block, eroding into a valley of overgrown forest. Nothing to the left or right but endless trees. There
are no neighboring houses in sight or fences to show the property's
boundary. We've walked through a portal into a secret forest.

We would need a machete to clear it.

Wesley says nothing. He knows there are no words to do the view
justice. He also knows us better than we know ourselves.

"That's a damn steep slope," Cam says.

"A slippery slope," I answer.

"It's a gardener's dream come true," Wesley says. The colors in-
tensify, brighter and brighter. Sound disappears, and only his statement floats in the air.

"Who owns an acre of ravine in the middle of the city? It's un-
thinkable," I say. But I am thinking about it.

"You could," Cam says. "I mean . . . we could."

I'm hypnotized by the vista. I notice some buildings visible in
the far distance, southward, and the tips of a few downtown office
towers: their glass facades reflect the watery Toronto sky, making
them, thankfully, nearly invisible. And among them, the iconic CN
Tower.

"Almost Manhattan," Wesley says, following my line of sight.
"Best view in town."

"It is hard to believe we're a few minutes from downtown," I
agree.

"This is a unique opportunity," he adds. He's no longer an agent.
He's a friend, desperate for us to buy the house.

"Exactly how far does this land go?" I ask. "How much is an acre, anyway?"

"Bigger than a football field," Cam says.

"It flattens out at the bottom. It's L-shaped. That roof down there is the vertex of the L, where it turns," Wesley says. "It's some sort of garden structure. Maybe that's wisteria on the roof?"

What is that roof? A beacon at the bottom of a ravine. Blood rushes through my head; I've been obsessed by ravines since I was ten years old.

"It's a complete mess," I say. I *love* it. Could I finally put all my gardening books to use? I've collected hundreds from bookstore sale bins. From bulbs to grasses to trees, I have the perfect manual. I read them for pleasure like I read my cooking magazines, which are full of aspirational recipes that I'm never actually going to prepare.

"It used to be a formal garden," Wesley says. "It was part of a prominent family estate, you know, about a hundred years ago, but it fell into the hands of some nongardeners, I guess, or maybe they were too busy renovating the house."

I think he said "estate." We've gone from ravine to estate? This property is our parents' dream, the next generation's betterment of their lot, literally. Now we stand in front of it, not believing our good fortune, and struggling between the guilt of our opportunity and our fear of not knowing what to do with it.

"But the old mansion is halfway down the street." Cam interrupts my thoughts.

"Yes. This house was built in the sixties when the land was subdivided. I think all the land below was part of the estate," Wesley explains.

"Looks like it's been decades since it was tended to," Cam gestures downward.

"Imagine it cleaned up," Wesley says, with false enthusiasm. Even he sees that the project is overwhelming. "You guys have always wanted a garden?"

This isn't a garden. It's the fucking Amazon.

"This is crazy," I whisper to Cam. "We don't have the time or money to take on something this big. Who'll help us?"

"It's been on the market for a while," Wesley says. "The price is down. Deals like this don't come along often."

Never, I think. But it's still out of our league.

"Have you even been down there?" I ask him, pointing at the mysterious roof.

"Too overgrown," he says. He's selling something that he hasn't even seen.

"Forget it," I say. "I don't like the house. It has shiny gold door-knobs. It's a box. Boxes are for dolls, not humans. And I just finished renovating our current house."

"And you did a beautiful job with it. It'll sell in a second at a tidy profit for sure," says Wesley, ready for a double trade. "Let's look at the rest of the house," he adds. "You'll love the kitchen."

It's hard to pull away from the view of the trees, but we follow Wesley to the kitchen. The contemporary gray cabinetry is at complete odds with the ornate hallway. It's elegant, but unfinished, making me more miserable. Its owners ran out of energy. Maybe the house is an energy sapper.

"You could easily finish this up," says Wesley, as he leads us down a short stairway to the lower level and into a peach-colored room. The paint shade reminds me of retirement homes.

"The view could be fantastic down here," Cam says, staring out the window to a vast flagstone terrace, with three-foot weeds tow-ering from the cracks. As always, he is drawn to the light.

"You should know there's a couple from Florida looking at it," Wesley says. "It's a great price for Americans."

I digest this new information. Could it be true? We turn a corner into an adjacent room with three walls of windows.

I catch my breath. The marble floor is smooth and graceful; the subtle bluish-gray walls mimic a spring sky. It is the outdoors magi-cally brought inside. My eyes wander to the right to find another sensational landscape: the entire wall is a painted canvas. A fresco. A single tree starts on the right, and its branches fill the wall up, down, and to the left. Translucent white flowers cover the branches, each with five petals and a blush of pink that creates the faintest rosy haze. The tree is alive, with a gentle personality that knows its role is to be beautiful at a time of year when everything outside is gray.

"Sour cherry," I whisper.

"What?" asks Cam, stopping beside me. "Wow," he adds when he sees the mural.

"Mom's tree." The smell of fermenting fruit fills my memory.

"Your mom has this tree?" he asks.

I walk closer to the wall and touch the canvas fabric that covers it. It's rough under my fingers as I trace the circular brushstrokes that make up the flowers. Something deep down, unrecognizable, summons me, taunts me, implores me. This room is what the entire house could be. An ode to a garden. To history.

An ode to Mom.

"We need to think about this," I say. I don't want to take my hand away.

And that is all Wesley needs. He runs off with his mobile phone, his shoes clicking on the hardwood.

I open my eyes to see Cam's green wellies in front of my nose. *Nothing broken*, I think, on our first day of tackling the Amazon.

"You okay?" he asks as I look up past his soil-stained beige cotton shorts and tattered oxford shirt to his worried face. If only his partners at the bank could see him now—the gentleman gardener.

"I'm perfect." I press my hand against the raw scraped skin on my back. Who cares about an open gash full of dirt? Not me, because I can be a gardener, too.

"You look like you're dressed for war," he says.

"Unlike you, I'm wearing gloves. So I'm fine." Admittedly, I'm sweating in my gray-and-pink-polka-dot rubber boots and long-sleeved bug-repelling jacket. We're novices without tools and experience, and, to save money, we're not hiring help. But I've got my books and the hope that Wesley will sell our old house soon.

"Okay, let's go," I say, ignoring the perspiration—or is it blood? —trickling down my back.

"We're getting to that gazebo today," Cam says, snapping his garden shears. "Or whatever it is."

I pause to look at the roof in the distance. Definitely wisteria, loads of it. I inhale the verdant heat that wafts off the leaves. This is the smell of *green*. The sun glistens on the spiderwebs that crisscross the path ahead. We'll have to cut through those, too, the police tape the spiders have laid to keep us out of their territory. *I'm sorry*, I whisper to the gangly arachnids. I quash my guilt for wrecking "nature's course" of the past decade. We're returning the garden to its glory.

Mom still can't believe we bought the house, although she said she'd visit once Sonia gets the test results. Her dizzy spells have become more frequent.

"I hope you crazy kids know what you're doing," she said on the telephone. "So tell me about the garden." I sensed a hint of approval. "But is it too much for you?"

No, no it isn't, dammit. Mom, of all people, wasn't allowed to ask that question.

"It's been let go for years," I said. "It's an overgrown forest down a cliff, once owned by a famous family."

I told her stories about the family and their five children. Their old house still stands on the crest of this steep ravine, a few houses over, although it's been subdivided into three private residences.

"Really?" Her voice slurred a bit. I sensed she didn't believe me.

We have to clear this thing, I tell myself, before Mom gets too frail to travel. I want her to see it in all its glory, and to go home and tell Sonia and the old lady, "I didn't know she had it in her."

I survey our challenge through the haze of heat. The broken steps made of rough gray stones, three feet across, cascade into a winding path downward. The soil around them is covered with five-foot-high stems with delicate lime-green leaves, a sea of vegetation as far as the eye can see.

"This looks like bamboo," Cam says, trying to cut one. It resists the shears, so he tries pulling it out. "The stems are hollow," he says, and tugs harder. It comes from the ground with a fight, several shoots attached to one root ball.

"Shit, it's like they're cemented in," he says.

"This is going to take forever," I say, looking at the shoots, which appear to have pushed themselves between many of the broken stones. "There are thousands of them. We can't pull them all out," I say, but Cam is already ahead of me, wrenching them out as if his life depends on it and forging our path forward.

I'm left with no choice but to follow him. Over the next hour we move less than fifteen feet down the slope. My shoulders and arms hurt. Either the bamboo is getting taller or I am starting to droop.

To distract myself, I imagine savoring my Earl Grey tea in the mystery garden structure below, reading my garden journal and planning the next planting season. I'll listen to the jingle of the wind chimes I will hang on a nearby tree branch—the chimes Father created out of delicate copper pipes and the only thing I brought home after his funeral. I stop for a rest on a crooked step to take off my gloves and wipe my face with a crumpled paper towel from my pocket. How many footsteps have landed here?

"Break," I say, stretching my cramped fingers. Cam flops down on a nearby stone.

"Should've worn gloves," he says.

I look at his hands. Blisters cover his fingertips and raw pink skin peels between his palm and his thumb.

"You're going to get an infection," I say. "We haven't got far," I add.

"What the hell is this stuff, anyway?" Cam asks, sucking on a blister. "It's taller than Max."

"Will you please wear gloves?"

"No." He pauses. "Do you hear water?"

"No. Are you thirsty?" I ask.

"I hear water. Listen," he says.

And there it is. A faint tinkle. It's the sound that a picturesque babbling brook in a fairy tale might make.

"I'm finding it," I shout, abandoning my shears. I charge forward through the bamboo. It wraps around my feet, and dry sticks poke my face. I raise the hood of my jacket in defense and shut my eyes through the rough parts. Water. Is it possible? I open my eyes to see, fifteen feet ahead of me, shimmering black patches where the sun hits wet soil. Rapture grips my heart. The delicious odor of mud and soggy leaves floats to my nostrils.

"It's here, somewhere," I yell back to Cam, pulling twigs out of my hair.

Although I can hear the stream clearly now, I still can't see it. The ground is moist, muddy in parts. Where is the water? The bamboos become taller, maybe ten feet high, as I follow the sound. The ground is covered with more large stones, the same ones the steps are made of, although by now I am well off the path.

Without warning, a sort of swamp emerges. It's bordered with large rocks and covered with heaps of dry bamboo. A bog. I approach it with awe, noting the moss that covers the perimeter. Several feet farther, the water deepens and spills over some rocks, gurgling, and into a stream that meanders farther into the woods.

"Don't tell me," Cam says as he comes up behind me, "that we have a high water table."

"It's a bog," I say. "It's amazing." *Uh-oh, high water table?*

"It's groundwater," Cam says.

"Don't worry. We're way below the house. There's no sign of water up there." *Please don't be up there.*

"It comes from somewhere. Usually downward," he says. "We better call Wesley. And our lawyer. We paid way too much for swampland. And when is he going to sell the other house?"

His words disappear into the breeze. I walk a few feet forward toward the stream and sit down on a wet rock. My tears mingle with sweat. Cam has to be wrong. This is an unexpected gift from the garden; it is the ravine river I walked along in my youth. I dip my hand in the water, which is cold and fresh, and splash my face. I tuck a smooth pebble into my pocket and look up to see Cam at the edge of the bog, staring into it with anxiety. His boots are sinking into the lush green blanket of moss. He looks like a crazed outdoorsman, covered in mud, with his hair sticking up and outward.

I laugh, feeling delirious.

"We can wrap your hands in the sphagnum," I tell him through my tears. "You're standing in it."

"For God's sake, this is serious."

"It is," I agree. "It's moss. Absorbent and antiseptic. They used to use it for bandages."

"They?"

"Red Cross, in World War I. Canadian women picked it and sent it overseas. Even here in Toronto."

"How do you even know that?" he asks, hiding his blistered hands in his pockets.

"Just do," I say. "This may be one of the most exciting days I've ever had."

"It may not be if there's water under our house," he says, although I catch him looking at the moss with more interest. "Okay, Mother Nature, we need to go up and check the basement. I've had enough today."

No more spreading yogurt on concrete urns to grow moss. We've got buckets of it. "We have moss *and* a babbling brook," I tell Cam, as we trudge up the stairs.

"We have a high water table and a shitload of work," he says.

"The water's a good omen," I tell him. "You said you wanted to buy me the ravine of my childhood. That one had a river."

He isn't enthused. He is hot, sticky, and covered with a fine film of dirt.

"We didn't even make it to your gazebo. We need to move faster than fifteen feet a day," he says. "I've only got two weeks off. We're going to need help, starting with a soil engineer. And if Wesley can't sell the house, we're hiring someone else."

He's right. Two city slickers plowing an acre isn't logical. I'm going to have to find some experts. We're in so much debt already we may as well drown in it.

My phone buzzes from my pocket.

"Sonia? Hi, you'll never believe it. We found a stream," I tell her.

"That's nice. Listen, I've got the results. Mom's dizzy spells are because of a blood clot in her neck. She's had some small strokes. I'm hoping you can fly in for the operation."

The day of clearing and the news of Mom have left me exhausted and emotional. After dinner and some computer time with Max on *Toontown*, I buy an online ticket for the next day. Cam will spend the rest of his two-week vacation with Max, not gardening, and taking care of Benji, our sixteen-year-old mutt whose old age is slowing him down to a near standstill.

"Mom's ministrokes are called TIAs—transient ischemic attacks," I tell Cam after we put Max to bed. "She has a clot in the carotid artery in her neck. They need to remove it."

"She's pretty old for major surgery," Cam says.

"According to Sonia, she wants it. It's risky, but doing nothing is a death sentence."

"I guess we respect her wishes, then," Cam says.

"She'll be fine. She's as tough as they get," I say, not believing my words. I head for my computer to do more research. "Besides, she's coming to see the garden."

Do you want the good news or the bad news?" I ask Cam as I drag myself into bed a few hours later, having Googled myself into fatigue.

He looks up from his latest book, *The Garden: An English Love Affair*. "Good," he says.

"Toronto's full of old underground rivers. Looks like our garden might be over part of the old Castle Frank Brook. I found a website that explores lost rivers. Amazing, huh?"

"Fascinating. Do we need a lawyer?"

"No, it's flowing from the west, from what I can see. We're good up here."

"We'll see," he says. "Although a swampy yard isn't what I had in mind." He closes his book and shuts off the reading light. "The bad news?" he asks into the dark.

"*Fallopia japonica*," I say.

"Is this a woman's thing?"

"The bamboo weeds. That's the Latin name," I say. "Common name is Japanese knotweed."

"That's not what I've been calling them, I assure you," he says.

"It's one of the world's top one hundred invasive species," I say.

"And we're covered in it," he sighs. "Did you at least find out how to get rid of it?"

"They say to tarp it for several years. But sometimes it'll grow through the fabric. It can even break through concrete."

"Jesus."

"Yup. Or major chemicals," I add, "although they will probably kill everything else, too."

"What should we do? We haven't got an acre of tarp. That's ridiculous, anyway."

"One article said to keep pulling out the roots and it will thin out over the years."

"You're kidding, right?" he asks.

"You're going to have to be more positive," I say. "Especially in front of Max."

"I'm positive I'm not going to spend the next year pulling that stuff out."

"We're not going to clear the garden this year, are we?" I sigh.

"Probably not, although I hate to lose the season. Why don't we interview some people and plan for the spring," he says. "Maybe we'll be in less debt by then, too."

"Oh, I forgot, we can eat the knotweed shoots in the spring," I say. "They taste like rhubarb when they're young." I'm pretty happy with this because I see pies in our future.

"Are you crazy?"

"If you can't beat it, eat it," I add, proud of my humor, but he's already snoring softly.

I sneak out to Max's bedroom, where the telltale light from an electronic device casts a glow. I see his hands dart under the covers.

"Still up?" I ask.

"No."

"Is that your Nintendo under there?"

"No."

"Won't you be tired for your tae kwon do lesson tomorrow?"

"No."

"I might have to go visit Grandma. Will you be okay with Daddy?"

"Yes," he says. "Is Grandma sick?"

"A little. We're going to fix it." I shouldn't let him get away with the game, but I'm too tired to lecture. I'll get him into the garden soon enough, and when I'm finished with him, he'll be falling asleep with memories of the trees he climbed that day.

JAPANESE KNOTWEED CRUMBLE

Japanese knotweed (*Fallopia japonica*) has a tart rhubarb flavor. The plants are best foraged in the spring. Use only when shoots are under 10 inches high, before they become too tough, and before they develop an undesirable sap. Peel the shoots if they are picked longer than 7 inches.

Knotweed:

2 pounds young knotweed shoots, washed and chopped
⅓ cup sugar
¼ cup flour
4 tablespoons raisins
½ teaspoon vanilla extract
1 teaspoon lemon juice
Pinch of salt

Crumble:

1 cup flour
⅓ cup oats
¾ cup sugar
6 tablespoons butter

- Combine the knotweed ingredients (excluding those for crumble) in a deep, 8-inch pan.
- For the crumble, mix together the flour, oats, and sugar. Cube the butter and add to this mixture, using fork or pastry cutter, until the mixture resembles coarse breadcrumbs. Scatter the crumble on top, and bake in a preheated 375°F oven until golden and bubbly, about 45 minutes. Let cool for 15 minutes. Serve warm with ice cream or whipped cream.

See page 267 for information on safety and sourcing of plants.

CHAPTER 3

Lily of the Valley

"I brought you french fries." Mrs. S, as we call her, pushes the greasy white McDonald's bag under Mom's nose. The odor of stale oil fills the new assisted-living apartment. She's Mom's only healthy friend left—a buxom, smiling woman with boyishly cropped short gray hair.

"Thmmkoo." Mom musters a half smile, which is all she's willing to give without her dentures. Sonia, ever the retired dentist, works on the nearby sofa with a small pair of pliers, adjusting them because they have been bothering Mom since the surgery.

I'm mystified as to why these two elderly ladies love McDonald's fries. For years they fed their families from their gardens or freezers; women who went to the farm to kill their own chickens didn't eat at McDonald's, but here they were. Two old conspirators having fun being *bad*.

"Remember our neighbor from the church? Two great-grandchildren now." Mrs. S is determined to drag Mom out of her sadness. Their gossip centers on the widowed friends still alive, what nursing homes they are at, and which children are divorced.

"We're still married," I say to Sonia.

Mom grunts. We haven't delivered enough grandchildren, I'm pretty sure is her thought. Only one between us. Yet she never even told us about our cousins; we weren't exactly raised to be natural mothers.

"Okay, this should feel better." Sonia hands her the denture and Mom struggles with a shaky hand to fit it in. We don't dare insult her by offering help.

Although her surgery went well, and the big stroke was averted, the doctors discovered that Mom's arteries are in sorry shape. They will continue to cause small strokes, and with her slurred speech and failing memory, she had no choice but to sell the house. Sonia took her around to look at assisted-care apartments, and Mom picked this one because it has a garden. Once the decision was made, transplanting Mom was easier than we'd expected. She seemed to have moved on.

I supervised the garage sale on the driveway, and we baked in the sun waiting for at least *one* passerby to buy *one* item. *Please*, my eyes begged, as a neighbor sorted through dishes and books. Suddenly I was selling more than junk—I was selling two lifetimes, and no one appreciated them, including Sonia and me. We didn't get a sale, not even one. We put a "free, help yourself" sign out at dinner, and the next morning still nothing was taken. So we sold the house with most of the contents to Don, the same guy who'd bought Father's car. It was as if his family were looking for an existing but different life: ours. It unnerved us, so we boxed some personal things, the intricately decorated Ukrainian dishes, and Father's tools, and carefully stored them in Sonia's basement, now loaded to the rafters.

Then there was the problem of Father's safe. He installed it himself years ago, under the basement stairs, under the floor, accessed through a secret hidden panel in the linoleum, encased in a concrete foundation.

"How can she not have the combination?" I asked. Sonia and I stared at the round black knob, its white numbers and ticks guarding the answer.

"She doesn't know what's in it. Doesn't seem to care."

"We'll have to call someone."

The mystery contents of the safe haunted us for days, as we

searched for the combination. We finally gave up and hired an exorbitantly priced safecracker, who arrived with an enormous black equipment case and thick glasses that didn't hide the curiosity in his eyes. Soon, a successful click broke the silence, and I paid him and led him out. He looked terribly disappointed as he shuffled out the door, but we were afraid of the secrets we might find. Sonia emptied the contents:

5 pairs of leather gloves, price tags still on, in original store
    boxes
6 leather wallets, new, also in original boxes
$5,000 cash
New gold cufflinks and tiepins
Old silver quarters in a Mason jar
2 new screwdrivers and 4 new pocketknives

A wave of sadness overwhelmed me. Who was this man? He had created Fort Knox for these items? Everything was new and unused, except the quarters. Yet everything was *old*. There was no mistaking it—these were Father's black market bartering items for the next big one.

After that, we all wanted to get out of the house. Mom reminded us that it was only "stuff"; she was satisfied with the proceeds of the house sale.

"I have a nest egg," she told us. "I can still pay my own way."

"What's this?" I asked, as we were packing Mom's clothes the day before the move.

A crumpled plastic bag I found at the back of her top closet shelf contained ladies' underwear, white shiny polyester in a large size that Mom hadn't been in years. Price tags dangled from the seams. I walked the bag over to where Mom sat and opened it. She peered in with a half-grin.

"For my funeral," she said. "And pack the purple dress."

My hands turned cold as I shut the bag. This stuff was at least ten years old. When was she going to mention it?

"Mom says this is for her funeral," I said, opening the bag to Sonia, who was working in the kitchen. She sighed, put down the dishes, and sat on a nearby chair.

"She doesn't have much faith in her daughters getting it right, huh?" I asked, and I tucked the underwear into yet another box destined for Sonia's basement.

It was when I watched Mom look at the garden for the last time that I knew she was leaving behind a part of her soul. Her eyes gazed forward, unfocused, as if she was reliving the seasons and the years and the life and death and rebirth of each of her plants. She stooped in sadness over the bars of her new walker, and I somehow knew it was one of the saddest moments of my life, too.

"Neighborhood's going downhill," she said. "I got my money out just in time."

Okay, maybe she wasn't as sentimental as I expected.

I followed her to the car.

"And at least I don't have to crawl to the bathtub anymore," she said. *Crawl?* I reeled at the thought of her on her hands and knees struggling up the stairs and around the second floor. *Now* we find this out? What else had she been doing before we moved her? Well, at least now she's safe in her recliner.

"That's quite the chair," Mrs. S says, bringing my thoughts back to the apartment. She pats the crimson velvet of Mom's La-Z-Boy on steroids, with control buttons and a side table for juice and a tissue box, the same way a car salesman pats a shiny new car.

"Sonia found it," Mom says proudly. "She's my boss now. She takes good care of me."

Mrs. S gives Sonia a nod. She likes her, while she seems to dismiss me.

Sonia smiles. She has undertaken the role of caregiver with a vengeance. Cam and I offered to move Mom to Toronto, but neither Mom nor Sonia agreed. Sonia feels a sense of duty as the elder (eleven years older holds a lot of clout), and she has a relationship with Mom that I don't understand and can't replicate. I'm the less important sibling, the one who can't fix dentures and order around nurses. I tell myself I'm fine with it, although I'm not sure one ever accepts one's role in a family. Sonia thinks I deserve it because I moved away—she's hinted as much. She still doesn't understand that I *ran* away.

"We're taking her on an Alaskan cruise—the whole family," I tell Mrs. S. "To get her used to her walker. The ships are designed for it."

Mrs. S looks surprised. "You want to go?" she asks Mom.

Sonia looks up at Mom.

"She's never told you how difficult her passage to Canada was?"

"No," I say. She's never told us anything.

"There's a casino on the boat. She's excited about that," Sonia says. She has no desire to delve into history.

"Do you need a nap?" Mrs. S asks Mom, grabbing her hand. I realize why Mom doesn't want to move to Toronto. I'm her daughter, but this woman is her *friend*.

"Nooo," Mom answers in a childish whine. She struggles with her extra-big-button remote control and turns on the television. *The Price is Right* fills the screen.

Mrs. S turns her chair to the screen, grabs Mom's hand, and says, "Okay, perfect. My favorite show, too."

That evening, I ask Sonia about it.

"All I know is that I was born in a small town in England where they had jobs. And then they came here," she explains.

"Why? With who?"

"No idea," she says, shrugging her shoulders. "Not that it matters anymore. She still wants to go to Alaska."

• • •

It's a relief to get home and have my Saturday morning chats with Cam. I tell him about Mom's move and how weird it is that a new family is living in our stuff.

"Apparently she doesn't like ships, but she's up for Alaska." I pour my Earl Grey into a travel mug for the garden. "They had a rough passage to Canada or something."

"Really? What happened?" Cam asks.

"No idea." It's hard for him to understand the silence of our household.

"Why don't you do some research? I think I saw an old ship register in that box of photos you brought home for Max," he says.

"Maybe. So what?"

"So aren't you curious?" Cam loves history, and I don't. Especially mine. We opened that safe and got a glimpse of Father's mind. I can't handle more.

"I have zero interest in their past. I've got enough to do going forward. If she wanted to share her stories, she would have."

"Okay," he says. "I've never understood why you girls don't explore your history."

"You didn't grow up in our household. *Drop it.*" This is where Cam and I separate, like two branches from a trunk, farther and farther apart, with no hope of mutual understanding.

"Well, okay, let's get out there, then," he says, nodding toward the garden.

"Max and I are going to the bog," I say. I've convinced Max to help me find the source of the stream.

Because I can garden *and* be a mother. I stop short in my thoughts, shocked by the resentment that still surfaces. I resolve to do more, be more, love more.

"Mom's gonna help me glue moss onto my LEGO model for grass." Max walks into the room with a pair of garden clippers. Some leaves are revealing hints of yellow and the air feels cooler, so I insist he wear a jacket over his white tae kwon do uniform. He doesn't want to take off his new green belt, another rung toward the ultimate black.

We set out while Cam heads for the garage to retrieve his beloved pruning loppers. He relishes the immediate gratification of each snip, while I'm still hesitant to cut large branches, fearing I might create a trail of miserable deformed shrubs.

"Call us for lunch?" I yell over my shoulder. "Let's go, Max."

I adjust my small camera and give it to Max, putting him in charge of plant pictures for Grandma. He stares at the buttons in awe. He's young, I know, but I'm on a mission to cure his nature-deficit disorder—NDD. I've read it's the disease that ails our techie children. I'm thinking my camera is better than the Nintendo, and at least he'll have to get closer to the plants.

As we get to the bottom of the slope and onto flatter land, I can barely see where Max has run ahead of me. We are at the lowest part of the ravine, surrounded by forest. It's eerie, yet beautiful, as my sense of aloneness surrounds me and all sounds disappear into the moss-covered boulders. I savor the moment, letting my thoughts fade. This must be what they mean by mindfulness. Quiet bliss.

Then I remember my wandering son. Parenting and mindfulness may not be an easy mix.

"Max?" I yell.

"Mom," I hear through the branches. "Mountains!"

I turn right and shove my way through the brush. We are now at the bottom of the L, an area of the garden that isn't visible from the top of the slope. I walk with my head down to protect my eyes, moving branches aside with my hands.

"Where are you?" I yell. The knotweed has come to an end. My stomach lurches when I realize I am facing an enormous clearing. A small mountain sits in the center, about eight feet high and twenty feet in diameter, covered with beaten-up plastic tarps. Max sits at the top.

"I'm the king!" he yells.

"What the hell is that?" Cam asks, surprising me from behind.

"Kilimanjaro." I head for one corner of a tarp. "Sand," I yell as I lift it up.

How did that get here?

"It gets worse." Cam's voice floats from the other side of the mountain. "Bags of cement."

"Why here?" I ask, looking around. Only to notice several stacks of wooden shipping palettes nearby. Dismay weighs me down, more than the cement.

"It's the only area of land that's flat," Cam says. "They must have used this stuff to build the stone wall that supports the terrace."

"This got trucked here," I say. "But how?"

The bottom of the garden is street level for houses below our block, but those streets are far away, through a swath of city-owned parkland and more forest. Did construction workers drive through it?

"This is a disaster," I say. "We'll never get this stuff back up. We have a problem."

"We have tableland," says Cam.

"What?"

"Flat land. We can have a gently rolling hill of grass one day." I hope he's kidding. We're at the bottom of a ravine in the middle of a forest. No grass will grow here, nor should it.

"Tableland is storage land. They used it as a junkyard," I say.

"Mom," Max yells, "a secret path! Come!"

I race toward Max through the earthy heat. Another path? What else lurks in this mysterious garden? On the way, I notice a mass of green leaves, about eight inches high, at the base of a large tree. My throat constricts with emotion. *That's* what else.

I've never seen so many, so densely close together. I walk toward them slowly, as if speed might turn them into a figment of my imagination, and lean down to pick two pointed oval leaves on a stem, one sheathing the other at the base. The stalks of white bells are missing, long gone since the first days of spring, but these are definitely the pointed green leaves that I used to doodle on my schoolbooks.

"Mom?" I whisper to the warm breeze, as I walk around the patch to see how far it goes. It extends westward, below the shade of several trees, where the knotweed thins out. I take a deep breath, hoping to inhale some of the oxygen the plant leaves have released.

Until about the age of ten, I did homework at the kitchen table, where the vase with the ruffled glass rim, like the collar of a clown's costume, graced the off-white crocheted tablecloth. In it, deep green leaves surrounded delicate stems of white flowers. The fragrance permeated the kitchen, battling the aroma of leftover smoke from Father's cigarettes—John Player's Navy Cut. He smoked a pack a day.

Mom loved the lily of the valley that grew along the shady side of our house. The fragrance still reminds me of her. I've read that it's a tough-as-nails perennial, and that suits her. It will survive in deep shade or full sun, is resistant to insects, and can be transplanted anytime. It will keep going after many others fail to thrive. Yes, that's her.

❧

"Where's Mom?" I asked Sonia one day when she'd walked in with an armload of books. I was devouring an after-school snack, the air thick with the flowers' fragrance.

"Days." She opened the fridge to look for food.

Mom worked two rotating shifts at Celanese, a German-owned chemical factory. She worked on manufacturing machines for twelve hours at a time. Days were 8:00 a.m. to 8:00 p.m.; nights were 8:00 p.m. to 8:00 a.m. Father worked outdoors as a pipe fitter for the Canadian National Railway on three rotating shifts. Days were eight to four, afternoons were four to midnight, and nights were midnight to eight in the morning. They were rarely home at the same time, and if they were, one of them was sleeping off their shift. I became skilled at eating alone and developed the habit of reading while eating to keep myself company — books, comics, and cereal boxes.

"She's smart," Mom told the principal of the local school when I was five. She was eager to get me into school, because her work schedule needed a place for me to be. The school relented, and after she showed me the way a few times, I walked by myself, about a mile, over railroad tracks and through busy streets, to grade one. I didn't question my independence, or that Mom was always too busy to walk with me.

At night, on the rare times that both Mom and Father were home, Sonia covered my ears with her small hands as we lay in our shared double bed.

"Don't listen," she would say. But I was old enough to understand unhappiness.

They fought after we went to bed, thinking that we didn't hear them. They argued, in harsh Ukrainian syllables, about money, work, and our behavior.

"I'm never getting married," I promised Sonia. I curled into a fetal position under the warmth of our quilt.

"Me either," she said. "Let's read."

And she made a tent out of the bedcover, where, with our books and an old black flashlight with a CN logo on it, we ran away into our stories.

The shift work paid off, and we moved into a newer, more spacious house. Mom began sending monthly parcels to the Ukraine: lipstick, hosiery, and candy — *worth lots on the black market*, she explained, and then the discussion was over. Our new house was six streets east and had a wooded ravine behind its alley instead of my playground of railroad tracks. It was quiet — no more bellowing train horns and slightly less fighting, because Mom and Father were busy in the larger yard. If they were occupied, things were better between them, although, for me, at the age when teasing the skinniest kid in grade school was my fellow students' priority, my parents' increased activities became a source of constant humiliation. I was a child of immigrants in the city, and they were farmers without a farm.

I dreaded the annual delivery of a truckload of manure that Mom spread over the garden. She tilled it into the arid soil and ended each day reeking, her clothes covered in brown smudges.

"Sheep is the best," she lectured one day, as if I cared. The stench covered the neighborhood like an invisible cloud.

"No, I don't smell shit," I said to my friends, as we played in the nearby park.

Even worse, the same farmer delivered our annual meat supply.

"What's that?" I asked in horror, the first time I came home from school to find Mom stretching the end of a long beige mass of rubbery tubing around the kitchen faucet.

"Intestines," she said, turning the water on so that a large balloon formed and ran through the endless miles of guts. "To make the garlic sausage."

"Sausage?"

"We bought half a pig and half a cow. The Panchyks are going to take the other halves."

"Halves?" I knew that meant dead. I tensed, prepared for the rest of the answer.

"Mr. Panchyk will help us butcher them in the garage. Our freezer will be full for the winter. It's cheaper." Worse than I imagined.

I followed Mom into the garage, which had been transformed into a meatpacking plant. Two carcasses hung from the ceiling. Huge rolls of pink butcher paper and plastic wrap sat on a long portable table, and Mr. Panchyk was sharpening a cleaver. Father was wiping blood off the floor. Over the next week, cubes of fat, bacon, and steaks were packaged and labeled with a thick black marker and neatly piled into the freezer. Mom ground pork, mixed it with spices and garlic, and stuffed it into the intestine casings. Father built an outdoor smoker and hung rings of sausage from the garage ceiling.

"No, I don't smell garlic," I said to my friends, who scrunched their noses as we cycled around the block.

My family produced embarrassing smells. I hated them.

Adjacent to the stocked freezer in the basement was a larder with a rough gray concrete floor. Mom stored the glass jars of fruit, beans, beets, and jellies there, like the rows of my cherished Crayolas. I loved to hide in there when I was sad. It was impenetrable, and I imagined surviving forever by candlelight and melted snow. At the back of the cold room was a hook that held some clothes in cloth bags. I opened them one day, curious.

"There's a fur coat in the cold room," I told Mom, who was washing laundry on the old wringer machine. She still hung clothes outside on the line.

"That's mine. The cold keeps it from drying out."

"I didn't know you had a fur coat." It seemed expensive for a family who butchered their own meat.

"I bought it for myself as a gift."

Mom never explained herself, never told a story. I held my breath, ready to listen.

"When I was pregnant with you, your father told me if you were a boy, he would buy me a fur coat."

I let this sink in, my hands clasped together and held to my chest.

"You were born. No coat."

My hands rose to my face, fingers covering my cheeks, icy against the hot skin. Was this why my father never spoke to me?

"So I saved my money and bought my own coat. Although I have nowhere to wear it."

After that, I stopped playing in the larder.

I found a new place to hide. The ravine wasn't the safest place to be, but those times were different. My parents didn't care, or worry.

I went out after school, often with Megan, and came home by dark. During northern Alberta summers, that meant 11 p.m. If I add it up, I spent more time in the ravine than I did at school, or at home.

Long trails led to the North Saskatchewan River, and I walked along the river to downtown, or jogged the other way to the eastern tip of the city, through the four seasons, watching the trees on the riverbank lose and gain and lose their leaves and the water freeze and melt and freeze again.

I didn't know at the time that there are sixty miles of trails along the river and that the valley is one of the longest urban parklands in North America. But I knew I was free.

❧

"It goes back up to the top." Max's voice pulls me away from my patch of lily of the valley. "Come, Mom!"

I follow the cracking of branches as he pushes forward. It truly is a secret path, about three feet wide, made of dirt held by old railroad ties so that the ascent is a series of tiered steps. It rises steeply upward in a switchback curve and turns sharply east, where it flattens and is lined by the trunks of towering trees. The railroad ties are rotting and the path is overgrown, but cleaned up, it will be phenomenal —every turn provides a different perspective of the garden. Large boulders line the path here and there; someone created this enchanting trail, and I vow to restore it someday.

"Mom," calls Max, his voice eager, "can we call it the Secret Path?"

"Sounds perfect."

"I love it down here," he says. "It's a giant forest full of secrets. Is it really ours?"

"It is," I say. "I love it too."

That evening, we glue our collected moss, twigs, and leaves to LEGO pieces to create a bizarre town where plastic meets nature in the most unnatural way. Max goes to bed without argument, overwhelmed by his day. I am dead tired, yet restless. Cam is deep into *Pruning: A Practical Guide.*

I open the side cupboard in the small den where I have my desk and computer and sift through the bags of photos and boxes piled inside. I find Father's box of photos and flip through the contents. There it is: the ship brochure. Booklet actually. I pull it out and cram the box back into the cupboard.

In the lamplight on my desk, it looks old. *Canadian Pacific* is written in thick gold cursive bubble letters on a navy blue background. A red-and-white flag floats above the words *Passenger List.* I'm captivated. I've never heard of a passenger list. Would we get one on the Alaskan cruise? I doubt it. I run my fingers over the dry paper, feeling as if I'm about to open more than a tattered brochure.

I need a cup of Earl Grey. With extra milk, the way I love it, and the way Sonia's properly-steeped-black-tea-drinking husband deems disgusting. This brochure represents their coming to Canada, to the new world to create a better life for their children, and yet I witnessed misery. Did their marriage start that way or did it become that way? It would be better for Sonia if it *became* that way so that she would have been born into good karma. It's too late for me. I'm the product of too many drinks at a party. An accident *and* a girl.

Why should Mrs. S know Mom's history, but not us?

I open it to the first yellowed page: "*Empress of Canada,* From Liverpool Wednesday, February 20, 1952, To Saint John N.B." A faded black-and-white rendering of the ship shows tall, wide steam stacks above the boilers—it doesn't look as glamorous as the front of the brochure implied. In fact, it looks like an army ship. The first few pages contain strangely lighthearted advice about ocean travel, such as "Seasoned travellers lay the foundation for a pleasant voyage soon after they have been shown their rooms," and "When the seasoned traveller heads for a country he has never visited he opens his mind as carefully as he closes his luggage."

What?

These bizarre tips are not for immigrants who can barely speak

English. I turn the page to the first-class passengers. They are the tourists who were likely on the boat for pleasure — seasoned travelers. The Andersons, the Marcottes, and the Wilsons. The lower class seems to be a mix of tourists and immigrants with foreign names, including my parents and Sonia: Mr., Mrs., and Miss, from Ross., England. What does "Ross." stand for?

It is a motley crew of rich and poor, vacationers and homeless foreigners. How many times have I experienced a mundane landing on a plane, not knowing that I sat beside new immigrants who were terrified as to whether their new country would bring them what they were searching for? I hope I helped them with their overflowing luggage in the overhead bin or gave them a small smile. Will they keep their ticket stubs and not show their children?

I research the ship because now I must. The *Duchess of Richmond* was built as a transatlantic cruise liner in 1928. She was one of four Drunken Duchesses, aptly named because of how they rolled around on the high seas. During World War II, she was retrofitted to a troopship to carry soldiers to North Africa; she survived, while long-range German bombers sank her sister *York*. She was renamed the *Empress of Canada,* and retrofitted back to an ocean liner. She was a survivor ship, providing service to survivor immigrants, although it didn't last long. Maybe she was tired because the war had taken its toll on her, or the hopes of newcomers to Canada were too much to bear. When an intense blaze broke out, and explosions caused her to take on water, and lean, and then lean more deeply into the ocean, she gave up and lay on her port side like a wounded warrior until her remains were scavenged by Italian ship scrappers.

My parents sailed on one of the last voyages she made — they reeled through violent seas with a newborn and not much else. I open the brochure back to their names on the list. As I scan the page, I see the names of another of Mom's friends and her husband, and Miss and Master, their young babies. Blood rushes to my head. Mom had *friends* on the boat. They nursed their babies on the ship together. Why do these old friends hold hands and share fries and their secrets? I want some of those secrets to belong to *me*. I should have asked more questions. I wasn't brave enough to break the silence.

I close the brochure, my resentments rising to the surface, pushing away my guilt to where I can safely ignore it. I have no idea who my parents are, or why I have to learn about them in a brochure.

Suddenly, I don't want to go to Alaska.

LILY OF THE VALLEY POTPOURRI

To dry flowers:

- Pick fresh flowers on a sunny morning, after the dew has dried.
- Flowers may be dried in bunches hung upside down in a dry, warm location, or scattered on a cookie sheet lined with cheesecloth and set in the oven at the lowest temperature with the door open. Flowers must be completely dry to preserve their color and fragrance. Any moisture in the potpourri jar can cause mold.

Potpourri:

1 cup dried lily of the valley* flowers
2 cups dried violet or viola flowers
¾ cup dried rose blossoms
1 teaspoon vanilla extract
3 tablespoons orrisroot† powder (available at specialty natural food stores)

- Gently blend dried flowers in a clear glass container with a tight lid. Sprinkle in orrisroot powder and blend. Sprinkle in vanilla, one drop at a time, stirring after each drop.
- Seal and store in a warm, dry, dark place for six weeks to cure.

See page 267 for information on safety and sourcing of plants.

---

* Lily of the valley should not be ingested by humans or pets, as it can be toxic.

† Orrisroot may cause dermatitis in some individuals. Please do not breathe in dust, and handle with rubber gloves.

CHAPTER 4

Cattails

"Where did you find this guy?" Cam asks, handing me my gardening gloves. He still refuses to wear them despite the cuts and blisters.

"Stan? On the Internet. Stan's Pond Management."

"What pond are we managing, exactly?" Cam doesn't trust my hiring process, but we need all the help we can get.

"Max and Shelly were exploring. They've found water, apparently. They were telling fish stories."

"It's dangerous for him and his babysitter to be down here unsupervised," says Cam angrily, as we make our way down the steps, which are finally navigable with some care.

A voice travels over us. "Hello there?"

"Hello?" I call.

A tall slim man, wearing a plaid shirt and high black rubber boots, wades through the weeds toward us.

"I'm Stan," he says, putting out his hand. "Hell of a place."

"Hello," says Cam. "I'll leave you guys to it. I want to figure out what's over there." Cam stomps away, probably to plan the borders of his rambling lawn.

I start. "We've got water down here, and a stream. I don't know where it's coming from. No one had any information for us, not even the real estate agent. Can you figure out how—"

Stan wanders off through a dense area of shrubs and trees while I am speaking.

"Whoa!" he shouts. I've lost sight of him.

"Stan?" I yell.

I hear his voice through the bushes. "You've got yourself a pond! And two smaller ones down there, from the looks of it." I follow his tracks, stopping in wonder when I reach him.

An enormous pond shimmers beyond the knotweed, maybe thirty feet long and fifteen feet across. The water is deep green, turning to black closer to the middle, and the perimeter is bordered with a plant that looks like watercress. Jade-colored algae float at the top; more of it is visible a few feet down, a green respite against the murkiness. It looks like a layered underwater village, perfect for fish and frogs. Dead leaves float on the surface and fallen tree branches protrude from the depths, asking to be saved.

"Cam! Come here!" I yell. My eyes are riveted.

"It's amazing," Stan says. "What a property. You're downtown, and I feel like I'm in the country."

"What the he—," Cam says, coming up behind us. "Is that a pond?"

"Three ponds," says Stan.

Cam is speechless. I see pond lilies in my mind.

"Is that koi?" Stan asks, darting forward and pointing to an orange flash in the water.

"Koi?" Cam asks.

Shelly wasn't kidding.

"Type of ornamental carp," says Stan. "This thing's gotta be deep."

"Impossible," I say. "How did they get here? No one's been down here in years." My words roll together, as if that might answer my questions faster.

"Koi live twenty, thirty years," Stan says. How can he be so calm?

"But what about food? Don't they freeze?" A large silver fish surfaces, with a smaller orange one and a spotted one following.

"They'll eat the water plants and hibernate at the lowest part in winter. This must be a spring-fed pond. Bet it doesn't freeze in the winter."

The muscles in my chest tighten.

"Koi," I say.

"Koi," say Cam and Stan simultaneously. I feel the need to hug someone.

"You okay?" asks Stan.

"Not sure," I say. "I think this is too much for me." The ravine garden was already a dream come true. Mix in a spring-fed pond and silvery fish, and I might require resuscitation.

"Is she crying?" Stan asks Cam.

"She does that," Cam says.

"You've even got cattails over there," says Stan.

The brown-tipped spikes are hardly visible through the mess. Cattails? That does it. I'm going to die of pleasure.

"I used to play with them," I say. "Gordon Lightfoot, you know. 'Pussy willows, cattails, soft winds and roses . . .'"

"She gonna be okay?" Stan asks.

"Yeah," says Cam. "Give her a minute."

"'Rain pools in the woodland, water to my knees. . .'"

"How can we be sure it's spring-fed?" Cam asks.

"We need to find a place where the water is flowing out. That keeps the volume pretty steady all year round. Moving water doesn't freeze."

Stan heads through the brush, around the pond. We follow behind him like eager ducklings.

"It feeds this smaller pond here," he points. "Look at this old bridge. It goes right under it."

I follow his finger. The bridge curves in an upside-down smile, a broken balustrade and flaking concrete pillars at each corner.

"This doesn't look safe," says Cam, pulling away fallen tree branches that block our way. He's dumbfounded. Cam, master of total control and advance preparation, has no game plan.

The sound of rushing water intensifies near the bridge, which is about ten feet across and looks solid despite the eroding balustrade.

"I don't care if I fall in," I say, walking onto it. I am on top of the world at the bottom of my garden. I want to sit on the edge of the bridge with Max and dangle our feet over it while we count the pond lilies I will plant here. Benji will chase rabbits across the rolling lawn where Cam will pick dandelion leaves for my salad. A nearby squawk startles me.

Ducks. Two ducks, one brown and one with an emerald-green neck, flutter away.

"Mallards," Stan says. "A pair. Nice."

Mating ducks? We have a secret zoo.

"Will they eat the fish?" I ask.

"Nope, don't worry. Their nest is probably in the shrubs out there somewhere."

"It appears we have a fully stocked yard," Cam says. "What's that?"

"Looks like a city fence that's been here a while. It's tall enough." Stan points to a chainlink fence that demarcates the property.

I look over the bridge, beyond the fence, to see a small waterfall, about three feet high, on a base of large boulders covered in slimy green algae. The amount and velocity of the water is surprising, especially considering that same amount must be entering the pond consistently from some mysterious place underground. The small brook we found isn't even a tenth of the flow.

I try to see beyond the fence, but it is overtaken with cascading heart-shaped leaves. I peek underneath them to find thin curling tendrils and clusters of wild grapes. Vine wreathes are in my future! My eyes follow the glistening water until it disappears under broken branches and clusters of vines. Where is it going?

A whitish object to the side looks to be a washed-up skull. It's too pointed to be a raccoon's and too small for a hare's. Maybe a fox. It occurs to me that this garden is alive with more than plants. Our responsibility suddenly takes on a new dimension. We have wildlife. We can't just show up and tidy their house. Yet the historic bridge is crumbling. Do we let it fall in and float away with the garden's legacy? What the hell are we doing here?

"There you go," says Stan, standing beside me. "I bet that feeds the Lower Don. There are lots of underground aquifers in this area. You're incredibly lucky to have one springing up on your property."

"Can we clean it up?" I ask Stan. "Without harming the fish?"

"Hell if I know. It's gotta be deep. It needs aeration. We can't drain it. Hard to get the debris out. Really, never seen anything like it in the city."

The next morning, I'm up early. Two cups of Earl Grey, a flip through RHS's *Grasses* and *Wetland Plants*, a few hours online, and I am a cattail expert. Their shoots are edible, and they grow faster than corn. In some regions, they are considered invasive and are eradicated by burning. I'm appalled, especially because birds use the seed hairs to line their nests. I'm about to fall into a slumber at the table, into my imaginary pillow stuffed with the fluff of the ripe cattails, when the boys walk in.

"Good morning, Mom," says Max, as I look up and accept a kiss on my cheek. He's already wearing his tae kwon do uniform. "Can we go check on the fish and ducks?" Since we brought him down to visit the koi yesterday afternoon, he's talked of nothing else.

"Let's eat first, and then we'll go before your class. Can you retie your belt evenly?"

As Max struggles with his belt he announces that he named the fish: Fishy #1, Fishy #2, and Spotty.

"How are those patterns coming?" Cam asks Max. Max has been practicing his eight tae kwon do patterns—*poomsae,* as they're called —in front of the full-length mirror. I'm mesmerized by the fluid sequences of kicks, punches, and blocks of a warrior's dance.

"I think I'm ready for blue stripe," he says, chewing his toast carefully. He knows his master will not forgive a soiled uniform. "Can we build a tree fort on the Secret Path?"

The conversation moves to yesterday's adventure—the ponds, the bridge, and the question of fish food.

"Come on, let's go," says Max.

"We need to bring up some cattails," I say.

"Mom keeps finding weird plants for us to eat down there," says Cam. "We better look out, buddy."

"It's called foraging," I say. "It means searching for food in the wild."

"Like animals do?"

"Exactly. We're animals. There's lots of cool stuff out there. Did you know that cattails are useful from top to bottom?"

"Your mother is going to make us eat weeds," Cam says.

"Don't," I say to him in a low voice. "Did you know cattails are called Cossack asparagus?" I continue. Why didn't Mom tell us about this eastern European delicacy?

Cam rolls his eyes. Max ignores me. Benji opens his eyes and delivers a slow yawn.

"Benji will eat anything," I say, looking at the pup for unconditional approval. The dog lies down on his side, stretches, and goes back to sleep.

"Maybe we can rake out some of that algae," Cam offers.

"We can't hurt the fish," Max says. "Maybe they like it messy." For a computer nerd, he's pretty intuitive.

"They need oxygen," I say.

"They have oxygen now or they'd be dead," Max says, his arms crossed, his eyes determined. He loves animals and he is protective of his pets.

A heated discussion ensues with no resolution. Do we clean the pond or leave the pond? Feed the fish or leave the fish? We need to clean the paths but can't disturb the paths until we find the duck's nest. I'm upset, yet content. We will argue our way into agreement about any minutiae the garden throws at us for as long as it takes. At least we're talking.

𝓏

Up until about the age of twelve, I would walk into the kitchen most mornings, still willing to try. "Good morning."

Silence. Father would sip his coffee, with sugar and milk, and eat his oatmeal, always oatmeal, without looking up. The same slight pain, the feeling of rejection, would grow in the middle of my chest.

Mom would be at the sink, peeling vegetables. "Good morning," she'd respond.

I could sit at the kitchen table for an hour, and Father wouldn't speak to me. He'd make a few comments to Mom concerning work or the garden, but necessities only. Then he would escape to his luxurious garage, which was beside Mom's garden—two parallel universes where each would go to their personal refuge.

The garage was finished with polished wood cabinetry and paneled walls. It had a pristine cement floor, straight storage shelves, and a furnace for winter. Father built it himself from the ground up. He was a natural carpenter, welder, plumber, and electrician. Self-taught, except the welding, which he learned at CN.

"Why won't he talk to me? Does he hate us?" I asked Sonia one day during a ravine walk. I carried an armful of cattails from the swamp. Mom coated them with hairspray to keep the seeds together and displayed them in arrangements in the living room.

"I don't know. Maybe something happened in the war," she said.

"What? Mom was in the war too. She doesn't act like him."

"Who knows? Mom doesn't discuss it."

"She married him."

"I think she was in love with someone else. Some boy in the village."

"What boy? How do you know that?" I asked, breathing harder.

"She told me. She tells me stuff when she's angry at him."

I walked faster. How come my mother and sister had a secret relationship? How come they shared personal things with each other and not me? All Mom discussed with me, and barely, was my report card. Bad enough Father was silent, but Mom too?

"C'mon. Let's find some leaves," Sonia said. "We'll press them when we get home."

"How did they meet?"

"I don't know," she said. "It was wartime. You could ask her."

This was an impossible answer. As if in our house anyone would ever ask a question like that. Wartime was the catch phrase meaning "we don't talk about it."

"Forget it," I said.

So I didn't know how my parents met. So what? It wouldn't change the way they were.

"Is that our father?" I asked Sonia, as we returned from the walk, leaves in hand.

"Yup." He was at the end of our block, rummaging through the neighbor's garbage, a pile of junk beside him in a box.

"Why do we have to have a father who's a garbage picker?" I asked. "That's what my friends call him."

"He must be out of projects," Sonia said.

We kept walking, knowing that stopping to talk was not an option.

The neighbors eventually noticed Father's scavenging. At first it was a mystery; after all, we were not visibly in need. Eventually they came to realize he liked fixing broken things. If our iron broke, there would be a selection of five rescued ones to choose from, stored neatly in the garage. It was like a department store. Soon the neighbors gave broken appliances to Mom, to pass on to Father. He would fix the appliances with spare parts he had collected from garbage cans and junkyards, and then have Mom return them. Not because he liked the neighbors or was a generous man. Simply because if something was broken, he needed to fix it. And he knew he did it better than anyone else.

So why didn't he fix us? I wondered. Or himself?

Sometimes he needed help on the table saw, measuring long distances or holding parts that were being welded. It was only then that he would ask Mom, or sometimes have her send me, because his need to build outweighed his need for solitude.

"Your father needs help," Mom would say, and I would put my homework aside and walk to the garage, not knowing what would be in store, cursing myself for not being a boy, but determined to prove myself worthy of whatever project was underway.

"Hi." I always acknowledged him. I still hoped for "Hello" back, maybe because we were on his turf and he might be more inclined. It never happened.

Father mostly pointed to the large planks of wood that I was to balance on the table saw as he maneuvered them through. The whirr of the blade would mask the silence. I loved to smell the sawdust as a clean cut emerged. Then, my usefulness over, he would nod to dismiss me.

"What's that?" I asked one day after school, when I found Mom and Sonia pressing what appeared to be a doorbell, oddly placed in the kitchen near the phone.

"Your father installed a buzzer. To the garage."

It suddenly buzzed loudly. Mom waved through the window.

"What for?" I asked.

"If he needs help, he'll buzz," said Sonia. "If it's time for dinner, Mom will buzz once. If she needs help, she'll buzz twice."

And that was the beginning of even less conversation in our household.

Buzz your father, Mom would say. And I'd push the doorbell, and he would come to the house, wash his hands, and sit quietly at the table until his plate was put in front of him. Meat, mashed potatoes, a green vegetable, and canned fruit for dessert. Apple pie on Sundays. When we were buzzed for help, whoever was free would take their useful pair of hands over to the garage, and work in silence until Father nodded.

✦

Cam's hand touches my arm as he puts a bottle of wine and a glass on the scuffed leather of my old desk. He pushes aside the pine-scented candle I've kept on my desk for years because it's my favorite fragrance. Who knew that someday we would have a real forest that smells infinitely better? My feet are tucked under Benji's belly because his basket consumes most of the space under the desk. I'm watching a YouTube video of the "Pussy Willows, Cattails" song and the photos of woodlands look just like our garden. Gordon (as I call him) is *so* profound.

"You don't find his songs a bit melancholy?" Cam asks. He's being diplomatic. He hates Gordon Lightfoot's music, although he tolerates my being his loyal fan because he says I'm one of the few left living.

He still teases me about a fundraiser we attended last year, where Gordon was a celebrity guest. I bought an autographed book, and one for Sonia too; after all, she introduced me to his folk-rock in the seventies. Those days of hiding in the ravine and my loneliness must have made me the perfect flypaper for Lightfoot's lyrics; they stuck and are forever imprinted in the part of my brain that activates when I am alone on a wooded trail. I even had my picture taken with him at the fundraiser. *He used to live down the street from you, maybe two blocks away,* someone had told me that evening. I now realize Gordon Lightfoot and I shared the same ravine. The same view. I can pretend to see it through his eyes.

"They're not melancholy. They're thoughtful. About nature."

"They bring me down."

"He's a poet. A national treasure." Why am I getting defensive?

Cam doesn't get it. He doesn't even know the lyrics to "If You Could Read My Mind." I turn off my computer and change the subject.

"We've got a lot of bills." The pile overwhelms my desk, and Wesley still hasn't sold our old house; every dollar spent is significant. Beyond the household expenses, there are bills for Max's activities: photography camp, computer camp, and tae kwon do. When will there ever be time for plain old-fashioned nature? This garden could not have come soon enough, I decide.

"Are we living vicariously through our son?" I ask Cam, as he settles into the sofa facing my desk.

"We're giving him what we didn't get," he says, as he sips his wine.

"Expensive hobbies?" I ask.

"Time," he answers.

Easy for him to say. He had devoted parents as a child, despite their being hard-working immigrants. If he didn't get their time, he definitely had their attention. And love.

"I suppose," I say, admiring the colorful wall of gardening books behind Cam. Punctuated with several small bronze bird statues, these are the shelves I first set up when we moved in. The books are categorized by type of plant or gardening advice. I have a full shelf each for trees, roses, and herbs. Several plant encyclopedias. They have been my virtual garden and my virtual friends, traveling and growing with me through the years. Cam makes fun of the more interesting ones, like my *Backyard Birdsong Guide* with a built-in audio player of seventy-five birdsongs. His loss. Even Max likes listening to the warblers, loons, and chickadees. Cam prefers books about historic European gardens, like *The Garden at Chatsworth*. A pretty dull read if you're not English royalty.

I also have several books about the human relationship with nature. Cam hasn't read these. In fact, he rolls his eyes when I talk about biophilia (love of nature and living things), and he laughed when I told him soil is the new Prozac because some soil bacteria produce serotonin. It infuriates me, but "Never give up" is our family motto, and I'm determined to convert him, and especially Max, to a deeper understanding of the natural world.

Since he's a captive audience on my sofa, I stand up and open Richard Louv's *Last Child in the Woods* to read him a quote by Robert Frost: "When I see birches bend to left and right . . . I like to think some boy's been swinging them."

"Max told me you guys want to put a tree swing on the Secret Path," Cam says.

"Did you know eighty percent of North Americans live in cities?" I ask him.

"You've mentioned it once or twice." He looks at my orderly arranged shelves. "So those are finally useful."

"Very."

"How are we going to take on this project?" he asks. "It's bigger than I thought. We have to respect the ravine, too."

"The remnants of the estate are pretty much destroyed," I say. "I guess we save what we can. We haven't even checked out the gazebo yet. And we need to get all the construction debris out."

He stands up to pour more wine. "This is going to cost a fortune. Did Wesley get back to you?"

"There have been a lot of showings. It'll sell by Christmas for sure," I say.

"Well, winter is coming—let's focus on the interior and start again next spring."

That night, I sleep and wake fitfully, dejected that we've gone as far as we can with the garden, which seems to be nowhere. Although I'm the first to lecture Max about patience in his world of immediately responsive video games, it seems I don't have much myself. Waiting until next spring will feel like an eternity.

CATTAIL FRIED RICE

Please note:

Young cattail shoots may resemble poisonous daffodil (Amaryllidaceae family) or iris shoots (Iridaceae family). Use cattails only with absolute positive identification.

To harvest:

- Select large shoots (*Typha latifolia* or *Typha angustifolia*) that haven't begun to flower, in early spring. Separate the outer leaves from the core to the base of the plant, grab the inner core with both hands as close to the base as possible, and pull it out. Peel and discard the outermost layers of leaves from the top down, until the soft, edible part is reached.

Ingredients:

1 tablespoon toasted sesame oil
½ cup peeled and chopped cattail shoots
1 cup shallots, chopped
2 cloves garlic, chopped
3 cups cooked rice
2 tablespoons soy sauce
1 tablespoon chili paste or ½ teaspoon cayenne pepper

- Heat the sesame oil in a large skillet over a medium flame. Add the cattails, shallots, and garlic, and sauté for 5 minutes. Add the remaining ingredients and cook until the rice is hot. Stir frequently to prevent sticking.

See page 267 for information on safety and sourcing of plants.

CHAPTER 5

 ⌁

Apple Trees

SPRING HAS ARRIVED, and it didn't take as long as I expected because I was *busy*. With gas lines, electrical work, and cabinets, the interior renovations are a full-time job and remain a work in progress. We were mesmerized by the garden's cool-weather personality; the leafless trees allowed for a perfect view of the downtown skyline. Twinkling lights filled our evenings, and when the snow covered the slope, I felt I was in the foothills of the Canadian Rockies.

The trip to Alaska was ideal for Mom; she and her walker rolled around the ship's casino with Sonia and Dennis while Cam and I went on wilderness hikes, and Max played in the kids' computer center. Wesley sold our old house to a charming couple while we were away. They love it, so I love them.

Today, on this sunlit March day, I am renewed. My part of the earth is tilting toward the sun, and the light is falling directly, densely, warming my hair as I wait on an outside deck chair. A friend's contractor, Bill, will examine the mysterious garden gazebo. I decide, as he approaches, that he looks expensive.

"Did you bring some boots?" I ask, shaking his hand. "It's still pretty muddy down there. The snow hasn't fully melted."

"I'll be fine," he says. Not likely. His brown leather shoes are immaculate.

"My husband's been clearing the rest of the path to the gazebo all morning," I tell him. "The last bit may be rough going. We've never seen it close up."

He smiles. "How bad can it be?"

"Okay, then," I say. Goodbye nice shoes.

We dodge mud and soggy piles of weeds from last year as we head down the stairs.

His shoes get dirtier, and his appreciation of the garden grows, as we head lower and lower into the ravine. He is shocked, as most people are when they first enter the garden. It's an extraordinary contrast from the unassuming house at the top.

"What the hell is that up there?" Bill asks from behind me.

I stop, paralyzed. The smell of rotten wood and sweet fragrance fills my nostrils.

We've caught up to Cam and are finally in front of the gazebo. But it's not a gazebo—it's a small *temple*. I'm finally standing at the base of the beacon that haunted me from afar all last summer. It's immense. I crane my neck upward, dwarfed by eight stone columns. This structure, in its graceful position at the bottom corner of the L shape of the garden, is definitely the heart of the property.

"That's," I answer, "the gazebo."

"I thought you meant some small wooden thing," Bill says.

"This belongs in the English countryside," says Cam. "I'm Cam, by the way," he adds, reaching out for a handshake with his filthy, blistered hand. Bill looks appalled, but shakes it.

"So what do you think?" Cam asks me. He's as overwhelmed as I am.

"Jesus," says Bill. "This thing is two stories high. And, that's the biggest wisteria I've ever seen."

I look up, adrenaline coursing through me. Excitement and intimidation compete in my heart.

"It looks thirty feet high. The vines have destroyed the roof," he adds.

The wisteria branches wind over the octagonal roof, obscuring much of its graceful tiered design. I quickly count the tiers.

"Nine levels," I tell Cam. "It's going to be okay."

"What?"

"The roof has nine levels. It's a pagoda." The smallest tier is at the top, and subsequent levels cascade downward and outward. From this moment on, that's what we'll call it. A pagoda!

"Odd numbers belong to the living, even numbers to the dead," I explain.

"Pardon me?" asks Bill.

"In Asian culture," I say. Cam should be grateful I know these things.

"Okay," says Bill. He looks confused.

"Okay," agrees Cam. He looks skeptical and drifts off to the other side of the structure.

The thick concrete columns, about fifteen feet high, are disintegrating at the top where the damaged roof allowed the rain to seep in.

"This is massive. The floor's got to be twenty feet across," says Cam.

I step into it. My heart pounds in my ears, its rapid rhythm quelling the sound of Cam's comments. The original family must have built this. Garden structures were popular status symbols for the wealthy. This one holds its own against any in my gardening books. An elegant grande dame, despite the cracked orange terracotta floor covered with debris, branches, rotten apples, and brown heaps.

"Is that shit?" asks Bill.

"Look up," says Cam.

I look up to notice several pairs of eyes staring at me from between the rafters of the soaring wood ceiling.

"Raccoons," I say. "A whole family."

Well, who could blame them? It's quite the nest. Mother Nature has taken this pagoda for her own. To the side, I see a tree from my childhood—a crabapple. Right outside their door. I can taste the tangy jelly already, although we'll need to convince the raccoons to abandon their snack bar.

"That's the least of our worries," says Cam from behind the back pillars. "It's built right beside the bog. This side is sinking. I'm ankle deep in mud."

"But it's old," I say, looking at the fractured railing — it matches the one on the bridge. "Why didn't it sink by now?"

"Yup, this thing is headed downward," says Bill. "It needs a total overhaul. And my guys need to get up there to take down that wisteria ASAP. If the roof is safe, that is."

"We need to restore this," I say to Cam. Before it sinks into the quicksand. "Or where will we have tea and crumpets on a summer afternoon?"

"Better be sooner than later," says Bill. He pokes a tree branch at the foundation under the surrounding balustrade, and stone and cement dust crumble to the ground. "The foundation's compromised."

"My wallet's compromised," Cam whispers to me. "Crumpets?"

"You may want to consider taking the whole thing down," Bill says. "This is a pretty inaccessible spot. And it needs so much work. It would be easier to rebuild it from scratch, except we can't get any material down those stairs." He looks down at his now muddy shoes with a wince.

"This is a historic structure. We can't change it. We need to restore it." I say.

"Are you saying you couldn't do it?" Cam asks.

"I can do anything," Bill says. "I'd need scaffolding and lots of trades. Roofer, masonry, carpentry . . . To rebuild most of it, under these conditions, will cost a fortune."

A fortune.

I sit on a broken step to digest the news. Cam slumps down beside me.

"We need to talk about all this," he says. "This is a five- to ten-year project." He looks dejected. His concern about the garden's potential as an endless pit is now a reality. Except the pit is more like a chasm.

· · ·

My parents never hired help, and wouldn't have, even if they could afford it. They did it *themselves*. Even at the age of twelve, I understood the simple division of labor between them. Mom was the gardener; Father was the builder-fixer. Sometimes they crossed into the other's territory, but only with permission, and they still argued. Mom grudgingly put Father in charge of tree grafting, because it was a natural extension of his carpentry skills. She tended to two apple trees in the yard, and thanks to Father's handiwork, each tree incorporated at least three large branches that produced different species of apples.

"Some for eating fresh," she explained to amazed visitors, "some for pies."

I liked to watch Father graft—he was a surgeon. He selected a sturdy main branch to accept a graft, chiseled a clean cleft, and cut the tip of the incoming new branch into a blunt edge. Then, holding open the cleft with his yellow-handled screwdriver, he inserted the new appendage and filled the open joint with shiny black tar to seal the wound. I wondered if the tree was pleased to adopt the new apples that were forced upon it. It looked painful.

One grafting season, I faced an epiphany: if trees are living wood, then the planks on the table saw are dead. The next time I helped Father cut some two-by-fours in the garage, I felt we were dismembering a dead body. I stopped enjoying the sweet smell of sawdust. It was the first time I realized that we didn't only eat from our trees—other uses required that we kill them. Given my tendency to anthropomorphism, this was probably the moment I became a tree-hugger.

Father loved apples, especially in Mom's pie. He stored them through the winter in a cold spot in his garage. This was the kind of collaboration that worked for my parents—it had to be mutually beneficial. From pies to sauce to oven-dried, Father ingested enough apples that the antioxidants should have kept him alive to eternity. Who knew they would lead to his death?

Apple-raisin yeast bread was one of Mom's signature dishes. On Saturday mornings, I watched the bread dough bubble and grow in the enormous baking bowl, the chipped white ceramic one with blue trim around the top edge. The fermenting yeast smelled foul and at the same time delicious as it grabbed the sides of the bowl like quicksand moving backward.

"How much flour?" I asked. Fine white powder rose from the bowl and tickled my nose as she tossed in cup after cup.

"It's always different. I *feel* it." Mom's gnarled gardener's hands kneading the smooth dough spellbound me. The raisins floated around unincorporated, unable to adapt to the slippery surface.

"Why don't the raisins mix in?"

"They'll mix in, in their own way."

She brushed dark yellow melted butter on the unbaked loaves that covered our cracked laminate counters and the kitchen table. Mom baked in bulk, freezing the extra. Time saved meant more time with her plants. Father's regular spot at the table was covered in loaf pans so he was relegated to a small corner for his coffee break. He'd sit as silent as the bubbles in the dough, forever sealed in their cage of flour and water.

To my surprise, our apples had a host of uses.

"What's this?" I asked Mom one day, lifting an old pink towel off a contraption hidden in the back of the basement on a shelf behind the furnace.

"It's to make alcohol. Don't tell anyone. It's illegal."

Illegal? My back stiffened. It had to be really illegal given the way the distiller was hidden. The stylish pot with a long thin tube became my Big Family Secret.

Until then, I hadn't even known fermented fruit created alcohol, and this was no humble cider. Fermented apples became juice, which was then boiled in a distilling pot. The alcohol vapors were collected and condensed to create a 50-proof spirit in another pot.

One more time through the distiller yielded 80-proof and it was ready for the sour cherries.

The liquor was hidden in the cold room in large unlabeled wine jugs, and Father sneaked down to get some when they entertained. Their friends, fellow Ukrainians from the church and the community center, became adopted family members brought together by their escape from Russian oppression. They drank appreciatively and quietly, as though the *Militsiya* were lurking outside, ready to pounce.

I watched from the stairs; it was like a foreign movie. I didn't understand the language well, but the faces were expressive and captivating as they shifted from sorrow to merriment. And Father actually sat with them and silently drank his rye.

Sometimes the women brought food, each one proud of her specialty. Mom made marinated beef and pork from our well-stocked freezer. After dinner, while one of the men played his accordion, they whirled around in wild polkas across the polished square wood tiles Father had installed. They celebrated occasional wedding anniversaries, although most of their marriages appeared to be the union of uprooted souls in troubled circumstances, making the best of things. And they sang. Songs in Ukrainian about the homeland. Whether or not they were, those songs all sounded sad to me.

🜲

"Watch out," I say, as Max races into the kitchen holding Benji. He runs a few circles around the table, Benji still in his arms, as if they are dancing.

"I'm taking Benji for a spin," he yells. "What's for dinner?" He sets the dog down on the floor and rubs his neck. They used to chase after each other, but since Benji can't run anymore, he gets carried. The dog looks a little dazed, but satisfied.

"Fish for us, steak for you, canned food for your friend." Benji looks up with distaste. He doesn't prefer his special prescribed diet from the vet, but he has digestive problems as well as arthritis. Myself, I don't eat much red meat thanks to our garage butcher shop.

Max grabs his brand-new iPod, a product of my capitulation during a poor parenting moment, and sits on the vacant lounge chair in front of the kitchen window beside his father. I wish I could have held out a few years, but his proficiency with electronics astounds me. *NDD, NDD,* I reprimand myself. Benji sits at his feet, ready for squirrel patrol. He manages the rodents from the window, whimpering whenever they get in his line of sight.

I sip my pinot grigio. "Bill's crazy. I need to get a few more opinions," I say to Cam.

"He's right about one thing. We need experts. We've already got a pond specialist, God help us," he says. "We need an arborist, carpenters, stoneworkers. Who's going to manage all these people?"

He's right. We could quit, just let the garden go. It's halfway gone, anyway. We knew it was a crazy idea from the beginning, and the house requires enough work to keep us busy.

"Yes!" Max says, as he scores another hit on his game. I look out the window at the pagoda in the distance, and think of Mom, stuck in her recliner.

"I'll manage them," I say quickly.

"You?"

"Me. I'll be the contractor. It's less expensive that way."

He looks at me suspiciously. "I'm giving you a budget," he says.

"Of course."

"Can you install a small swimming pool on the terrace while you're at it?" he asks.

"Not now," I say.

"Why not?"

"It's not part of the garden." The truth is, swimming pools were something the rich kids had when I was growing up. Along with shag carpets in sunken living rooms and mothers who smelled like expensive perfume. Pools made me uncomfortable for more reasons than being unable to swim.

"We're getting a pool?" Max asks, looking up from the screen. "When will it be done?"

"I think we need to finish the house first, and then move on to the garden," Cam says. "There's my library to do, the chimney repairs, and the unfinished stuff."

"We'll see," I say.

During dinner, we tell Max about the pagoda. He wants to see the raccoons first thing in the morning. New zoo members.

"They ate all the crabapples last year and made a mess on the floor," I say. "That'll have to stop." It occurs to me that raccoons also eat fish; I better let them have the crabapples. "Or you guys can plant some real apple trees for me, closer to the house," I add.

"Do you have your Mom's pie recipe?" Cam asks.

My shoulders sag. I haven't told him yet that Sonia called earlier to tell me that Mom had a bad fall and needed a few stitches on her scalp. Worse, she doesn't remember any of it. Her pie crust secrets have likely disappeared with her failing memory—not that I wanted them.

"Nonna's apple tree grows pears," Max interrupts. Indeed, Cam's parents have an apple tree and a few pear trees with varietal grafted branches. His childhood yard produced embarrassing smells, too—fermenting wine grapes and boiled tomatoes.

"Your mother would like an apple tree with different apples on each branch," Cam tells Max. "Maybe I should learn to graft. Can you find out how it's done?"

"Okay," says Max, always obliging if the task involves the computer.

They walk to the small desk tucked into the kitchen corner. Strangely, Max has never eaten an apple. Not fresh, not in a pie, not in a sauce or as juice. It's as though he's allergic to them. But a few minutes later they come back successful. A website shows them how to create a fruit salad in a tree, with different branches of apples and pears.

"Let Dad show you how to bookmark that website," I tell Max.

He sits back at the computer, which happens to be a Macintosh. At least *that's* an apple.

Benji lets out a sudden growl. We look out the window to see two huge black birds on one of the tree branches.

"Are those vultures?" Cam asks. "In the city? Wow."

"Awesome," says Max.

More pets in the yard. We've now adopted squirrels, raccoons, fish, ducks, a speedy hare, umpteen birds, including sinister vultures, and the dead fox's family, yet to be seen. I'm not sure if it's because he's an only child, but Max has embraced the entire wildlife family, and I suppose I have, too.

🦋

At nine years old, I was becoming an only child; our eleven-year spread seemed larger when Sonia was twenty. Saturday mornings were the limited time I spent with her, now that she was busy with her university friends. One Saturday, Father came into the living room after working the night shift. This was unusual, because normally he hung his coat, washed his hands, sat at the kitchen table, and ate his oatmeal. Instead, he loomed in the doorway, his hands hidden in the enormous patch pockets of his grease-spotted work coat. The odor of engine oil wafted around him.

Sonia and I had just turned on the television for Saturday morning cartoons. The glowing dot in the center of the television screen spread sideways as the electrons of the cathode ray tube performed their magic. We loved television programs, although we were limited to three Canadian stations in black and white: CBC English, CTV, and CBC French, which in Edmonton was promptly ignored as some frightening foreign invasion. A few American shows had infiltrated national broadcasting, and we were infatuated with their stars, starting with Ed Sullivan and culminating with Bugs Bunny.

Sonia sat on the nubby brown sofa; Mom was half asleep on the rocker, because she was also on night shift but had to do the weekend baking before she took a nap. I lay on the floor in front of the television set, leaning on my elbows, poised for escape into a fluorescent world of animated animals. Now we all looked up in surprise. Father was not there to say good morning, so what was he doing? And with his coat still on. Worry crossed Mom's face as she stared at him.

"What?" she asked, not rudely, not warmly. Something was wrong.

Father walked to an empty section of the sofa and pulled his right hand out from behind the flap of his jacket pocket. His blackened fingers held a tiny blonde puppy. He put it down on the sofa and silently left the room.

During the quiet shock that descended, I marveled at the tiny curled tail, the ears that flopped forward, barely the size of quarters, and the frightened brown eyes that resembled dark almonds against the fur. A puppy? We stared at it as if it had been dropped from a hovering spaceship. Was it real? Its fur begged to be smoothed as it radiated from a small, shiny, spotted snout. Then, without ceremony, the Martian puppy squatted, as much as a short-legged little thing like that could squat, and it peed. And peed and peed — so much for such a tiny bladder. The puddle spread, until puppy was in the middle of it, and then the pee seeped through the fabric and into the foam of the sofa, where it would undoubtedly smell forever.

It's the first and only time I heard Mom shriek.

"What is that?" she yelled toward the kitchen.

Sonia and I reached for the puppy, ready to protect the miracle that now lay upon the soggy sofa. We didn't stop to wonder where it came from, or to deal with the incredulity that Father had brought it home. We had a puppy despite the vicious fight that ensued in the kitchen. Apparently someone at Father's workshop had brought a box of unwanted puppies to the rail yard in order to get rid of them, and Father brought one home. He was a hoarder — we already knew that; so many peculiar things made their way into his garage and our house. But a dog? Mom wanted none of it. It would be messy, and she would have to feed it and clean up after it. Between work and the garden, there was no time for a puppy. For the first time in our lives, we were on Father's side. She yelled, and he said nothing, as he sat at the kitchen table and ate his oats.

Sonia and I had already named and washed the puppy before Mom finished her tirade. While Father went to sleep in the bedroom and Mom rinsed the dishes, Kaboobie, as my sister christened him, became our best friend. Kaboobie was a television cartoon character, a flying camel that carried two teenaged siblings through a fictional Arabia, and now, in his dog transformation, Kaboobie was about to transport me to a land of canine intimacy and devotion that would last a lifetime.

"Do you bark?" I asked the puppy. "Can you say hello?"

He gazed up at me, his eyes nervous. His nose wiggled at the aroma of cinnamon and baking apples.

"He's still scared," my sister said. "He'll bark when he's ready."

Kaboobie sighed and settled into my lap. I fell in love. I had an adopted brother and suddenly I felt less lonely.

....

CRABAPPLE JELLY

Equipment:
Large, deep stainless steel pan with a heavy base
Cheesecloth or a jelly bag for straining the pulp
Funnel
Preserving jars, sterilized
Water bath canner

Ingredients:
8 cups fresh crabapples
3 cups white sugar

- Wash the crabapples. Remove the stems and cut off the bottoms. Do not peel or core. Put the crabapples in the saucepan and just cover with water. Bring to a boil, reduce heat to medium, and let simmer for 10 to 15 minutes. The apples should soften. Strain the apples and liquid through 2 layers of cheesecloth, to obtain approximately 4 cups of juice.
- Discard pulp and pour the juice back into the pan. Simmer for 10 minutes, stirring occasionally. Skim off foam. Stir in the sugar until dissolved. Continue cooking at a low boil until the temperature reaches 220°F, or until jelly thickens on the back of a cold spoon. Remove from heat.
- Using the funnel, fill hot sterilized canning jars, leaving a ¼-inch headspace. Cover with prepared lids. Boil in water bath canner for 10 minutes. Store in a cool, dry place.

See page 267 for information on safety and sourcing of plants.

....

CHAPTER 6

 ❦

Maples

I'M DISCOURAGED AND DETERMINED, having come to accept these conflicting emotions.

The steps loom above me, no longer a romantic passage into a secret garden, but an excruciating outdoor StairMaster that is responsible for my burning thigh muscles, stiff calves, and the unusual tingling around my kneecaps. Max is almost eight years old now, and we're stuck on garden cleanup. Cam insisted, and he won the battle. The house came first, and we postponed a year of outdoor work. At least Cam's library is finished, the room of his dreams, with his hundreds of books finally out of boxes and settled in the floor-to-ceiling shelves.

The garden paths are still roughly clear, but the knotweed has resurfaced, the pagoda is still sinking, and I'm still tackling the weed cover. The steps are so ingrained into my muscle memory that their form pulses through my arteries as well as my nightmares. I could navigate them in the dark and avoid every crack and broken corner, and in my dreams, I do—up and down, up and down, shoulders hunched as I carry at least thirty-five pounds per trip. Yet the pile of debris must go somewhere, and I've amassed enough biodegradable waste bags at the top of the driveway, as required by the city's curbside waste program, that they are spilling onto the front of the neighbor's property.

Five feet away, the chainlink fence that divides our property from the neighbor's wild ravine undulates in the haze, beckoning me. Why not dump the waste over the fence? It's organic. Good for the trees. No one will care. Or know. I stiffly stand, take a deep breath, and slowly drag my heavy garden trug to the fence. One, two, three, and I hoist it over my head, pain shrieking up my arms and down the side of my back. From the top of the jagged fence top, I push the trug to empty the debris, only to watch it fall to the other side. Shit!

Too lazy to go up the steps, into the neighbor's property, and down their ravine, I push the wide toe of my rubber boot into a diagonal hole of the chainlink. It doesn't fit. It rests on the wire, barely in, as I hold on and jam in the other boot. I manage to get to the top and get one leg over, straddling the sharp top of the fence, with wire sticking into my pants in ways that are too close for comfort. I decide to swing the remaining leg over and jump. As I fall, one of the fence wires punctures a vein on my inner arm, about two inches below the ideal spot for taking blood samples.

Blood gushes like river rapids, soaking my garden glove, which is all I have to stop the flow. I envision bacteria swarming into my body as I bolt home through the neighbor's yard.

Rubbing alcohol and an hour of pressure stops the bleeding from what the Internet informs me is the antebrachial vein. I also learn how to identify sepsis, and decide, although I'm a likely candidate, I'll take my chances because I'm too tired to go to a medical clinic.

"You didn't think to get it checked out?" Cam asks when he examines the raw skin around the wound that evening. "You've probably got dirt in it. It's deep. And it'll be a nice scar."

I don't mind the scar. My physical body has unexpectedly meshed into this garden project as much as my emotions.

"I bled all over the place. Like blood meal fertilizer, but fresher."

"That's a bit gross, Alex."

"It's as if the garden and I are oath brothers," I say. "Exchanging dirt and blood."

"It's as if you were punished for dumping into the neighbor's property," Cam says.

"I'll be more careful," I assure him.

His eyes flicker with understanding. He's also learned that the grueling physical work brings us closer to the garden. It makes us feel we deserve its beauty.

A new day. While I give my sore back a rest, Chris, a friend's beloved arborist, will evaluate the trees and decide which need removal. She promised me he is reasonably priced, and that he won't be another contractor running away up the steps, so I'm hoping for a long-term relationship. There are dozens of trees in different stages of life or decay, and some are enormous and terrifying, with dead branches ready to fall on our heads.

I search for Cam and Max to join me. They are in the playroom, newly christened the "iLounge," where they spend way too much time on electronics. An oversized tool cabinet sits in one corner, full of Father's old tools. The rest of the room accommodates a twenty-seven-inch computer screen, a flat-screen television, and a new Xbox. There are wires everywhere that make up the circuits of a brain that Max already understands. The room freaks me out, but it's clear this will be their man-cave into Max's teenage years, and they don't want my opinion.

I try to distract them, but they're playing Max's latest obsession, the land-building game *Minecraft*. The rectangular digital trees and cubes of purple dirt called mycelium horrify me, and it's disconcerting that my son thinks plants can grow at night with fire-lit torches. All the more reason to get him into the real outdoors.

"Do you want to meet Chris?" I ask. I launch into my explanation of the Japanese concept of *Shinrin-yoku*.

"There's finding a language he'll get," says Cam, as he moves a cube of trees across the screen.

"It means forest bathing. Japanese scientists have been tracking its health benefits for more than twenty years."

"What?" Max looks up from the screen.

Cam stares at me blankly, brows furrowed.

"The chemicals from plants and the sun make you healthier and happier." Would it kill these two to open their minds?

"Okay, Mom, I'll come outside later. I promise."

"Forget it," I say.

Holy woodsman, what a handsome arborist!

Chris seems pleased to meet me, too, and is enraptured by the garden. His windburned face and earnestness disarm me. He knows a lot about trees, and I'm an eager student. He's about thirty years old, healthy-looking in a lumberjack kind of way.

"We've got some pruning to do here," he says. "Lots of decay, dead branches. Downright dangerous." He whistles a long low whistle. "Lookit there."

We trudge through the bushes, and he identifies one issue after another. His handsomeness is wearing off.

"Problem is, where will we put all the deadwood? My guys can't haul it up those steps. Some of these huge trunks are dead."

"Firewood." Cam startles me from behind. I guess he didn't want me to be alone in the garden with an attractive stranger. "Cam." He extends his hand to Chris.

"Chris. Treescapes, Inc. Nice to meet you. We've got some work here. I'll need my best team."

"He has a team, at least," I whisper to Cam.

"Is it expensive to take the dead trees down?" I ask, holding my breath.

"You're looking at some spending here. It's dangerous work; the guys climb on ropes and send the pieces down in sections. They're experts, but I need safety backup for them on jobs like this."

I exhale. Not good.

"We can start with the most dangerous areas first," he says, noticing my distress. "Why don't I scope out what needs to be done?" He wanders down the slope.

"What did we expect?" Cam asks. "It doesn't sound like this can wait, and the trees on the driveway are hanging over the house, too. Those will bring the roof down."

"Is that a redwood over there?" Chris yells back at us, seconds later.

We follow him down to examine the tree.

"Stunning," he says.

The three of us look up in awe, dwarfed by the green umbrella of branches.

Its lower limbs are dead and covered in vines, but the delicate needlelike leaves are intact higher up. It looms about seventy feet above us, although it's small compared to the giant ones I've seen on the West Coast in California and British Columbia. But here? It must stay warm enough near the pond during the winter.

"Not indigenous." Chris checks the redwood's trunk. "Someone planted it. Beautiful. And look at those Norways. Disaster. Those maples have been banned in most places. They should do that here." He shakes his head.

"Banned?" I asked.

"They're invasive. Kill other trees with their crazy roots. You've got a problem."

"You don't know the half of it," says Cam, staring at the delinquent maples.

I walk Chris back toward the steps with a heavy heart.

"Those old mulberries will need a good pruning," he says, pointing at enormous drooping branches. "And look at that Japanese maple," he adds. "It's magnificent."

"Of all these maples, Chris, do you see any sugar maples?" I ask hopefully.

He scans the trees. "No. They don't typically grow in urban areas."

I'm disappointed. The talk of maples reminded me of my first Québec *cabane à sucre* and of autumn in Montréal, where sugar ma-

ples with scarlet leaves brush the city with a red hue. Chris breaks
my reminiscences with a yell.

"Wait a minute! There are two big sugars right over there." He
points to two symmetrical trees on the Secret Path.

"Really, are you sure?"

"Let's take a look. I can't believe it." He clambers down the slope
and examines them.

"Yup, these are nice sugars." He runs his hand on the bark.

My heart beats quickly as I look up to the trees' canopy.

"How can you tell?" I can already taste the pancakes drowned in
syrup. Max will love this. Gordon's song "Love and Maple Syrup"
plays in my head.

"The bark. Look how the ridges form." Chris points at it like a
schoolteacher.

"I see." Not really.

After Chris leaves, I examine the bark of some oaks. It looks
pretty much the same to me.

"I want to read bark too," I lament to Cam.

"We live in downtown Toronto," he reminds me. "You'll have to
trust Chris."

That afternoon, Max and I search through Father's old tools for a
drill and a large bit strong enough to bore into trees. Our next step
is an online order: four aluminum buckets, lids, and spiles. One filter the size of a pasta pot.

"Cool," Max says as I fill our online shopping cart. We ask for a
rush delivery because ideal tapping weather is imminent. We also
order an assortment of bottles shaped like maple leaves, log cabins,
gingerbread men, and old-fashioned jugs.

Cam comes up behind us and surveys the screen. "What are you
guys doing?"

"Tapping for sap."

"Really, Alex, we have so many other things to worry about
right now," he says.

I can't answer in front of Max, but I'm furious. Doesn't Cam see that I've finally got Max involved? That I'm *present?*

❦

"Are you sure it won't burn?" I watched Sonia's hands as she pressed a brilliant yellow maple leaf between two pieces of waxed paper, the kind Mom used to wrap Father's ham sandwiches. In those moments, she was my teacher, surrogate mother, and role model. She was my hero who gave me a pair of rose-colored glasses that matched hers.

"Don't worry," she said as she guided the blue-handled iron. As the two sides of waxed paper melded to the leaf, the veins that ran through its five narrow sections appeared in relief.

"See, it looks like a hand with five fingers," she said as she held it up to the sunlight that streamed through the window. "And where the stem meets the leaf looks like the top of a heart. Now press it in one of your books and you can keep it forever."

And the maple leaf found its way into the latest Nancy Drew mystery. I had plenty of books in which to press leaves, because Sonia took me to the local public library on Sunday afternoons. I loved the basement children's room. The live petting zoo in the corner held a few baby chicks and a bunny that slept in the sawdust strewn on the floors of the wooden pen. "Remember, your limit is seven books," Sonia would remind me, and I always took out the full seven. Then we went upstairs to the gray metal stacks that made up the adult section, and Sonia wandered around in no discernible pattern. She picked up books here and there while I peeked through the lower stacks and spied on people. Sometimes I sat on the wheeled, rubber-topped footstool and rolled down the aisles, smelling the dust and musty paper as I whizzed by.

I learned later that the special yellow leaves we sought, with the silvery underside, were those of the Silver Maple, one of the few maple species that thrive in frigid zone 3. They favor the riverbanks of the North Saskatchewan River. I adored that bright shade of yellow, and later Sonia sewed a quilt for my bed in exactly that color. At night, snuggled under it, I dreamed of fields of golden leaves that protected the forest floor from the coming cold, like my quilt protected me as I read my books under it. Most maples have, in botanical terms, palmate leaves, but for my sister they were hands with fingers reaching from a heart. And that's what she was to me. Until I became a teenager, and she became an adult.

Puberty was a lonely place. Sonia was busy with university life, and Mom was in the garden. No one to give the dreaded sex talk or to explain menstruation and its delicacies. I was saved by information from the school brochure, and when I started, I was too embarrassed to ask for help or go to a pharmacy on my own, so I bought sanitary napkins from public restrooms with quarters I took from the "change jar." I think Mom thought I was buying candy with the diminishing coins, but she never asked. When the girls at school got training bras, whatever that meant, I was the only one whose mother didn't take her to get measured at the local department store. I became increasingly resentful and miserable at school, where I was alternately called Ukey and Flatsy. Nowhere to go but up, I decided I needed to change.

Change meant smoking and drinking with the so-called cool kids, even if they were the ones who called me "the accident." Next came bush parties on farmers' fields, where we lit illegal fires and drove home on dirt roads in the prairie dark.

By the end of high school, Megan and I had a gang of older friends who were regulars at the local nightclubs. In those days, age requirements were lower. Driver's learning permits were given at fourteen because someone had to drive the tractors at the farms, and bars were lenient, to say the least. Country music bars or discotheques were the flavor of the day, so we chose the more glamorous. It was the era of Farrah Fawcett, and we proudly took our winged hair out at least five nights a week.

About the same time, I decided to move my bedroom into the basement to facilitate sneaking in late. If Father had issues with my behavior, he screamed at Mom. If Mom had concerns, she talked to Sonia. No one talked to me, so I did what I wanted to.

The other issue of late-night returns involved negotiating Father's homemade trip alarms in an inebriated state. The alarms had gone up at the same time as the kitchen buzzer. Father was his own security company. Paranoid that someone would rob his garage of its tools, or steal the fur coat from the larder, he laid invisible wires here and there near windows, doors, and randomly in the yard. When tripped, they set off an alarm that sounded like a school fire bell. I became adept at jumping over these, as if I were a horse jumping random hurdles in the dark.

When new wave music hit the airwaves, I went for a radical change.

"What happened to your hair?" Megan asked me as I snuck into her basement bedroom. "It looks pretty scary."

"It's cool."

"It's purple."

"Yup."

"And a brush cut," she added.

"Father told Mom I had to get out of the house. Can I stay here?"

"Okay. But we can't let my parents see you."

"The bus driver wouldn't let me get on the bus," I said.

"The Number One?"

"Yeah. He said no punks allowed. I walked home."

"I guess it'll grow," she said, handing me a baseball cap. No way was I going to wear that thing.

I went home that evening because Mom called Megan's, assuming I was there.

"You're going out a lot," Sonia said the next evening as I slipped on my gray high-heeled boots.

"So?" I asked.

"You can't let your marks suffer if you want the scholarship," she said.

"Thanks, *Mom*," I said. The scholarship wasn't on my priority list. When had Sonia become a parent?

❧

"Are you sure we got it right, Mom?" Max asks during Sunday breakfast eggs.

Max and I waited only a week for our box of supplies and perfect tapping weather: warm days and cold nights. Max drilled the holes while I watched nervously, and now we obsessively check them every day. But the sap hasn't been running.

"Are you sure you didn't drill into the oaks by accident?" Cam asks.

I'm starting to question Chris's bark-reading ability. Maybe he's just a pretty face. Were they in fact sugar maples?

Max and I run down for the morning bucket check. They're full of water.

"How much water?" Cam asks. "It didn't rain that much. Don't they have lids?"

"There's a little hole in each lid," I explain.

"It's impossible," he says. "How did they fill up with rain? I think you got your sap." Does he look excited?

I run down the path. Three squirrels chew the base of the maples. *Shoo*, I say as I dip my finger in a bucket. It looks and tastes like rainwater. But according to my *Backyard Sugarin'* book, at this point the sap is only about 2 percent sugar. It's worth a try.

Max helps carry the gigantic canning pot to the outdoor burner of the barbecue. It's far too heavy for him, but he struggles with his side anyway. With a forty-to-one sap-to-syrup ratio, we should get about one cup.

It boils all day. And boils.

"It's rainwater," I insist to Cam. "I'm taking a nap. Max can keep an eye on it."

I wake up two hours later and the water is still boiling. It's reduced somewhat and turned yellowish, probably due to the dry oak leaf that now floats amid the bubbles. I turn off the barbecue and Max helps me move the liquid to a large pasta pot in the kitchen. I may as well finish evaporating the water, just in case. Meanwhile, I go back to my books.

An hour later, Cam yells from the kitchen, "Smells like something in here."

I run over from my desk. He's right; it smells like cotton candy.

I look into the pot. "Oh my gosh, it's syrup!" The liquid in the pan has reduced into a golden sticky solution.

Cam grabs a spoon and dips it in, gives it a taste. I hold my breath.

"Absolutely delicious," he declares. "Max, come up quick," he yells.

"The first sap is called the Robin's Run," I say, my voice cracking. "First sign of spring. It's the sweetest and mildest."

From that Robin's Run we get about six ounces of delectable syrup. I pledge to keep tapping and to put more syrup by for the year. It will be the first harvest from my garden. I look at my lonely jar on the counter, remembering Mom's larder. No comparison. Except that I did this with Max, and I realize we *must* finish the garden restoration if only to have more moments like these.

We have pancakes for dinner. Even Benji gets one, mixed into his food. I watch Max lick his fork, smacking his lips precisely the way I've told him not to. Today, I don't mind.

"Pretty good, huh, Dad," he says.

Bet they don't tap on *Minecraft*.

It's as good as a *cabane à sucre*. "Québec makes three-quarters of the world supply, you know," I lecture. I've been researching, and I share my discovery that squirrels will score the tree with their teeth to lick the leaking sap.

"Squirrels need food, too," Max says. "We should drill mini-holes for them."

It's as if he understands my soft spot for rodents.

🍂

"Put it down the hole with this," my foreman said one morning, handing me a large spoon with a three-foot-long handle and a yellow bucket of poison. I pushed my cropped burgundy hair off my face, the purple a distant memory.

"I'm *not* killing any gophers," I told him. Maybe university wasn't such a bad idea?

"You are," he said. "Can't have them burrowing around this place. A hole in a pipe around here will blow this place sky high."

After high school, Mom secured a summer job for me with the maintenance crew at the chemical company. I was the only summer student, and one of only two women. We were given the worst and dirtiest jobs in order to appease the full-time men. On the plus side, I did learn how to double-clutch a dump truck. My female counterpart used to smoke weed and drive the tractor in crazy circles to mow patterns onto the lawn. I collected stickers for my hard hat and got to keep my steel-toed boots, which came in handy with my punk rocker look.

But I was not going to kill innocent gophers. I found a place on a ravine pitch near the factory and disposed of all the poison, and then wandered around for the rest of the day with my spoon and empty bucket, pretending to look for holes.

Through the gossip in the lunchroom, I heard from Mom's friends how disappointed she was that I didn't win the scholarship. She was hoping to show off another genius daughter. I resented her embarrassment; it stiffened my resolve not to try to live up to Sonia's perfection, and being indignant was easier than admitting I could have worked harder.

The $2,500 I earned that summer went straight into the purchase of a used burgundy Triumph Spitfire. It was a lemon. Father was furious and yelled at Mom constantly about the car. He never said a word to me, but I would frequently pass his legs on the driveway, the only part of him visible as he lay under my car, trying to fix its many problems. I didn't know what they were, but it had them. Maybe he was happy to have that lemon to fix because it was an insurmountable challenge. His intervention allowed Megan and me to cruise around for a year, a trail of burning smoke behind us, thinking we were hip, until one day the engine seized up for good. We were back on the Number One.

Father's car wasn't an alternative.

He used his salary from the railroad, much to Mom's fury, to buy an enormous gold Oldsmobile. "We could have bought a *house* with that money!" Mom had yelled, but he didn't care. They had separate bank accounts, and it was his money. He covered the seats in thick uncomfortable plastic that smelled in the summer heat, and took the car out once a week on Sundays. He never opened the windows, nor were we allowed to, as if keeping it hermetically sealed would make it last longer. Sonia and I never thought to drive it — we called it "the boat."

Although it was new, he tinkered with it incessantly. Once, I found a yellow envelope of photographs of close-ups of parts of the car. The doors, the interior, the exterior. The engine, the trunk, the bumpers, the dashboard. I screwed up the courage to ask Mom about them.

"Your father thinks that if he ever takes the car to the dealer, they are going to switch out his new parts for older ones. This is his proof," she said.

That's why I didn't ask questions. When I got answers, I usually wished I hadn't. I vowed never, ever to drive that car, under any circumstances.

Mom found me in my room. "Can you go pick up your father? You'll have to take his car."

"What? Where is he?" His car? No way in hell.

"At Marko's. They've had too much to drink."

Marko was Father's only friend, as far as I knew. He often walked over to our house, about a mile, and he and Father would sit in the garage and drink. I used to wonder if they talked. They had some mysterious history that bonded them enough that they drowned their sorrows together. Then Marko would stumble home.

I was terrified to pick Father up. Would he get into the car? I shook all the way there, unable to judge distance, too scared to adjust the long front seat or the mirrors. The plastic crinkled under my legs and the click of the turn signal was as loud as a hammer. I rolled up to the small house, its width about the same as the length of the car.

They were in the yard when I arrived. Two empty bottles of rye sat on a small table.

"Let's go home," I said to Father. Marko slurred some words. Father didn't look up, but tried to stand. He couldn't get out of the rickety wooden chair. That's when I realized that I would have to actually touch him. Had we ever physically touched? I couldn't remember. When I was a baby? Maybe our fingers had brushed once when I handed him a tool in the garage? It was bad enough I drove his car. Fear and responsibility overwhelmed me. *Pretend he's a stranger*, I told myself, to make it easier. *He won't remember anyway*. I walked over, took a deep breath, took his arm, and pulled him out of the chair. The fabric of his checkered work shirt was damp and he reeked of cigarette smoke and alcohol. I held his arm up to the car and eased him in.

I drove in silence, my hands in perfect position on the large wooden steering wheel, while he stayed inside his abyss. The twelve blocks ended quickly, and I helped him into the house and onto the floral couch, where he laid his head on the flat brown-velvet pillow. He didn't shut his eyes: they stayed open in a vacant stare. Mom didn't look up from the sizzling frying pan in the kitchen, nor did she say anything. I wanted to ask about Marko but didn't have the courage. For the rest of the summer, Marko came to our house and Father didn't go there, and I crawled back into my disillusionment, wanting to escape the factory and the family.

I decided to go to university. My first year as an English major delighted me, as books became my lifeline. Mom was disappointed, again, assuming literature studies wouldn't pay future bills, but at least I was in university. Unfortunately, not for long.

....

MOMIJI TEMPURA

In Japan, this treat celebrates the harvest. The leaves are usually preserved in salt for a year prior to use, but botanist James Wong suggests brushing with maple syrup as a delicious alternative.

Ingredients:
1 cup tempura flour (available at Asian supermarkets)
½ cup ice water
Fresh untreated red Japanese maple leaves
Maple syrup
Vegetable oil for deep-frying
White sesame seeds

- Clean maple leaves thoroughly with a wet towel. Using pastry brush, brush with a thin layer of maple syrup.
- Preheat vegetable oil to 350°F in a pan suitable for deep-frying. Oil has reached the right temperature when a small drop of batter sizzles and floats.
- Add ice-cold water to flour, stirring gently. Do not overmix; batter will be slightly lumpy.
- Lightly dip leaves in batter and fry immediately until golden brown. Drain on rack and sprinkle with white sesame seeds while hot.

See page 267 for information on safety and sourcing of plants.

....

CHAPTER 7

❧

Periwinkle

"WHAT THE HELL are you doing? Get out of there before the roof falls on you." Cam comes up from behind me in the pagoda as I am adjusting the battery-operated radio to 680 NEWS. I've done my research. Apparently, raccoons hate talk radio. Who doesn't? They also don't like light. The old CN flashlight, balanced between two rocks, points upward. Father would be proud.

"I'm encouraging the raccoons to move out," I say.

"Have you gone mad? Where do you expect them to go?"

"Don't know." You'd think he would appreciate my ingenuity.

"This is your priority in this whole mess?" he asks, waving his arms to encompass the garden.

"I'm waiting for my next landscaper interview."

"Well, come see what I found," he says.

The gate is at the bottom of the property, behind the footbridge. Beyond it is an unused tract of city land and a busy street. Equally exciting is the periwinkle that grows at its base. My mother-in-law Rosa calls it *centocchio* in Italian. *One hundred eyes*, because that's what the abundance of blue flowers look like when they twinkle in the sun.

"It's not even locked," I say. "This is how all this construction material got in."

"Across the city land," adds Cam. "I'm surprised that was allowed."

"They must have applied for a permit. At least we have a route to clear out all the junk." This is a good find. A doorway out of our mess.

Joe from Joe's Landscaping is speaking to me when the bird shits on my head.

"That's good luck," he says.

"Please continue, Joe." I pretend not to notice the warmth dripping down my scalp.

"You've got a lot of crap down here," he says, looking at the piles of debris.

"A lot," I agree, wiping my hair with a tissue from my gardening vest's pocket.

"Bylaws say we can't cross parkland. For any reason. Those alone—" he points at the broken palettes "—are several truckloads. No way that shit is goin' up the steps."

Joe could use the exercise. His belly, encased in a tight green T-shirt, protrudes over his jeans like an enormous peony bud.

"What do we do, Joe?" I ask. "It got in here somehow."

"Probably at night," he says.

"Excuse me?"

"I'll have to let the guys work through several nights. Weekends only, when the city inspectors aren't around."

"You're kidding, right?" I ask.

"I'll have to charge you extra, for night shift. And the risk I'm taking. We're gonna have to park our small trucks in the park."

"We're not doing anything at night. I'm not interested in breaking the law."

"No other way I can see doin' it," he says, scratching his chin.

"Let me talk to my husband and call you," I say.

I follow him up the steps and watch his truck speed away. Another one down.

"I've got my last landscaper coming by tomorrow, with a landscape architect. These guys are supposedly the best in town," I tell Cam after dinner. "I can't take another Joe."

"So they're expensive."

"Maybe. But you get what you pay for. This is too important for amateurs."

"Agreed," he says. Wow, and the bird didn't even shit on his head.

Before I can reply, the phone rings. It's Sonia, distressed. Mom's residence manager requested a meeting. Mom has been falling more, and her instability is beyond unacceptable. To make matters worse, her memory loss is increasing. Her doctor explained that it's the beginning of dementia.

"They're going to move up her care level at the apartment to the maximum," Sonia explains, "although because it's only assisted living, she'll need to leave if she gets worse."

Dementia. The word rolls around in my head, twisting around neural pathways that carry fear, guilt, and sorrow. We saw her increasing forgetfulness. No cure, a slow decline of her mind. Dementia. It's a death sentence for a woman who never stopped learning.

❦

"I'm sixty," Mom said. "Is it too late to learn?"

"No." I tried to sound convincing. "You can buy yourself a small car." Terrifying, but it had to happen.

"Your father will say no."

"We won't tell him," I said. "It's not his decision."

"That's true," she agreed, and I began her secret driving lessons.

She was a good driver when she was the only one on the road. Unfortunately, she didn't recognize the presence of other vehicles, and unwittingly left chaos and frustrated drivers in her dust. She failed the driving test over and over, and I insisted on more practice and another try.

"Hello, Stefanie, today's going to be the day!" said Tom, the clerk at the Motor Vehicles branch, when we arrived for her third time. He settled on her first name after she gave him apples from her garden.

"Hope so," Mom said, and headed off with the evaluator.

Ten minutes later we watched from the office window as she parked.

"Not this time," I said to the clerk.

"Don't think so," he agreed, as she hit the pylon.

A month later, after the fifth test attempt, she rushed into the office with a grin.

"You did it," I said, trying to hide my relief.

"We'll miss you, Stefanie," Tom said, and hugged her.

I took her to a nearby pub to celebrate, and we shared a gin and tonic. We rarely went out together, let alone to a bar, but it was an unconventional day. And I learned something about her that afternoon. Mom was not only a resilient lily of the valley; she was a heroic vinca, from Latin *vincere,* meaning to conquer. "It's never too late to learn something new," she said to me, admiring her picture on the license card. Words I'll respect for the rest of my life.

Mom told Father, and of course he was furious, but she bought herself a green (her favorite color) four-door Oldsmobile (Father's input) and drove it anyway. She bought me a string of pearls as a thank-you present.

"You've given me independence," she said, as I examined the traditional necklace. Far too sophisticated for the likes of me, but she was living her dream, and I had no right to be anything but grateful.

She loved her car, and it became the Ukrainian shuttle bus for all the non-driving women. Mom drove it at regular intervals between the church and the community center. The car became her life, representing freedom from everything that tied her down—the war years, her factory job, and her silent husband—so I shut my eyes to the regular fender benders. She was so thankful that she offered more gifts.

"I'm going to buy you some china," she told me.

"What for?" I wasn't interest in dishes. I still hadn't worn the pearls.

"Every woman needs to have a china set," she said. This coming from an immigrant factory worker. "I can afford to buy you the best now. Twelve place settings." Her wages were high in blue-collar terms.

"I'll never cook for twelve," I said. Where was this mother when I needed a training bra?

"You need extra in case it breaks," she said. A short drive in her new car, and we were scrutinizing plate patterns.

"I guess blue is nice. It looks like *barvinok*," I said to her, and with that three-second decision, I ended up with twelve place settings and a gravy bowl and coffee pot. *Barvinok* is the Slavic name for common periwinkle, which grew in abundance in her garden. The china came finely wrapped in hordes of boxes, was incredibly expensive, and intimidated the hell out of me. It was some strange coming-of-age ceremony that I did not understand. Was it a dowry? The last thing on my mind was marriage.

"Maybe you can sell it someday if you need money." The china also mystified Mandy, my new friend in the architecture program. After one year in university, Chaucer's Middle English sent me running to the local technology institute. My new plan: design buildings. I had discovered Frank Lloyd Wright.

"How can you leave the university after one year?" Mom was devastated, still upset about the scholarship, and that I'd stepped down to an inferior institution of learning.

Father yelled at her about my decision that evening, but a few weeks later I caught him looking at my drafting table. I was surprised by his curiosity, although I knew his interest wasn't in me but in the beauty and balance of the mechanical arm.

I became a naive Ayn Rand admirer, like most of the architecture students. After reading and superficially memorizing *The Fountainhead*, I followed my selfish soul in the pursuit of true design. I embraced Rand's realism. It appealed to my scientific side. Man is hero; his happiness is the moral purpose of his life. Sounded logical to me.

That June, the only summer job I found was one drafting plans for government liquor stores. The design was consistently rectangular except for the changing square footage based on the neighborhood demand for spirits and beer. The parking lot was always on the same side, near the checkouts. Rand's objectivism was on hold for a few months.

After two years of architecture, Rand was a distant memory. I noticed the work of students in urban planning. Their models of city plans and landscaping were fascinating, as opposed to the building plumbing and electrical systems that I had designed for the past two years.

"What is urban planning?" Mom asked when I announced the change. Her voice sounded normal although she dropped a mug into the sink when I told her.

"Designing cities, neighborhoods. Parks."

"What about architecture?" She checked the Pyrex mug for cracks.

"This," I assured her, "is a perfect combination. I will be a landscape architect."

❧

Lisa is a well-respected landscape architect, and my last lead.

"Forget about the garden; frankly, your entire house is off-side. It shouldn't be built beyond the slope of the land," she says. We stand on the terrace, peering over the sun-dappled forest.

"But it's been here since the sixties," I say. Lisa has brought along Ben, from Ben's Landscaping and Design. He has the most immaculate navy blue truck I've ever seen.

"Yes, it's been grandfathered. But you certainly couldn't build it here today. And you'll never get permission to make additions or major changes. You're in the ravine, and shouldn't be." Lisa is unequivocal. "And no pool." She looks at Cam.

"You guys been clearing this yourselves?" she adds, looking down the slope with awe. "Pretty big job."

Cam nods.

"Ibuprofen and determination, mostly," I say. And it occurs to me that somewhere in between the dead shrubs and struggling peonies, it's become more than about saving money. Whatever we can master alone, we will, because that's what happens when love and challenge cross paths.

"But we know we still need some professional help," I add.

Ben isn't encouraging. "You can't haul construction materials through the city park below. It's a protected wetland, adjacent to a bird sanctuary. You'll be heavily fined, shut down, and who knows what else. And any new plants we add must be indigenous materials only—"

"We're okay with that," Cam interjects. "We want to restore the garden to its original beauty; we're not interested in being destructive or off-side."

"But there's a historic garden under here," I say. "We've seen the signs—a few surviving lilacs and peonies. A magnolia."

"Well, we don't need to take out something that's here. In fact, we can't remove large trees unless they're dead, and only then with approval. Lucky you haven't touched any trees."

"Has the Conservation Authority been here yet?" Lisa asks as she appreciates the view.

"No," I say. *Who?*

"Doesn't matter. If they were here, we know what they would say," she says.

They both look at me, waiting for comments. I have nothing left.

"You can't do much here," Ben says. "Although, I see your point. It was a developed garden. It's an unusual circumstance."

"All that construction debris needs to be brought up to the top by hand. The cement in buckets. How many steps up?"

"Eighty-one," I say. "I know each step personally."

"My guys won't do it," Ben says. "They're too expensive to be hauling debris."

"I know the City," Lisa says. "I have a relationship with them. I can't compromise that, I'm sorry."

"Not sure we've been much help. It's an unfortunate situation," Ben says as he tackles the steps. "You won't get approval for much here," he adds over his shoulder. "But, good luck."

I take a break from the garden that afternoon. I convinced Lisa to think about possible options, but I'm not hopeful. Cam decides to do some pruning, and I decide to spend some time with Max.

"Do you want to go bike riding?" I ask Max as I sip my Earl Grey, with extra milk today. He is perched on a kitchen chair with his iPod in his hands.

"Nope, I'm on a mission," he says.

I look over his shoulder to see aliens shooting each other.

"Are you playing a violent game where people kill each other?" I ask.

"They're simulations, Mom. I'm hunting robots, not humans. No blood."

A rush of anger overtakes me. I can't control my son, the garden, or Mom's dementia.

"That's it," I say. I stand, walk to his chair, and wrench the iPod out of his hand. The kitchen window is handy. I open it and throw the iPod down two stories to the stone steps, where it lands, smashes, and its pieces spread into the garden like shattered glass.

I turn away from the window to see Max's eyes wide with shock, and then with realization. And then pain, as his cheeks flush and his eyelids squeeze shut over the escaping tears. He leaps out of his chair and runs to his room, slamming the door behind him. His muffled sobs flow through the hallway in a low fog of sorrow.

I turn back to stare out the window. *What did I do?* The vision of Max's wretched face floats in front of me. *What's wrong with me?* My mother never broke anything in a fit of anger, even in the most vicious of arguments with my father. I'm supposed to be a *better* mother. I can't tell Cam. He mustn't know, until those pieces of motherboard genetically mutate with the periwinkle and make iPlants that will strangle me in my Little Garden of Horrors.

My guilt compels me to check on Max, to muster an apology, to overcome my embarrassment, when I pass Benji in the hall, sleeping on his side.

"Come on, buddy, let's go see your brother," I say to the dog.

Benji lifts his head to look at me, but his body doesn't follow.

"Buddy?" I lean down to pet him. He's hot and his fur feels damp. My heart races. "Benji? Cam!" I need to find Cam.

"Cam!" I yell out the window. "Cam!"

Cam races inside, not noticing the iPod fragments on the steps.

"We need to take him in right away," he says, petting Benji's forehead with love in his fingers and fear in his eyes. We leave Max with the neighbors, telling him Benji is sick. His sadness takes on another layer of grief as he pets his puppy goodbye.

I clutch Benji's tattered chew toy as we lift him into the car. I hug him on my lap, searching his eyes for reassurance, but he's practically unconscious.

Cam can't speak. Benji is his first pet. The emergency vet wants to keep him overnight. He's found a suspicious lump so he'll start some blood work, and will transfer him to our regular vet in the morning. I can't bear to leave him, but at least he'll be monitored this way.

"Don't let him have pain," I beg, feeling helpless.

🖎

The situation seemed hopeless. I didn't find work after getting my diploma in urban planning and I was a wayward twenty-something with nothing to do. A global recession created high unemployment, and no building or planning was going to happen for the foreseeable future. No one had taught me that I would be vulnerable to economic cycles. I thought education equaled employment.

"I think I should learn French. Another language is useful," I told Mom. "And maybe I should study business. I'll always be able to get a good job." My creativity had shifted to practicality.

"Will you live at home?" Mom was hopeful.

"I'm thinking Montréal," I told her. "I'll study business in French
—how hard could that be?"

Father was not pleased, although who knew why. Sonia thought
I should study and live at home like she had. Mom gave up, overwhelmed by a daughter she didn't know and couldn't figure out. I
was overcome by a need to reinvent myself into something better
than I was, and all I knew for sure was that this had to happen far
away from anything I knew.

Luckily, I wasn't seeking approval, since I had none.

Within a few months, I was ready to leave. I didn't want anyone at
the airport, and this offended the family. I was the one leaving, so I
insisted we say goodbye at home, which is why we were assembled
at the kitchen table. Easier for all of us, I decided. Quick and un-
complicated on familiar ground. Father sat in his usual spot, silently
staring into his coffee cup. Sonia sat across from him, arms crossed.
I traced a pattern on the crocheted tablecloth with my index finger, sticking it through larger holes and moving around the breadcrumbs trapped underneath. I decided that a tablecloth with holes
defeats the purpose. The smell of fried fat hung over us because it
was a rare day that Mom didn't fry something in lard.

"Your father made you something," Mom said.

"Me?" I asked. Made me something? I squished a crumb.

"Yes, it's over there." She said it gently, which was unusual when
she communicated on his behalf.

A large red toolbox, about a foot high and two feet across, sat on
the adjacent living room carpet.

My throat constricted, tighter and tighter. Impossible.

"For me?" I asked Mom. My father still looked down. I wished
he would look up, look me in the eye just once. *Say "Yes, I did,"* I
willed. Nothing.

"You might need it out there on your own," she said. "Although
it's pretty heavy."

I peered at Sonia's face for something. Nothing there either. She looked down, too.

I stood, walked to the box, and touched the rough metal. I knew right away he'd welded the pieces together himself, because the seams were perfect. I recognized the red rust primer paint; he used it on most of his ironwork—our rain barrel, Mom's plant stands, and the fence. Sometimes he added a black shiny finish coat, like on the fence, and sometimes he didn't.

I imagined him in the garage with sparks flying around his enormous welder's helmet. He had never made me anything. Hardly spoken to me, and now I was getting a fucking toolkit.

As I opened the lid, the smell of tar and iron and oil filled my nostrils. It was the fragrance of his garage, bottled in a metal case. An assortment of used tools filled the kit, collected from the railroad shop and the neighbors' garbage cans. The black rubber flashlight with the CN logo was there. I shut the lid, locking in the perfume of his solitary life.

"Thanks," I said, looking up and over to the table. *Look at me,* I willed. And then he did. He raised his head slowly, and his eyes, grayish green, met mine squarely for the first time in our lives. Then he looked down again. What a remarkable color. The rest of us were born with such dull brown, boring eyes that my sister called them hazel to make them more appealing.

My father made me a toolkit.

Sonia uncrossed her arms and rummaged through her handbag. She withdrew a small conical figurine made of straw, and handed it to me. An angel with delicate wings. A tiny piece of paper was attached to it with a miniature pearl string. It said, "Sisters are special angels who always carry a spare set of wings in their pockets."

An angel? My sister shunned religion as much as I did. An angel, even a symbolic one, made no sense coming from her. She was Einstein. Who was the angel? We both knew it wasn't me; it must be her.

"Thanks," I said. I wasn't sure if I could handle any more. Everyone was acting out of character.

She said nothing. She slumped into the same position as Father, two bookends across the table. An epiphany then: she *is* Father. Her hands, her talents. Her studying to be a dentist, her soldering jewelry and stained glass windows as hobbies, the sewing, the crocheting. All the Barbie clothes she made for my dolls. That's why she never discussed anything personal with me. Instead, she made me things with her graceful hands. She is Father. The realization hit me like one of his hammers.

"Are you okay?" Mom asked. "I have something for you in the bedroom."

I couldn't wait to leave the room. To leave the two soul mates who faced each other, but had never really met.

Mom handed me an envelope. "It's from me. And your father. You'll need some money to get started."

"Thanks," I said. Guilt, heavy guilt, weighed me down and made me feel every inch a failed daughter. "I know you guys are disappointed in me. That I'm leaving."

"I left my family younger than you," Mom said. "It was the war, and I survived. You'll be fine."

What? Was I getting her blessing?

"Always use what's between your ears," she continued. "It's only dirty paper in that envelope. That's what money was during the war. It was dirty paper lying in the streets. Study hard. That's worth something."

The envelope suddenly *did* feel dirty in my hands. I needed to be alone somewhere to think. Mom was giving me advice? It was the toolkit all over again. I was speechless.

"I've always wanted to travel, to see some of the world. You and me are alike that way," she said. "We take risks." Now? *Now* this personal revelation?

"And your sister is like your father—that's how you two turned out," she said. She knew. She knew all along. I suddenly understood that I was her adventurous sentimental favorite despite my short-comings. I felt sick.

"I think I'll take a last walk in the ravine," I said, and I raced out the back door, the screen slamming behind me. I didn't see Mom's garden, the garage, or the rain barrel through my streaming tears, as I ran into the trees.

❧

I rest my tea mug on the step near the fading old magnolia. I want to be alone to think about my mother and my dog. The setting sun creates shadows in the forest, blurring the beauty into a dark fog of shapes. It will be harder for Mom to see this garden now. The garden of a lifetime, of a dream, and the woman who would have understood its essence might never see it, and if she does, will she recognize her plants? And Benji will likely never run through it.

Poor Benji. He was a filthy, untrained ragamuffin when I picked him up at the Montréal SPCA so many years ago. He listened to me during walks and he curled into me when we slept.

"A dog?" Mom had said when I told her I had adopted him. "Why? Don't you think it's time you thought about getting married and having children?"

Which part of her unhappy marriage did she think I missed? And what would I do with children? I didn't even know how to hold a baby. She told me to study and get a good job, so I did. I didn't want a family, because I didn't know what I was missing, but I sure as hell knew what I was avoiding. Somehow the gods sent me Cam and Max anyway.

I take a last look at the rustling treetops, pick up my teacup, and head up the garden steps.

PERIWINKLE SKIN OINTMENT

Please note:

Do not eat. *Vinca major* is considered poisonous when in-gested. Always test a small patch of skin for any adverse reactions before using any herbal treatment.

Ingredients:

¾ cup fresh periwinkle leaves (*Vinca major*) and flowers
1 cup almond oil
1½ tablespoons beeswax

- Clean the leaves and flowers, ensuring they are free of dirt, in-sects, and mold. Rinse with cool water and let dry.
- Place leaves and flowers in a double boiler with the oil and warm on medium heat for about 20 minutes, without boiling.
- Strain out the leaves and transfer oil back to top of boiler. Add beeswax and heat until the wax has melted.
- Transfer to a sterilized jar and let cool. Store in the refrigerator.

See page 267 for information on safety and sourcing of plants.

CHAPTER 8

Primroses

BENJI HAS CANCER.

In my cozy bedroom chair with the best view in the house, I'm broken. My friends without pets don't understand why I feel like I'm losing an appendage, while the dog owners are keeping their distance, taking slightly longer walks with their pups, and giving them extra pats lest it happen to them. The morning sky is red: sailor's warning. Dark gray clouds are sliced by uneven striations, as if someone brushed them with a rose petal. My trees are dark silhouettes; the calming green I crave is still invisible at dawn. I clutch my warm teacup for comfort and try to plan my Saturday.

Benji, in his basket now moved beside my bedroom chair, shares my perch, listening to the squirrels rustling through the leaves, since he can no longer walk. Our vet recommended euthanasia. We took him to the university teaching hospital for a second opinion. The two-hour drive to the country town was short for a dog who journeyed many miles with me over more than fifteen years, through cities, heartbreak, marriage, and childbirth, without a whimper of protest. Now he lies on his side, suffering quietly. Take a few days to say goodbye, the second vet said; his time has come.

It hasn't, I tell myself. But my heart knows different.

"I can't kill my dog," I tell Cam. "He'll go naturally."

"You do know it's the humane thing to do," he says. "The right thing."

I press my left arm into my chest to stop the pain.

"That's what *they* say." I won't do it. Never.

Now we are barely speaking to each other. Cam is in his library, nursing his own broken heart, underlining passages in his latest book and turning his emotions into scribbled notes in the margins. I leave my chair to kneel on the floor near Benji. It's not close enough so I curl myself into his small basket, putting his front legs around my neck. His shallow breath crosses my face, drying my tears. Better.

No word from Lisa and Ben this week, which has made me surer than ever that they are the experts I want. I think they're playing hard to get, and it's working. Cam suggested perhaps they're simply busy. I suppose they need to think about it. It's a difficult job because of the ravine slope. No large equipment will fit down the narrow staircase along the side of the house or the neighbor's equally steep lot. There are the city ravine bylaws to work around. And after all that, it's not even a showcase garden for them—who will see it back here? I get their point. Not much upside. Maybe they'll be motivated by the challenge? They don't seem to need the business. Although, maybe Ben's truck is *too* nice, like a too-clean desk. Einstein said an empty desk means an empty mind.

Maybe I should fire Lisa and Ben.

Meanwhile, I'm stuck waiting in a tailspin of things I can't control. So while they decide, I will *do*. The first step will be to remove the construction debris in the garden. Nothing like a tidy outside world to hide a messy inside one.

The dumpster arrives in the afternoon. Or should I say "rust bucket."

"You ordered the cheapest one you could find, didn't you?" asks Cam, surveying the corroded steel.

"It's going to hold cement and junk," I say. But now that he's mentioned it, is that a hole near the bottom? Imagine the garbage this dumpster has seen. It has *experience*. I pat it like a new car.

"So where are your rugby players?" He sounds jealous.

"They're coming next week." Cam kicks the bin's corner and rust flakes fall to the ground. He heads back into the house without a word.

Stephan, the owner of our alarm service, provided a remarkably simple solution to clear the garden junk: his son's university rugby team friends are home for the summer and looking for work. I trust Stephan, a tall, broad-shouldered man who speaks with quiet confidence.

"They're not doing anything," he explained. "They'll haul that stuff up to get some exercise and a few cases of beer."

"Beer?"

"Yeah. You want me to send them by?"

"Well, maybe they should look at it first?" I asked.

"You get yourself one of those big bins and park it in the front. They'll fill it in no time."

"Can I give them cash?"

"Okay, they'll just go buy the beer themselves," he laughed.

Today, the bin looks too small as well as decrepit. The construction junk will fill it ten times at least. It's all that would fit down the driveway so I'll have to get it picked up and redelivered. Cam's relieved the neighbors can't see it — he's a private guy who feels a family's dirty laundry, or dirty dumpster, should never be aired in public. I don't much care. Rebuilding is a messy business, whether it's a garden or a broken heart, and everybody knows it.

I head down the steps to examine the pile of debris, and to formulate a plan for the boys. On the thirtieth step down, I pray for an entire team. They will be army ants attacking Kilimanjaro. How much concrete can a guy carry, even if he has rugby shoulders? This is, perhaps, a dumb idea.

I follow the rear city fence toward the pond, where a clump of towering pines smell like Christmas, when I spot the mass of chartreuse cabbagelike leaves. Fluorescent circles, large and small, spread outward like raindrops on a lake, lighting up the shade under the overgrowth.

A rush of air enters my lungs. Primroses!

The weeds are dense here, and there's no sign of a path—no wonder we missed them. But they'll be striking when we clear the overgrowth. Mom's had bright yellow flowers, and leaves similar to these, but they were tiny. She loved them, probably because their first spring bloom was an escape from the ugly rubber houseplants. I edge closer. No, these are not Mom's primroses. Long stems tower from the center of the leaves, some three feet high, holding dried clumps of burgundy flowers sequentially, like spindly topiaries. They dominate the three-foot-wide space between the city fence and the back of the pond.

I clap my hands together like a child. We have Shakespeare's primrose path!

I run up the stairs two at a time and into my den, wishing I could tell someone. It's there, between *Clematis* and *The Practical Encyclopedia of Orchids*: a hefty book call *Primula*. The cover, graced with pink flowers, fills me with hope that ours will look this way in the spring. I learn that we have candelabra primroses that love cool, shaded bogs. I run my fingers over the pages, savoring the intricate blooms, even though they're two-dimensional. Mom will be thrilled when I tell her. Then I come to my senses. It's unlikely she remembers her primroses.

Cam walks in, carrying Benji in his arms. The pup looks peaceful, although his eyes are red and listless.

"We have a primrose path," I announce. Finally. I said it out loud.

"Huh? I thought you were working on a garbage strategy." Honestly, who uses the words *garbage* and *strategy* in the same sentence?

"Shakespeare," I explain patiently. "He mentions it in *Hamlet* and *Macbeth*. To follow the primrose path was to follow a tempting road to self-destruction."

"We didn't read Shakespeare on our side of the tracks," Cam says.

"Hi." Max walks in and immediately cradles Benji's head in his hands.

"Let's take him for a walk. I want to show you guys something," I say. "Max, you can carry Benji."

The boys follow me outside and down the steps, with Max hugging the dog to his chest.

"Here it is," I say. Cam's expression is impatient, probably because the flowers are not in colorful bloom.

"These flowers have a lesson, Max. To walk on a primrose path means to take the easy way out. Or it can mean that sometimes things aren't what they seem."

"Do we have to eat the leaves?" Max asks. Cam looks up in fear.

"Maybe. They taste like lettuce."

"Again, Mom? The garlic mustard leaves you made us eat were *awful*. And I hate lettuce."

"I'm out," says Cam.

"Primrose flowers have five petals," I say, determined, showing Max a dry flower. "They represent the passages of life: birth, youth, family, rest, and death."

A long journey in the short-lived petals. I look down into Benji's clouded eyes. *I'm ready,* they tell me. The petals are spent. Time to let go.

I pick a few stems that still have some open flowers. I'm ready too.

"I'll make the appointment for Monday," I whisper to Cam. I barely see his nod.

"I can't wait for the primroses to bloom next year," he says to Max cheerfully. Only I notice the catch in his voice.

"You know Darwin studied them?" I ask.

"That's interesting," Cam says. He's not interested, especially now.

I try a more compelling story. "Max, did you know certain primroses bloom faster before a volcanic eruption?" I watch his back as he walks ahead of me.

He keeps walking, no response. Dammit, Max, please listen. But he doesn't.

"Really?" asks Cam.

"Really," I say. It is amazing that the flowers that greet spring can also forewarn of disaster. Shakespeare *was* insightful. These flowers are the beginning and the end.

That evening, Cam suggests we tell Max about Benji. Honesty is the right answer, he says. I disagree. Eight years old is too young to deal with euthanasia. *I* can't even deal with it, for fuck's sake.

Cam begins over dinner. "We need to take Benji back to the hospital on Monday," he says.

Max's face crumples, and intense sobs come from somewhere I don't recognize.

Cam pauses and looks to me.

I shake my head. That's it. We will lie.

🐝

My first months in Montréal had me lying on a regular basis. I told myself that I was fine, and told everyone else that I was fantastic. The city split me right down the middle of my twenty-something self. I was starting a new life, ending an old, and wobbling around on the many paths the city proffered. They swirled around me in a cacophony of noisy bakeries, mysterious accents, and three-story walkups, spinning my senses into amazement on a daily basis.

It was an ideal age to live in Montréal, a city best experienced with naiveté and unrestraint. I was alone; friends from Edmonton who had also considered moving decided Montréal wasn't for them. I didn't much care because it isn't a city for everyone. It attracts or repels unequivocally. In my case, the dirt from the streets and the fragrance of smoked meat and shawarma entered my lungs and opened them up like an inhaler. The unrest between the French and the English, between the Jews and the Muslims, the cops and the dope sellers, along with the young girls in tight dresses, struggling students, and subway buskers woke me up after years of deep prairie slumber. I thanked everyone who encouraged my move, and hated anyone who hadn't. Montréal created my desire to simply be.

Then at night, I lay in bed, steeped in uncontrollable, illogical misery.

I didn't understand it. I didn't miss the silence of my parents' house. I missed Sonia, but the old Sonia, from my youth. The new Sonia was a grownup, with her own life. Yet sorrow overcame me, and I cried until sharp pains traveled from my neck to my temples. I drank water and took painkillers. I talked to myself rationally. What was wrong? I was young, healthy, and ready for university. I ate at restaurants alone and frequented sleazy bars on the infamous Crescent Street, where I made dates with handsome strangers who spoke French and fed me steak tartare with cornichons. I drank espresso and watched students argue about politics. I pretended I was part of the 1920s French café society. Yet my overwhelming sadness was inescapable in the stillness of the night.

I wrote letters to Sonia during the day, relating my adventures: my first side trip to New York City, the Formula One race, the sweet hand-rolled marzipan from my local bakery, and the handsome Moroccan man who served fresh mint leaves in a clear tea glass.

I told her about how I loved the blue-and-silver subway cars, the smell of their hot rubber tires on the rails, and the indistinguishable French announcements that everyone ignored. About rebellious Montréalers who spurned the stringent Catholic Church, as they cussed with sacred words in a slurred phrase of "*Hostie-calice-sacrament-tabernacle.*" I photographed two-hundred-year-old churches converted to condominiums and nightclubs, and dreamt of sleeping and dancing between murals and burial vaults. I wrote to Sonia with the romance that she taught me to seek, pages of it. And then at night I cried again, drowning, waking up some days unable to get out of bed. My new start was undoing me. Personal reinvention, it seemed, required a breakdown.

・　・　・

I saw a psychologist's newspaper ad one morning. Her name was Jeanne and she was looking for unpaid volunteers who were emotionally unstable or prone to mood swings to be part of a study. Was that me? I'm not the first to seek solace in a want ad, I told myself.

Her nondescript office highlighted her grace, her elegant suit, and her long blonde hair. She reminded me of my English professor, who read Chaucer with her perfect left leg hoisted on a platform through an endlessly high slit skirt. I adored Jeanne and believed she could help me.

"Are any of your family members depressed?" she had asked. My father came to mind. Was depression the same as fucked-up silence combined with occasional bursts of fury?

"No," I answered.

"What do you do for fun," she asked, "during the evening?"

She disapproved that I read only school texts and the newspaper. She was astonished that I didn't own a television set. I didn't tell her about my dating goal—Francophones and foodies only, preferably both simultaneously—and that I never wanted to marry.

"Buy a TV," she said. "Keep jogging, and let's try some mild antidepressants until your mood swings stabilize."

I took her advice, running through neighborhood after neighborhood, like I was running through a crowd of interesting people at a party, in circles and squares and zigzags. I tried the antidepressants, but they clouded my perspective and my magnificent city appeared boring. After a year, I gave them up and bought a TV. I kept dating and never discussed my feelings. I held on to moments of joy as I ran through the trees of Mount Royal Park, and decided I needed friends—or maybe a dog.

❧

"Goodbye, best friend," I whisper, as Cam gently puts Benji's ashes into the small hole under the serviceberry. The sun highlights Max's hair as he kneels on the ground, his hands splayed on the dirt. His sobs and the sight of his shaking body overwhelm me. I want to stop his first loss of love.

Suddenly, I remember being Max's age, looking through the wooden boxes in our living room, when I found a small white cotton bag, the type that might store fine jewelry. I opened the rough string to see dirt.

"What's this?" I had asked Mom, showing it to her where she stood over the sink, peeling potatoes.

"Oh," she said, "that's dirt from my mom. From her grave in the Ukraine."

Shock hammered my body. She had never mentioned her mother, or that she was dead. I put the terrifying bag on the counter, and ran to my room. When I came down for dinner that evening, the bag was gone. I never saw it again, and Mom never spoke of it. But the bag of dirt haunted my dreams.

I pull my eyes away from Max. I can't breathe. I remember my last night with Benji sleeping on his side, curled into my stomach. I rubbed his swollen belly, memorizing every inch of fur. I wished for another second of unconditional love. I told Max that Benji died peacefully in his sleep. I couldn't tell him that the vet gave Benji a sedative, and that Benji curled his lips and growled as the needle penetrated his artery, and that the next needle stopped his heart from beating, and that the vet wrapped him in an old red checkered blanket on the cold stainless steel table, and that we hugged his cooling body and cried our eyes out. It's enough for Max to know he's gone.

"This will be Benji's tree," Cam says, filling the hole with dirt, as if he is wrapping Benji in his favorite blanket. "We can see it from every window."

"I never want another dog," says Max, looking up through his tears.

"Me either," says Cam. "My heart doesn't have room for another one," he says to me. Okay, for now. But I need to rescue another dog someday.

We each share a Benji story, like when he chewed most of the sofa, and when he peed on Cam's mother's leg, because she had been standing still so long watering her roses that he thought her leg was a tree stump. We laugh, and I feel lonelier than ever as I lay the spent primrose flowers on his grave.

It doesn't matter where we are born—it's where we end up. I try to help Max to deal with grief by explaining that Benji had a good life, that he survived his early trauma, found us, and where he ended up is what counts. That he's safe under his tree, now, after giving along the way, teaching us about the generosity of dogs.

"I can see his tree from the iLounge," Max tells me. "And the kitchen."

"And?"

"I like remembering him," he says.

He's found comfort in memory. It's not terrifying. Mom's bag of dirt was not terrifying.

But it was.

"One took off his shirt," I whisper into the phone handset to my friend. It's Monday morning, and I'm hiding in our bedroom, slightly behind the curtain, watching the towering rugby players cart buckets of broken concrete. It's their second week, and they're still enjoying themselves despite the stifling heat. Their deep voices float through the open window, talking and laughing, and I wish for Max to have friends like this one day.

"Can I come see them tomorrow?" she asks. "I have to pick up the kids now."

Oh, did the cutest one just pour a bottle of water over himself?

"Okay, come for tea." I'll share my half-naked rugby players, because the bin is full, and there isn't enough beer on the planet to show my gratitude.

The boys make progress, creating an open patch of flat land covered with dead weeds. They also uncover an unfinished low retaining wall, about eighteen inches high, which follows the bottom of the L-shape of the property. It will need to be finished, I decide, because the land above it slopes down sharply from our neighbor's house. Looking up, it occurs to me that our immediate neighbors to the west have a perfect view of this part of the garden. I hope they're pleased with the cleanup.

The wall, made of dry-laid flagstone, matches the large retaining wall holding up the terrace. The grass could start at this wall; it's the perfect height to sit on while admiring the pond. I notice a pile of discarded flagstones nearby. No time like the present to set them aside for the wall repair. The first one's heavy. I pull my rubber gloves out of my pocket, put them on, and flip it over, removing the roof of dozens of ground beetles swarming underneath. The shiny mass of legs and wings frightens me, although they're a necessary part of the garden food chain, preying on the sticky slugs that eat the hosta leaves at night and leave their telltale slime route like a map. Still, I jump as the beetles head toward my boots. I drop the flagstone with a thud.

I've tried to overcome my fear of the garden's insects by reading about them, hoping understanding will bring appreciation, but nothing about multiple mouthparts, compound eyes, and spindly legs that end with miniature claws makes me feel warm and fuzzy. Bugs are tiny stealth machines that crawl up my sleeves, my pant legs, and into my hair. They bite, and the itching bothers me long after they've snuck away. I suppose I'm the one who's inserted myself into their domain, uninvited, and I do have a grudging respect for their emotionless sense of purpose. But still, how many times have I come into the house after working in the garden to hear Cam say, "Don't move, there's a bug in your hair"; or run into the house, having accidentally squeezed a buried wasp nest and had my entire hand stung, and walked around for two days cooling the burning welts in a bowl of ice. My relationship with the bug world needs work.

I can't lift the flagstone high enough to carry it properly, so I lean it on the front of my legs and struggle to the wall in a slow, contorted walk, banging the weight into new blue bruises across my thighs.

"We can do that for you," says one of the boys, as he passes by with a bucket.

"I'm okay," I tell him.

His eyes gleam with a mix of curiosity and respect. "Try to bend your knees a little more, then, and lift like this." He demonstrates with my flagstone.

His camaraderie fuels me for a few more hours, until I can barely lift my arm to wipe the sweat off my face.

I spot the bench while I'm sitting on the wall for a rest. It's perched about fifty feet upward and eastward toward the old mansion. I climb through the underbrush with excitement. What is it doing there, floating in the middle of the forest with no path attached to it? It's not easy to get to, but it's worth the effort. The old stone has been repaired, and the view provides a peek at the pond and the primroses, but not the pagoda that hides beyond. It's an enticing preview of what the garden once offered. Above the bench, a steep stone stairway leads to the balcony of the mansion. I realize I've found the original path into the garden. I feel the presence of past families at the bench, enjoying a bird's perspective, or perhaps continuing onward to picnic by where the pond water sloshes over the rocks.

We need more benches like this—the garden is a journey, and, like life, needs rest stops along the way, different vantage points to help our doubts morph into wisdom. I find a tree on the slope above the wall for the future swing, the perfect place for it to lull us into semi-sleep.

I race up to look for the boys. They need to stop immediately. I ask them to put aside extra-large stones and scrap wood so we can build benches. They roll their eyes, laugh, pick the biggest stones out of the bin, and start to bring them back down. More beer. And a place to drink it.

· · ·

My evening research brings me a surprise: a website called *Darwin Online*. I spend several minutes staring at a picture of a book's worn gray cloth spine of 1887, *The Different Forms of Flowers*. Chapter one is about Primulacae, and too detailed to keep my interest, but it's as close as I can get to smelling and touching the musty yellowed pages of a museum book. Primroses were interesting to Darwin because their two methods of reproduction helped him develop his theories of plant intelligence. The first is ideal: primroses have two types of flowers: one flatter, called a *pin*, and one elongated, called a *thrum*, adapted this way to achieve cross-pollination. This provides access to a greater variety of valuable traits over time. Less desirable, each flower is a hermaphrodite with both male and female parts. Darwin called this type of self-fertilization an illegitimate union. What would Darwin say about me, an unexpected product of two unsuited people?

I reach over to the cupboard and find the box of old pictures I brought home for Max. Ukrainian friends, my parents' adopted New World family, sit together at tables laden with food. A birthday cake here. A Christmas decoration there. They look happy. They look lonely. Where were Mom and Father's real family? Alive? Dead? Why didn't I know?

I lied to Max. Where we were born *does* matter—it grounds us. But after all the years of silence, my parents' unknown history is like a defective magnet that attracts and repels me simultaneously. I take a deep breath, tidy the photos, and put them back in the cupboard.

···

PRIMROSE MERINGUES

To prepare primrose (Primula vulgaris) flowers:
- Wash all flowers and let dry thoroughly. Remove pistils and stamens before using, separating the flower petals from the rest of the flower just prior to use to minimize wilting.

Ingredients:

4 large egg whites
1 cup granulated sugar
10 primrose flowers, chopped

- Preheat the oven to 300°F. Whip the egg whites and ¼ cup of the sugar in a large bowl until soft peaks form. Still whipping, gradually sprinkle in the rest of the sugar, beating to soft peaks again. Gently fold in the chopped flowers.
- Line a large baking sheet with parchment paper and pipe or spoon the mixture onto the paper in 8 to 12 mounds, leaving a few inches between them.
- Bake for 45 minutes, or until dry and firm to the touch. Leave to cool on the paper.
- Peel the meringues off the paper carefully; they will be fragile.
- Store cooled meringues in an airtight container.

See page 267 for information on safety and sourcing of plants.

···

CHAPTER 9

Sumac

"How many stitches?" I ask Sonia.

"Twelve. Lucky she pulled the call button down with her. She would have bled to death by morning." Sonia hasn't slept. This is her reality, dealing with increasingly common near misses. Mom forgot she couldn't walk and wanted to go to the bathroom. Or she decided to try it anyway.

I stare at the rectangular rust patch the dumpster left on the driveway.

"Why didn't you call me from the hospital?" I ask, controlling my frustration.

"I didn't want to worry you. There's nothing you could have done." She's right, of course. But it's not the first time I get news of a problem after the fact.

My anger turns to guilt. Sonia spends so much time at Mom's apartment, cleaning, doing laundry, and taking her on short field trips to the garden center. How frustrated she must be to have not been there when Mom fell.

"The apartment manager suggested we start looking for nursing homes."

"They're kicking her out?" I ask.

"She can stay for a while if she gets a wheelchair. But she's a liability. It was inevitable." Sonia's voice cracks. "Nursing homes are awful," she says. "She'll only have a bed and a chair."

My stomach churns. All those years of strength and digging in the garden. Dementia, a wheelchair, and a nursing home? Mom will never accept it.

"Can we move her here?" I ask. "There are more homes to choose from."

"Her doctors are here. So are her friends, and the church." Sonia stops short of saying burial plot. "She wouldn't want that."

Sonia wants to care for her until the end. And in my guilty, jealous, grateful heart, I know that's what Mom wants, too.

The rust shadow of the oxidized iron bin outside the window blurs. Time, water, and oxygen bring everything, even mighty steel, to its base. I need to finish the garden *now*. I'll fly Mom down when she stabilizes. Where the hell are Lisa and Ben?

The tree pruning team arrives after breakfast. Their leader, Adam, scopes out the day's work. I've lost my interest since Sonia's call. I breathe deeply as I follow Adam into the garden, hoping the earth will soothe me. Mom must miss this the most. Now she breathes the recirculated smell of bland food, adult diapers, and cleaning supplies. All I can do is hope the dementia has made her forget what she's missing.

"If a third of the branches are dead, it's a good sign it's in decline," Adam says. Wow, at least a third of my heart has been dead in the past, and I've come back.

"Don't be extreme," I tell him.

"Unfortunately, it's been years. Trees have a life span, too."

I suppose. Trees, dogs, mothers.

As he tilts his unshaven face upward toward two enormous oaks, his diamond earrings refract the sunlight into a colorful prism. The unbreakable gemstones, formed deep within the earth's mantle, suit him.

The oaks dominate the area above the pagoda. They are the garden's heart. Adam circles the trees, still looking up, his hands on his hips, his eyes squinting. *Don't you dare, Adam.*

"They look okay," he says. "Lots of deadwood, but we'll get it."
Atta-boy.

"We have nowhere to put the deadwood," I tell him.

"That's a problem, because this one is gone," he says, pointing to
a tree trunk about twenty feet from the majestic redwood. Dense ivy
covers the dead tree's base in a wide circle, and has also crawled up the
trunk from the ground. It looks like an upside-down tree with a rich
ivy canopy. I kneel at its base and throw my legs up into a headstand,
leaning my feet on its trunk. Yup, it's an upside-down tree.

It stays.

"Will it fall into the pond?" I ask Adam's shoes.

"Probably not—the trunk isn't heavy now that it's dead." He
looks above my polka-dot boots. "But those branches are dangerous. We'll just take those down . . . is that a light fixture up there?"

I flip back onto my feet, and feel the blood rush down as I peer
upward. Yes, a light, pointed downward. Uh-oh. Is there . . .

"Wiring." He finishes my thought. Adam points to more black
electrical wiring under the ivy.

"We can't touch this," he says. His look is accusing and angry.
"Do you have live electricity down here?"

"I don't know." Twinkling fairy lights around the pond are in my
future.

"You better call an electrician. I can't bring my crew here if you
don't know."

Adam points out another dead tree beside the sugar maples on his
way out, with an enormous trunk. Below it, a silver tube runs along
the ground. More wiring.

"Shocking," I say. Adam isn't impressed.

"I'll call an electrician right away," I promise. I'm reliving Father's tripwires, except these are warning the rodents that we're
coming.

"Looks like this one has some residents," he says.

It's the tree I see from the bedroom window. I follow his gaze
up about thirty feet to a large black hole in the trunk, about a foot

across and two feet high. Another hole, smaller, rests about fifteen feet higher.

"Raccoons, I bet," he says.

"Huh?"

"Raccoons love hollow trees. Have you seen some around?"

"Nope." So that's where they went.

It's a two-story raccoon condo with an excellent view. I circle the tree to find more holes on the other side. They have panoramic vistas of the entire yard. If I had to design their home, I couldn't have done it better.

"You've got to bring it down," he says.

"I'll think about it," I say. *This tree stays, scissorhands.*

"Those top branches have to come down, at least," he says. "They'll fall this way, right into those staghorns."

Staghorns? I look left and up into the forest. A leafy green canopy looks as if someone installed several giant garden umbrellas.

My pulse quickens. Staghorn sumacs! The velvety branches look like antlers. My fingers itch to touch them. I can't believe it. The possibilities. Native tea. Spice. Home decor. Peace pipes.

"I bet the raccoons feast on those berries during the fall," he says. "You may want to get a trapper to move them right out of here."

I nod at him. What's he mumbling? We have *sumacs!*

"Can you cut some of those berries down for me?" I ask.

🐝

"It's sumac," Yasmine said, scooping fattouch salad onto my plate. "It's in the zaatar on the pita, too."

The crimson powder tasted like dusty lemons. Peculiar. Did I like it? I wasn't sure, but I craved more.

Yasmine, my new flatmate, was the most exotic thing I discovered during university, so much so that I put getting a dog on hold. I was distracted in a math course when she smiled at me. She was bored, too. She wore auburn lipstick, the color a cosmetics company might call "Spice," and my love for her and all things Middle Eastern began.

"Eat up, tall skinny white kid," she said. I didn't see myself as tall or white, but maybe I was, next to her toasted skin, voluptuous body, and dark red lips. Maybe she thought I was exotic, too.

Yasmine fed me constantly. She made yogurt from scratch; it fermented in a dented old pot on our living room floor. She hand-rolled rice-filled vine leaves, and stuffed tiny zucchini and cooked them in fresh tomato juice. Babaganoush. Tabouli. Mysterious spice fragrances permeated our kitchen and my heart. I had a *home*.

"Coffee?" she asked after dinner. The unfiltered Camel's acrid smoke wafted over the table.

"Yup." I reached for my lighter and a long thin du Maurier, my preferred brand, milder and more elegant. Tall skinny white cigarette.

We chatted in our small kitchen nook that was enclosed with a cavelike rounded ceiling. Yasmine filled her crystal glasses with single malt scotch. It wasn't my style, but she made me love to feel decadent, irresponsible, and contrary enough to think I was interesting. She knew her priorities—imported cigarettes, lacy French underwear, and professionally honed chefs' knives.

Yasmine's parents were killed in Lebanon when she was a toddler, and she was the lone Muslim child sheltered by a Christian orphanage. She rebelled against her devout older sister via a stream of gorgeous lovers who provided our flat with much traffic. I loved it. I had an older sister, too, and my own rebellion going.

That early contradiction prepared her for a life of contrasts. She was completely bilingual and moved through the dichotomous Montréal culture with ease. She balanced her traditional Middle Eastern roots with Western values the same way the sumac, a native of the Mediterranean, has naturalized in North America. She was the most fascinating person I had ever met, and she filled my void of loneliness twice over. Her friends were varied and entertaining:

professors, hair stylists, chefs, and strippers. We were intrigued fol-
lowers, falling for Yasmine's intelligence, brazenness, and constant
references to the Qur'an. Most of all, we fell for her cooking. My
loneliness dissipated with every nourishing bite.

I was surprised by the suggestion from a senior finance professor
at the university. He called me to his office for a personal meeting
to present a compelling opportunity. My grades allowed me to ap-
ply to an elite combined master's/doctorate program in the United
States after the completion of my undergraduate degree. I had the
technical aptitude to understand the intricacies of the then-nascent
derivatives trading, he told me. It was the next big thing in the corporate finance world. Apparently, I needed to be in New York.

"But I just got here," I told him. I feared that if I woke up too
soon from the dream that was Montréal, I might forget it.

"They're looking for brilliant women," he said. "You'll have it
made."

After all these years, I'd finally found a mentor, a kind teacher
intent on opening up my future. I was floored. I was also strangely
grounded.

"Montréal is my home now," I told him. He tried to convince
me, but the potential of success couldn't replace my sense of attach-
ment. I didn't have the heart to tell him that I was starting to hate finance anyway. I chose, instead, to live inside the warmth and energy
of a spice jar.

"Sumac," the taxi driver said, nodding at the window. "They grow
like weeds."

Fifteen years later, relocated to downtown Toronto and missing
my Montréal home, I asked the driver if he recognized the large
trees that lined many city ravine roads, the trees with dark green
leaves and peculiar red spikes.

My heart stopped for a moment; it was as if Yasmine had entered the taxi and was sitting in the front seat, flirting with the driver, her cleavage and white teeth causing distraction. Her signature lipstick was the precise red of the triangular flowers that pointed upward, seeking attention in the sunlight. Red light's wavelength is the longest: it can't be ignored. I now knew where my precious powder came from. This new city could be home, too.

❧

Lying perpendicular across the garden path, dead at our feet, is the largest raccoon I've ever seen, about three feet long. The bog's fragrant forget-me-nots create a purple dawn haze around it. It's so big we'll have to step over it to continue.

"Dammit," I whisper. Its tail is stiff, and its black masked face is sweetly innocent. I feel sick.

"No, no, no. I cannot go farther. I cannot work here." Salvatore, the new electrician, already daunted by the job's size, turns around and sprints up the steps.

"But wait," I say, rushing behind him. "They live in the tree. It must have been foraging at night and got hit by a car. It came home to die."

"I'm not working here, sorry," he says as he shuts the door to his van.

"You told him it came home to die?" Cam asks over dinner. "Why did you say that?"

"Do you think it stepped on a live wire?"

"Your guy from the city didn't tell you?"

"I was afraid to ask." The official from City Animal Services had arrived within hours. He wore a cap, a blue windbreaker, and jeans, and he carried a regular dark green garbage bag.

"We don't climb fences or enter water," he droned, "or go under decks." This is the kind of guy Yasmine would have called a *fonctionnaire*, a robotic bureaucrat.

"Their masks have meaning, you know," I told him as we walked down the stairs. "We're never what we seem. We hide even from ourselves."

"Ma'am, I don't think too much about that in this job," he said. Maybe he didn't, going around town, picking up dead animals all day. He's the front line, seeing the carnage of our human transgression on the natural world, letting us hide from our roadkill.

Fonctionnaire simply wrapped the garbage bag around the carcass and bagged it. Pretty much the same way I pick up dog poo.

"Don't you wear gloves?" I asked. And I thought Cam was bad.

"Nope. Have a nice day." I didn't have the courage to ask what he did with the bodies. He was gone faster than the electrician.

"Shit." I gape at the green and black mass of old wire at Mauro's feet. Cam looks equally surprised, although we're pleased with Mauro, our newest electrician and landscape lighting expert.

"I took down as many old fixtures as I could." Enormous rusted spotlights sit in another pile.

"All this was in the garden?" I ask. Fucking Disneyland.

"They're many vintages," Mauro says. "From different owners, probably. I took it all out like you wanted."

"Thanks. You're absolutely sure?"

"All gone," he says. "I put a new receptacle by the pond for your future fountain." I didn't want to tell him about the fairy lights, although a fountain is a pretty good idea, if I do say so myself.

"A fountain?" Cam asks impatiently. "Don't make it Disneyland, Alex," he mumbles to me on the way up the steps.

"I'm going to check on the condo," I tell Cam as we enter the house. "The raccoons were out last night."

It seems my raccoon family is alive and kicking. I head for the bedroom with my binoculars. Normally I see darkness in the oak's holes, but today I am rewarded with a small face in the lower window. An adorable furry mug with his mischievous black mask, a short pointy nose, and white whiskers. He looks vulnerable as he peeks through the hole. I hope it wasn't his mother across the path. *You're safe,* I tell him, *except from my prying eyes, and the big city you live in.* Does he see me in the bedroom and wonder why I'm messing with his forest? *I won't cut down your home,* I promise him. Although my definition of home has been morphing over the years.

The raccoons sleep on a dried-leaf bed behind the lower trunk hole. I know this because sometimes I see their furry, unmoving butts protruding during the day. The upper hole is the front door, with a leafy branch above it like the canopy over the entrance of an expensive New York apartment. My neighbor has seen them on our flat roof at night. They jump off a tree branch that overhangs our roof, right above our bedroom, and head to and from the condo. Cam and I are accustomed to the 5 a.m. thud above our heads. It wakes us up and reminds us we live in a forest, and that we share our home with others.

Beyond the trees, the skyscrapers are dull gray shadows of themselves, their windows and balconies obliterated by clouds. The trees have won the contest while the ghosts, the human pinnacles of achievement, have diminished into nothingness in the thin air. Trees will prevail, no matter what we do to them.

Such as on days like today, when we will prune them.

In a natural forest, dead limbs decompose and give back to the earth. In our case, I've decided to leave the debris at the property's edge, stacked in a natural fence that will span the divide between the tamed garden and the neighboring forest. It's the best I can think of and I know it's not great. The garden is teaching me the art of compromise, one small trade-off at a time.

Adam pitches the sixteen-ounce "throw ball" up the tree. We watch the thin string sail up, then back down, five tries until it goes over one of the fifty-foot-high branches.

"Wow," says Max. He and I raced home from his tae kwon do

test to watch the pruning. He proudly wears his new blue belt, the second-to-last color before black belt, still a couple of years away.

"It takes practice," Adam says. "On a good day, I get it over the first time. On a bad day, well—"

Max nods, watching with rapture. He gets it. Not all of his classmates passed the test this morning.

Adam adjusts his gray knit cap. Sexy, but where's his helmet?

"Lifeline's next," Adam says, as he arranges the thick blue climbing line. "This is going to let me walk around the tree." He winks at Max.

"I want to do that when I grow up," Max says. Adam harnesses himself into a climbing belt that looks like a metal diaper covered with hooks and clips. If I were a squirrel, I'd be laughing. As a human, I'm freaking out. Do these cowboys really know what they're doing?

Maybe I should offer them some cookies.

"Adam's the best," one of the ground crew tells Max, as we watch Adam ascend the rope. "Although he's not wearing his spurs today. Hope he doesn't slip." Well, that's just *super*.

The two guys on the ground watch Adam carefully, following the orders he shouts down to them. Their bright yellow helmets bob as they discuss each step. Soon, with a few monkey knots and slipknots, there are a dozen different lines in the tree for climbing, rigging, and moving equipment. From below, the tangle of ropes looks like tropical jungle vines. I imagine Adam in a loincloth.

"Do I pull it up?" calls a guy from the ground.

"No, leave it. If I don't tell you to do it, don't do it," Tarzan yells from the tree, his voice laced with authority. He's calling the shots. The ground crew becomes silent; they know their place.

They send saws and blades up the tree, and Adam dances around the branches, tying up limbs, cutting them, and hoisting them down. Max and I hold our breath for the most part. A false move and Adam falls to his death. It's slow going. After an hour, we've had enough. No wonder pruning will take weeks.

The first deadwood branch is about twelve feet long, and heavy. Max and I drag it to the side.

"We'll use it for the tree swing," I tell him. "So we can float in the trees, too."

I would have climbed the tree myself to see his beaming face.

"I got an e-mail from John today," Cam says during dinner. "He wants us to host an evening at home with David Suzuki." He tries to look nonchalant as he slices his chicken.

"Who?" I ask. "*The* David Suzuki?" Here? "Doo-doo-doo-doo-dee-doo-doo-dee-ba-da-da-da-dum-da," I sing.

"What's *that?*" Cam asks.

"*The Nature of Things,*" says Max. "Remember the penguin episode? Is he really coming here?" I *love* my son.

"He is," says Cam. "John wants us to invite friends who might be open to his message." We're fundraising, in other words. I don't ask Cam why he's suddenly interested in David Suzuki. I know he's doing it for me.

"What the heck is that, by the way?" Cam asks, pointing to the large clear pitcher where my reddish-brown sumac heads are floating in light yellow liquid.

"Mom's making sumac tea," Max says from his computer. "I told her it looks like a jar of pee with you-know-what floating in it."

I stare at the jar. Yuck, now that he's put it in my head.

"No David Suzuki for you." I love my son less.

"Why can't I be there?" Max asks Cam.

"Of course you'll be there," Cam says. "It'll be in spring. We have lots of time to plan. Leave your mother's tea experiment alone."

No vitamin-C-rich sumac tea for them. Let them get scurvy. Although I've kind of lost my appetite.

Before bed, I download *David Suzuki: The Autobiography, The Sacred Balance,* and *David Suzuki's Green Guide.*

"Really?" Cam asks when I show him.

"He gets bad press where I came from," I say, "oil fields and all."

"Well, someone has to take a stance, I suppose," Cam says. "But I'm *not* reading all those books."

The autobiography surprises me. David writes openly about his family's experience in internment camps in British Columbia, and how the racism he experienced became a source of lifetime motivation. His writing is humble and thoughtful. I realize his first fifty years did not follow a clear path; they were a series of events that allowed him to discover the environmental issues around the world until he embraced them. I feel like I've met him in person.

"I *really* like him," I tell Cam a few nights later. "His father told him that if he wanted to be liked by everyone, he wouldn't stand for anything."

"Good motto for Max," says Cam.

"You know he's as iconic as Gordon," I say.

"Who?" asks Cam.

"Gordon *Lightfoot*."

"Oh, *that* Gordon. Aren't they about the same age?" asks Cam. "Don't you have any young heroes?"

I've never thought about it, but actually, they are only two years apart. Hmm. Why *am* I obsessed with these old guys?

Realization washes over me. I met their soothing voices on television and on the radio in my youth. When they spoke and sang about the ravine that was my escape, they filled the silence that was our house.

....

HOMEMADE ZAATAR SPICE BLEND

Please note:

White sumac (poison sumac, *Toxicodendron vernix [Rhus vernix]*) is extremely toxic. Don't pick or consume.

All sumac plants are related to cashew, mango, and poison ivy plants. If you have sensitivities to any of these, avoid sumac completely.

To prepare fresh red sumac (Rhus typhina, Rhus glabra, or Rhus copallina) berries:

- Pick the red sumac clusters in late summer or early fall. Ripe berries are firm and will have a fresh, tart flavor when you bite into them. Separate the berries from the stems and let them air-dry on a baking sheet for approximately 1 week. Grind in blender on low speed and sift through a medium-sized sieve to remove the seeds.

For spice blend:

¼ cup dried red sumac
2 tablespoons dried thyme
1 tablespoon toasted sesame seeds
2 tablespoons dried oregano
1 teaspoon coarse salt

- Crush all ingredients except salt with mortar and pestle. Blend and add salt. May be stored in airtight container in refrigerator for up to 6 months.

Serving suggestions:

- Brush on flatbread or pizza dough prior to baking.
- Use as topping on hummus or yogurt.

- Use as rub for roast chicken.
- Mix 2 tablespoons zaatar with 4 tablespoons olive oil to use as a dip for bread.

See page 267 for information on safety and sourcing of plants.

~

CHAPTER 10

Serviceberries

THE PAPER BAG splits as it hits the driveway about the same time my butt hits the asphalt roof. A twinge shoots down my leg as cold water seeps into my pants, sending a chill up my back. *Damn.* I hoist myself up with my soaked gloves and peer over the edge. Another broken one. Wet leaves and branches spill out of the dozen paper yard-waste bags already piled below. I'll have to rebag the mess. I look across the expanse of roof that is still covered in soggy leaves. This will take *forever.* I hate leaves.

Perhaps *hate* is a strong word.

I *love* leaves. I taught Max my perfect technique for crunching through piles in the autumn, just like I taught him how to shatter the thin sheet of ice that forms on puddles in the winter. This is nothing. I'll be done by the end of the day. I skid on another rotting pile into an excruciating muscle pull. Fucking leaves.

My concern about potential flooding from the dangerous combination of last autumn's leaves and melted snow is what brought me up here in the first place, and I was lucky to find the heavy wood ladder on the side of the house. Its wooden tips peek up over the roof, and I wonder if going back down will be scarier than coming up. I may have to ask my neighbor's garden maintenance crew for help, although I didn't want them up here in case they fell off. They agreed to help me clean up the leaves at the property's base.

Meanwhile, I have the world at my feet. From the roof's south side, I see the entire acre of garden sprawled in front of me, its steep descent downward and the tableland below. From up here, it's *enormous*. My head spins, and not because of the height.

What the hell are we thinking? We can't tackle this. We shouldn't even *own* this. We don't know a corm from a rhizome. Well, maybe I do, but I'm self-taught with books from the sale bin. Not exactly the right qualifications for the expanse of land at my feet. We're dead.

The boys are gathering the leaves on large tarps and dragging them up the stairs to their truck. They've already uncovered an old path I never noticed. I need to bring Cam up here to enjoy this aerial perspective. He's the strategic one who sees a blank canvas as a possibility.

"We'll need red by the pagoda someday," he suggested the other day, as he surveyed the view out the kitchen window. Typical Cam. Red. What does *red* mean? Does he mean trees, flowers, or pillows on the stone benches?

"Try to imagine the masses of color, Alex," he said, "the garden as a painting." I live with Monet.

"I can't think that way."

"You know, red, to offset the greens in the spring and the yellow irises," explained Mr. Bird's-eye View.

So I'm worm's-eye view. I look at things from the ground up, taking in details no one else cares about. I don't want to be a slimy detail-oriented worm. Worms are ugly. Boring and dull. Like the life of accounting that I ran away from. Am I really left-brained, detail-oriented, lacking big-picture perspective?

Yes. I exhale slowly, hanging my head in perfect wormlike fashion.

But that means Cam is right-brain: possibly creative, but messy and forgetful.

So there.

But don't birds eat worms? I'm giving myself a headache.

Our relationship isn't a competition, I remind myself, as I fling another bag over the roof. We're the perfect pair to restore this garden. He'll create the outline, and I'll fill in the blanks. His intuition will guide his ideas, and my practical approach will make it happen. Which is why I'm stuck shoveling leaves off the roof. My role in our relationship takes more work. But I keep coming back to it, don't I? I guess the path to self-acceptance is one of the many in our garden.

"Aaaaaah! Whoa!" I hear from below.

Panic punches me in the stomach. One of the boys is hurt! I peer over the roof's edge. Their blue plastic tarp, covered with leaves, lies near the pagoda. Did part of the crumbling ceiling fall on them? I *knew* it!

"Guys?" I yell down, paralyzed with fear. I will never forgive myself if someone got hurt.

One of the boys runs up the stairs. "Up here!" I yell, waving my arms.

He looks up at me from the terrace with wide, bright eyes. Is that shock or excitement?

"Deer," he says, out of breath.

"Dear what?"

"Deer. There's a deer behind the pagoda, lying down in the leaves."

Oh, *animal* deer. Okay, he's crazy. It's probably a fox. I think these guys smoke pot when the jobs are boring, another reason not to let them on the roof.

"It's probably a fox," I yell down.

"No. It's a spotted white-tailed deer. I know what a deer looks like." White tail?

I head for the ladder. *Impossible.* It needed to cross an inner-city freeway and several busy streets to get here. And from where? We're downtown. A deer can't wander around downtown. Yet my pounding heart knows this crazy garden is capable of anything.

We run down the steps to the other gardeners, now huddled in a group far away from the pagoda, whispering like excited schoolchildren.

"It's lying down on the leaves. It scared me," says one.

"How did it get there? Don't spook it," says another.

"Show me," I say, and one guy takes my arm. "Be quiet," he warns.

He won't let me get close, so I peer beyond the pagoda, adjusting my eyes to a dark corner under the pines.

From the leaf bed, a sweet, triangular brown face with dark eyes and a wide brown forehead looks toward me. It has the shiny nose of a stuffed animal. Yup, that's a real live deer.

I back away, overcome with emotion. "You guys have to stop right now. Quietly pack up your stuff. I'll call you when I figure this out."

"Fucking deer in the middle of the city. Wait 'til I tell the guys at the shop," I hear as they tiptoe up the stairs with their tarps and rakes.

"Shh," another one whispers.

They don't want to break the spell either.

In the house, I don't know what to do first. The strange heat in my chest isn't painful, but I'm disoriented. It's a deep, quiet pleasure. It's magic. A deer has come to grace us with its presence.

Cam is incredulous when I call him at work. And busy, so he cuts off my explanation midstream. I know he believes me, but he can't seem to accept the idea that there is a deer in our garden. I call the Humane Society, and they tell me to call City Animal Services, who can't help.

"It'll leave the way it came in," the clerk tells me. "We can't send our people down there and risk scaring it onto a road. It'll cause an accident."

"But it jumped a five-foot-high fence to get in here," I explain.

"They can do that. It's best to leave it alone. Don't scare it. It might be resting and eating. Do you have water nearby?" Yes, yes we do. A babbling brook, in fact.

So the deer is to stay. All garden work is off.

My research tells me the fence was no obstacle, and that the deer is probably nibbling on the serviceberry shrubs near the pagoda. They munch the twigs in the spring and the berries in the summer. Serviceberries grew wild in my childhood ravine and Mom used them for saskatoon pie, as we called it. Our blue-stained dishtowels were impervious to rigorous bleaching; no wonder Native Americans used them for dye as well as for making pemmican. And now in our garden, deer food—the noblest of uses.

I also learn that Celtics believed that deer cut paths through forests for fairy troops. And that people follow deer to find edible herbs as well as the road to spirituality. *Show me*, I whisper toward the deer.

I tell Max about the deer after school. We wait for Cam to come home, and then we look for it together, sneaking toward the pagoda. It's gone. Max and Cam look at me with disbelief.

"Are you sure?" Max asks, arms crossed. I eat dinner in silence, feeling I had unfinished business with the deer. Worse, Max and Cam think I'm imagining things. I'm devastated. I guess I can call the boys back to clean the leaves.

The next morning, I hide in the bedroom, phone against my ear, as I savor the green haze of leaf buds on the bare branches outside the window. They say that a green aura signifies harmony, but I'm not feeling it today.

"This is our last chance to decide," Sonia says, outlining her idea of Mom living with her instead of moving to the nursing home. "We'll have to put ramps on the stairs and find twenty-four-hour nursing help. Retrofit a bathroom on the main floor."

"But one person can't move her anymore. You'd have to help the nurse with the lift sling. I don't see it, Sonia."

"But a nursing home room is so small. What will she do all day?"

"She's only been in her bed and chair for years," I remind Sonia, desperately trying to make us both feel less guilty. But I know what she means. Mom's assisted-living apartment was a home. This will feel like a hospital—and the last stop.

"Look, Sonia. Your house won't work," I start. "You're not a nurse. You don't have a bathing facility with a lift. She's had countless strokes. She has dementia. She can't walk or use her hands. And all those meds. You can't do it. Neither can I. It's not safe, and it's going to get worse. We've been warned by her doctor."

To Sonia's credit, she's found a good possibility, but she's nervous about it. The Good Samaritan is a not-for-profit Christian full-care home near her house.

"Describe it," I say.

"They've got volunteers and crocheted blankets," Sonia says. "And a huge garden. They're close to the hospital and have twenty-four-hour nurses. It's homey."

A garden?

Sonia stops speaking and guilty silence fills the void.

"You can wheel her around that garden every day," I say. "She needs you to be a daughter now, not a nurse. Leave that to the professionals."

"I know," she says in a small voice.

Damn it. Mom would not want to be slowly withering away like a diseased perennial. She'd want to be telling us what to do in our garden.

"The flower beds are beautiful," Sonia adds. "Maybe we can request a room with a window that faces them." Her weariness and despair float through the phone line.

"Call them," I tell her quietly. "I'll be there soon."

I hang up the phone and push my left arm to my chest to relieve the now familiar pain. The morning sun shines into the bedroom, but today it can't help me. Mom's decline is in front of me, forcing me to ask myself what kind of daughter I've become. I've been obsessed with being a better mother to Max, showing him nature, and becoming the gardener that would make Mom proud. It's the only language she understood, and I want to speak it. Perhaps I've been so busy seeking approval that I've forgotten to be a good daughter. It's just so very hard, because she's sick, and Father's gone, and they're both still two strangers who raised us.

And what of the garden? So much more work, time, and money. I desperately want to tell Mom I did it, that I fixed an old, broken garden, and that her grandson helped me, and that someone's hundred-year-old legacy isn't forgotten. If I can't show her that, what can I show her? She wouldn't have been overwhelmed by our garden. She wouldn't be sulking in bed. Feet on the ground, I tell myself, as I stand up and walk to the window.

Standing perfectly still below me is the deer.

Right under the window, on the terrace, practically touchable, unmoving, as if it doesn't want to wake anyone.

Deer!

I run to the kitchen, grab Max's and Cam's hands, and drag them to the bedroom. We stand in a silent row, looking down.

"I can't believe it," whispers Cam.

"It *is* here," says Max.

We watch. Still. Silent. Mesmerized.

Finally, the deer turns its head toward the forest and saunters gracefully down toward the steps, as if asking us to follow. *Mom?*

"It's clearing our path," I whisper to Cam.

Garden work's still off. Which is why I get the email that afternoon. Now that work is on hold, Lisa and Ben said *yes* to the garden restoration. Yes, yes, yes. Except no.

Still, the project's weight, the concrete debris and pruned branches and wet leaves, falls from my shoulders. The tangled wires and prying neighbors disappear. We'll have help. I'll be worry-free.

Free as a bird. Or in my case, a worm.

The restoration proposal includes preparation, garden cleanup, and a planting plan that maximizes views and incorporates complementary indigenous plants. Lisa also drew up a plan for a compact pool and will present it to the city authorities. Cam and Max see themselves dipping in the forest, and Max dreams of snorkeling. *I'd like to scuba-dive someday,* he's told me. *As long as it doesn't distract from the garden work,* I remind them—and as long as I don't have to put my claustrophobic head underwater. I'd rather be hiking.

✣

I was speechless, again, and it was only the second day of our hike. At twenty-seven, I was meeting the White Mountains for the first time.

"Hard to find the words, huh?" asked the hut boy who sat on a rock beside me as I let the water's white froth bubble over my hands.

He wore a kiltlike skirt, beat-up hiking boots, and a knit hat. Oh yes, and since he was shirtless, a pierced nipple and a complicated tattoo. He was part caveman, part lumberjack, and downright gorgeous. His wood-and-canvas packboard, leaning against a nearby tree, had at least seventy pounds of food on it. My small twenty-five-pound knapsack appeared pathetic in comparison, although it was getting heavier because I was collecting unique rocks as I walked.

Hut boy was part of the Appalachian Trail cabin "croo," one of many that traversed impossible mountain trails carrying food and supplies for hikers. The hut girls were equally stunning with their long matted braids and strong legs.

Zealand Falls, one of the eight backcountry High Huts maintained by the Appalachian Mountain Club, was an incredible place, where a mountain waterfall, dark forests, and beaver-filled bogs delivered heart-stopping pure beauty. I was in Middle Earth. I was on top of the world.

"I'm looking for an answer," I told hut boy. My roots, maybe, although only alpine flowers grow on the boulders above the tree line.

He didn't blink. "You'll find it here," he said, picking up his pack and slipping it on like a shawl.

When the mind is not sure what the heart will do next, the rock becomes the master and the road becomes what's left, I told his back as he floated away up the trail like a sure-footed deer. Maybe rocks can be anchors, just like roots. Gordon's words fell into the ripples of water, spreading into the stream.

Friends from my new finance job had invited me on this hiking trip in New Hampshire. I didn't know then that this would be the first of many similar trips, that I would struggle to get to each hut through blistering heat and lightning storms, bringing friends whose lives would also be changed by the White Mountains' energy. They weren't the majestic rugged Rockies from my home province, but they felt like home. Older, rounder, and greener. Approachable. Conversational.

And I was on this trip to have a conversation. I wanted to come down from the peaks with an answer. My job was perfect, but I didn't like it. *Despised* it, actually.

My first position after completing university was at a prominent telecommunications company, *real* work. Different from being a teacher's assistant grading papers, until the teacher asked me on a date. Different from my debut as a bar waitress until an undercover policeman told me the salt shakers were filled with cocaine and that I should duck if I heard a loud noise. This job was professional *and* safe. It involved a burgundy leather briefcase from Sonia, a new apartment, a car, and overtime. My salary was generous. I wore a two-piece suit and crunched numbers. Crunched and crunched. The more I learned, the bigger the numbers got and the more bored I became.

"You've got it made," Yasmine said to me, struggling with her oversized pack.

"Why did you think you'd need giant towels? I told you there's no water up here," I said, putting her excess rolls of biodegradable toilet paper in my pack.

"You never told me we have to carry our garbage for four days," she said.

"I hate my job." There, I said it. I hated accounting. I hated balance sheets. I hated the spreadsheets spinning around in my brain.

"You're making good money. That's why you finished your degree."

I finished my degree simply to finish. To prove myself to my family. To get Father's attention — which I didn't.

Each peak I scaled strengthened my resolve. Up used different muscles than down, as I ached through each conflicted thought. Finally, above the tree line, staring down into Franconia Notch, which was buried in ice 50,000 years ago, I touched the tiny leaves of endangered alpine-tundra lichen that grows less than a millimeter per year, and the wisdom left behind from the Ice Age seeped into my mind. It was unavoidable.

When I got home, I quit my job. And while I was at it, I ditched my workplace boyfriend, sold my car, and called Yasmine. "Want to share a flat again?" I asked.

❧

David Suzuki and his wife, Tara, are captivating. David's smooth skin and thick white hair radiate the vitality of a young man. Tara disarms with greenish, wide-set eyes and a radiant smile. This power couple proves two halves can make a whole that is greater than one. I shouldn't have read both his autobiographies. Or re-watched so many episodes of *The Nature of Things*. I stammer foolishly. Did I just mention polar bears in my first sentence? I'm an idiot.

"We're excited to visit your lovely home," says Simone from the David Suzuki Foundation. She smooths my awkwardness with a grin. I mumble something about seals and ice caps and race for the kitchen, my heart pounding.

"The buffet looks phenomenal," I tell Chef Jason, as he garnishes the plates with edible flowers.

The Foundation recommended Chef Jason, a locavore cook, to prepare the meal for the evening. He's used our home-tapped maple syrup in several dishes, as well as some pink petals from the garden's rosebuds. I follow him around the kitchen like a loyal puppy, thrilled that our guests will enjoy my foraged goods. I picked the dandelion greens this morning, a symbolic offering of my first flower to David.

"Enjoy your night," Chef Jason says. "I'm in control here." He doesn't need me; he's got the sustainably farmed salmon artfully displayed.

I head back into the living room for cocktails.

David, wearing a red shirt with a black printed Native design, is calm and smiling as we sip cocktails in the living room. He has that rare charisma—the Oprah, Clinton, Mandela kind. The charisma that comes from knowing your path. Our guests are starstruck.

Tara, quiet and charming, lets her husband be the face of their work. She is a professor, writer, and the driving force behind the Foundation, a star in her own right.

Max is in charge of pictures, a job we gave him to help overcome his shyness. He's obsessed with new software that allows photo editing—it's complicated but he's determined to figure it out. Tonight, his technology obsession is channeled in a useful direction. In fact, I'm about to get hundreds of photos of David Suzuki.

I watch our friends smile as Max shakes their hands and makes eye contact, following Cam's instructions.

"He's so grown up," a friend says to me. "I can't believe he's almost ten."

She missed my earlier yelling, when he refused to put on a dress shirt and nice pants. And my nagging before that, when he didn't want to clean his room.

David agreeably puts his arm around people and chats as they are photographed. Soon, he inches to the back of the living room, drawn by the beckoning trees beyond the balcony doors. I follow him onto the balcony, where he leans on the railing and examines the trees below, the same view that enthralled us the first time we saw the house.

"It's a beautiful forest," he says. I flush with pride, proud to share it with a fellow tree-hugger.

"Why does that black fence cut the forest in half?" he asks, pointing down to the chain link. "Too bad it's there, making a black line through nature."

I'm winded. A lump rises in my throat. A black line, like a scar. He's right, of course.

"Black, five feet, unobtrusive," I had told the man from Firm Fence who repaired the old fences. They were necessary by law if we were ever to get a pool. But obtrusive they were. David has Cam's perspective, but bigger. He doesn't see the garden. He sees the garden in the forest in the ravine in the city in the landscape of the country. Did I think that David Suzuki was going to admire a contained city garden upon which we've imposed boundaries?

"A deer jumped that fence last month," I muse. A displaced deer met a misplaced fence in the middle of the city. Suddenly I'm sad. The fence isn't a barrier except in our own minds. It gives us a false sense of security. Ownership. The deer ignored it, an easy obstacle between it and the serviceberry. Nature will grow over and around it. So who and what are we walling off?

"Dinner is ready," I say. "Self-serve buffet in the kitchen."

He smiles, not knowing that he has, in one statement, deflated me.

"Where did you get the salmon?" David asks Chef Jason, and they have a long discussion about oceans. He's moved on, while I'm still collecting my thoughts.

During dinner, David asks me if tapping for sap damages the maples. Chef Jason has been promoting our maple syrup. I'm surprised that as an elder, he doesn't know the answer. I assure him we take only 10 percent of the sap, and I explain the process, and how the Natives first discovered sap when it froze into "sapsicles" from winter tree branches. He's fascinated, now that he is assured that the trees are unharmed, and the rest of the conversation flows because he respects the Natives' closeness to nature.

After dinner, we usher our guests downstairs into Cam's library for coffee, speeches, and a question period. David is inspiring, un-scripted, and passionate. He speaks about the interconnectedness of humans and nature, oxygen and water, bringing things down to the simplicity of our lungs and to the complexity of the entire planet. He is worm's-eye view, bird's-eye view, and every gradation in be-tween. The guests are enraptured. They realize that although he is in his early seventies, he's only getting started.

I should be pleased as I try to fall asleep that evening, but I'm not. After a restless night, it dawns on me that our formal garden is being *imposed* on nature. How can I continue?

SERVICEBERRY PIE

Ingredients:

1 uncooked 9-inch prepared crust for 2-crust pie

½ cup sugar

2½ tablespoons cornstarch (or tapioca, if desired)

4 cups fresh serviceberries or wild blueberries

1 tablespoon lemon juice (optional)

2 tablespoons chilled diced butter

1 egg, beaten

- Heat the oven to 425°F. Press the bottom crust into a lightly greased 9-inch pie pan; set aside.
- Gently combine berries, sugar, and cornstarch in a large bowl. Spread the mixture into the pie pan and sprinkle with the lemon juice. Scatter butter pieces on top.
- Cover with top crust, flute the edges, and vent the pie. Brush pie crust with beaten egg, and sprinkle with additional sugar if desired.
- Bake for 15 minutes at 425°F; reduce heat to 350°F. Bake until filling bubbles and crust begins to brown, adding foil around the edges if needed to keep from burning, about 50 minutes.
- Remove from oven and cool on rack.

See page 267 for information on safety and sourcing of plants.

CHAPTER 11

Roses

I wake up to find *The Trees of North America* beside me under the bedsheet.

"There's something coming between us," Cam says, picking up the book.

"It's a deep-rooted problem," I say, grabbing it from his hand. I fell asleep looking up Lisa's plant selections from the list on the bedside table. Beside it, burning a hole in my heart, is David Suzuki's book, *The Declaration of Interdependence*. I put *The Trees of North America* on top of it. Guilt washes over me. I move the book again, exposing the splendid artwork of David's book. The subtitle *A Pledge to Planet Earth* catches my eye. I look back to Lisa's list, comprising the Latin and common names of indigenous trees, including red maples, hemlocks, and white cedar. Dogwood, willow, and serviceberry. I've already memorized their history, edibility, and disease resistance.

"Do you want to talk about it?" Cam asks.

The tension in my neck radiates upward and shoots piercing pain into my temples.

"Maybe later," I say. I can't tell him David has made me question the garden restoration. I know David would advise us to let the old garden go, to let the knotweed overtake the paths, and to let the pagoda and bridge disintegrate as nature takes its course.

"Let's have some tea," I tell Cam, contemplating my options.

I decide to stall. While Cam prepares the tea, I write a quick email delaying the contract signing with Lisa and Ben for two weeks. Stupid David Suzuki, screwing with my head. I hope a few days with Mom and Sonia will put things in perspective, although I doubt it.

"And this is Max with the fish." I hold the photo under Mom's nose and am rewarded with a crooked smile. I'm showing her photos to distract her as we pack up her clothes.

"That's nice," Mom slurs, trying to lift her arm to point at the photo. She stabs at the air with her fingers instead.

I swallow over the lump in my throat. This move, from Mom's assisted-living apartment to the nursing home, is too simple. She's moving without her possessions—the small table and sofa, the microwave and the telephone. She won't need any of them. Every move, she's lost a little more of the earthly world and a little more of her memory and dexterity. I'm starting to appreciate Father's quick exit. He avoided the Good Sam's long-term care over three floors where as patients become more ill or more overcome by dementia, they move up, a little closer to the proverbial heaven. Lucky for Mom, she's on the active first floor, where music, crafts, and a chapel keep residents busy.

"Coffee?" Mom mumbles.

I hand her the sippy cup of lukewarm coffee and thickener. Apparently, the gooey sludge is safer, because it travels more slowly down her throat. She can't drink normal liquids because the muscles that control swallowing don't respond quickly enough, and liquid may enter her lungs. She's resigned to it, bending her neck awkwardly to take a slow sip from the cup in front of her, unable to fully lift it. All the things I cherish about the steaming cup of tea that warms my hands as I walk through the cool morning garden, the hot liquid coursing down my throat as I inhale the sweet bergamot aroma mingled with the morning dew, are gone for her. She is sipping a memory, if even that.

"I'll work on the closet now," I tell her, tucking in her feet and turning up the volume of the television set. Mom grins at the blaring box, as drops of coffee fall on her large plastic bib. I hold back from wiping them, walking the fine line between caring and highlighting her helplessness. This has been Sonia's constant struggle, and she's taught me to be sensitive. I say a quiet thank-you to the fate that gave Mom her eldest daughter — I seem to lack the nursing gene, although I can't help but compare Mom to a younger Max, when milk and cartoons from his highchair allowed me to do housework.

I try to ignore the cracked wall plaster between Mom's chair and the bathroom, a record of her falls when she tried to make it without help. Instead of the ascending pencil marks on the wall that track Max's height, these dents track her decline.

This is the reason she must move.

"I should have moved her in with me," Sonia says. I look at her slumped shoulders and tangled hair. She wouldn't last a week nursing Mom. I wouldn't last a day. We're pathetic. Mom must hate us. For the tenth time today, I feel like a failure.

"Keep packing," I tell her. "The sooner she sees her new garden at the nursing home, the better."

I empty out the rest of the linen closet. Most of the stuff has to go — old towels, large bags full of papers, old tax forms, and photographs. We had crammed it all in bags after Father died, but now it's time to pitch it. I grab a tattered mailing envelope and peek inside. A yellowed document with a passport-sized photo of my young father is on top. His smooth skin and dark hair belong to a twenty-year-old. It's written in Ukrainian and German. My heart pounds as I flip through the rest of the contents. Papers in Ukrainian, or is it Russian and German — faded and written in Latin scrawl with a fountain pen. One looks like a marriage certificate. What is UNRRA? What is all this stuff? Pressure squeezes my head as I consider the possibilities.

"Waaaaaahhh!" Sonia races to the living room, where Mom points to her old address book, her face twisted in torment. Sonia holds her hand and talks softly to calm her down. My heart races as I pause in the doorway.

"Should I call someone?" I whisper.

"It's okay, it'll pass." Sonia murmurs about flowers and television shows until the unbearable whining stops.

I clutch the envelope to my chest like a pillow. "Geez," I say.

"They don't know what sets her off," Sonia says. "That was a mild one."

We finish packing quietly. Sonia handled the panic attack perfectly, although her pale face highlights the dark circles under her eyes.

"I found some old documents in the closet," I tell her. "They look like they're from the Ukraine. Do you want to see them?" Do *I* want to see them?

"I can barely deal with the present," she says. "Do you want them?"

"Maybe," I say. Maybe not.

"Is that a rabbit?" Sonia pushes Mom's new reclining wheelchair, courtesy of the Good Sam, on the garden's paved path toward the far corner, where a small brown hare hops under the blue spruce trees.

"Rabbit." Mom smiles. It *is* a lovely garden. The nursing home's dining area has glass patio doors that lead to a large grassy space surrounded by a rainbow of flowerbeds and leafy shrubs. A tall wood fence encloses the yard—we are in a lush secret refuge right down to Alice's rabbit. My shoulders relax, and I notice Sonia's hands have loosened their grip on Mom's wheelchair handles.

"You made the perfect choice," I tell Sonia quietly. She stares into the spruce trees, refusing to meet my gaze.

We wheel Mom up the ramp and back into her room, where a burgundy curtain separates her from her roommate. Between them, two television sets at full blast create a thousand decibels of noise, but Mom is oblivious to it as she dozes off. Sonia sneaks out to do some shopping while I stretch my legs on the foot of the bed and open *1000 Gardening Questions & Answers*.

A patient's ringing call bell in the hall startles me. Mom opens her eyes as I put down my book. They are surprised, then confused, and then they change again. I stare into the hardened small brown circles. Bile rises in my throat. Her pupils are constricted with anger. Or is it frustration? Hate? I can't look away although fear grips me, and her milky irises etch themselves permanently into my memory. Mom closes her eyes and the moment passes.

"Good nap," I tell her. "Want to have some juice in the garden?" I need to get outside before I faint. What if we've made a mistake?

"Mmmhmm," Mom mumbles. I grab her cup, struggle with the chair brakes, and head down the hall. *It's okay*, I tell myself, suppressing my nervousness.

I don't know how to be alone with her.

We wheel through the dining area and onto the path, and the soupy cafeteria odor disappears as my nostrils are filled with the fragrance of floral honey and spice. I breathe deeply. Maybe Michael Cohen is right? He writes about nature astonishingly engaging fifty-three human senses. Here, as Mom and I roll along the wide asphalt path, even though she is unwell, I'm convinced that at least forty of those senses are probably operating just fine. The sense of season. Of space, and gravity, and the comforting sense of the earth's rotation. I lean around her to see her expression—her face is slack and her eyes are bright, fixed on the flowers that border the path. Her skin is surprisingly smooth, as if the lines of pain have healed in the overhead sun's direct rays. Peaceful. I stop at the gazebo and sit on a bench, parking Mom beside me in the ample wheelchair space, and pretend we are in our pagoda at home.

This is it, I realize, scanning the perimeter of the garden. This is all she needed to be connected—a path and some trees. A little bit of green — be it in a park, on a balcony, in a formal garden, or in a forest — makes us all feel better. I check Mom again to find she's dozing, her head tipped back and her mouth slightly open.

Why am I questioning our garden restoration? It will be *our* place for contemplation, I decide, and we should let it naturally unfold. We'll plant more trees, more than there were before, and replant everything the construction debris killed. We'll reforest around the walking paths and the pagoda. David understands the need to make nature accessible — his television show did so for millions of people. And the dreadful black fence? It's irrelevant. Although sometimes a sanctuary needs boundaries, I decide, glancing around, and back at Mom.

I remember when Father welded the entire black iron railing fence around our house himself, straight iron bars, and the occasional twisted one. It went up methodically, section by section, surrounding our house like prison bars. He painted it shiny black, and it was the envy of the neighborhood. It was low enough to hop over, and the bars were spaced far apart enough that small dogs and cats could circulate through, far too penetrable for such an introverted man, but it was his demarcation, his line in the sand. Our yard was his hard-earned space, and for him, the fence was necessary.

I relax back into Mom's new garden. *This is your place,* I whisper to her as I tuck her shawl around her. She wakes up and the skin crinkles around the corners of her eyes — they are smiling. And then she starts to cry. The crying turns to sobbing and then loud howling. I look around for help, but the garden is empty. I take her hand like Sonia did and start talking, not as a daughter, but as a friend.

☙

My new friend Robin's office was my workplace sanctuary, although I was elated, at almost thirty years old, with my new job at a consumer products firm. There were relatively fewer numbers to crunch, and customers were engagingly emotional and irrational;

I loved them. They gave me a reason to go back to the university, which had become my happy place, part-time, to study marketing.

I admired Robin's organized agenda and perfectionism, and she envied my bohemian life. Our corporate spokesperson, she wore flawless makeup and tailored suits while I was significantly less put together. No matter—I knew about the wacky side she hid under her polished exterior.

"You *what?*" I asked.

She hiked her tailored gray skirt above her hips. We were in her office, door closed.

"Got a tattoo in New York, after a few drinks. Do you know what it means?" Beneath lace-trimmed panties, on her right hip were three items in a diagonal line, each about two inches square: a hot-pink rose, a bright green four-leafed clover, and a peculiar cactus.

"English, Irish, Scottish—get it?" she asked.

"Not really." Holy shit, what was she thinking?

"My heritage. English rose. Irish shamrock. Scottish thistle."

"You tattooed a thistle above your groin."

Robin pulled down her skirt, smoothed her blouse, and sat at her imposing wood veneer desk.

"Yup." Her green eyes dared me to say more, although I recognized a smile deep behind them.

From our first meeting, I pegged Robin as an English rose. Her beauty and porcelain skin allowed her to carry the title, and she was prickly enough to scare off the faint of heart. The shamrock explained her flaming red hair. But the thistle? That evening I checked the Internet to find out more. Indeed, it was Scotland's emblem. Scotland was saved from an invasion by the Norwegian army, who ran screaming after stepping barefoot into a field of wild thistles in the middle of the night. I also learned that Wales's old emblem often accompanies Robin's three tattoos. Luckily she didn't have room on her hip for a leek.

"You went to the food market on your date?" Robin asked, leaning forward across her desk.

"Yup. I bought bagels and bananas," I said.

"What was he wearing?"

"Black T-shirt. Black jeans."

"Hmm."

"Yup. And then I said if he were a gentleman he'd carry my groceries back up the hill. And he said, 'I'm such a gentleman I'll carry *you* up the hill.' And then he crouched down for me to climb on his shoulders."

"No!"

"So I did," I answered.

"You rode on his shoulders all the way up Guy Street?"

My assistant Darlene tapped on the door. "They're waiting for you in the boardroom."

"Got to go," I told Robin.

"I'm glued to my seat." She always said that after one of my date stories.

Sharing intimate details at work became our pastime. I laughed when I later encountered the Latin words *sub rosa*. They imply strict confidentiality. Roman dining room ceilings were adorned with roses, symbols of secrecy, to remind guests that dinner conversation was to be kept private. Robin's office should have been wallpapered in roses.

"You should settle down," Maisie, another office friend, told me over lunch.

"Agreed," said Robin.

"I told you guys I'm never getting married. No kids, either. I grew up in an unhappy household."

They nodded, although I knew they didn't understand. They thought they were smarter, and when a complete stranger at a corporate function asked for my number for a blind-date setup, I said no, amazed at the woman's boldness—and behind my back, they said yes.

· · ·

I agreed to the date because Cam made me laugh during the phone call. Later, as I sat in the wingback chair in the Four Seasons lobby, I was embarrassed and wondering how I'd let this happen. My blind date was late. A man approached me as I stood to leave. Definitely not my type, he was lanky and awkward, with a shiny sweating forehead. Time to change my name.

"Mary?" he asked hesitantly. Why was *he* changing my name?

"Uh, no," I said. He blushed.

"Sorry, I'm here for a blind date. Don't know what Mary looks like," he stammered. He turned and skulked away across the lobby. *Good luck, Mary.*

Cam finally showed up, with his piercing green eyes, wavy dark hair, and unapologetic smile. I found myself forgiving him for being late. A perfectly folded white pocket square graced his pinstriped suit jacket—and was that an Hermès tie? Yikes, a tad conservative.

"Alex?" he asked confidently. "Sorry I'm late." All right, Cary Grant, one drink, and then I'm going back to artists who give me piggyback rides.

Surprisingly, our offices were across the street from each other. I had left my briefcase at the office so I would have a quick exit excuse, and I realized that Cam had done the same thing—he was empty-handed.

"So you're a good friend of Anna's," he said, as I sipped my first glass of wine. Odd—where did he get that idea?

"Actually, I don't know her at all. I met her for a few minutes at a work function, and my friends gave her my number."

Cam's face paled as he took a gulp of his scotch. He was aghast that I didn't know Anna. *I* was aghast that I didn't know Anna. Cam was friends with her brother-in-law and had only agreed to come because he thought he was meeting her close friend. I was horrified, and ready to kill Robin and Maisie.

We filled the awkwardness by discussing work. I told Cam that I'd worked at a telecom company for two years and then quit, and was pursuing an MBA part-time. His shade of white returned.

"I worked there, too," he said with wonder. "I left after two years to do *my* MBA."

What? He must be teasing me. Besides, I would have heard of him.

Cam added more detail. It seemed we *had* worked at the same company, had essentially done the same job rotation, *and* had sat in the same cubicle.

Impossible coincidence. I ordered a second glass.

We shared a few laughs about the old-timers we both knew from the job. We talked about our current jobs as well, and Cam mentioned his visits to his company's New York office.

"Where is it?" I asked. "I'm there a few times a month myself."

"399 Park Avenue."

"We're at 345 Park," I said. "That's—"

"Across the street." He finished my sentence. "Strange," he said as he ordered a double. So both our Montréal and our New York offices were on the same block. Probably happens all the time.

"Do you want to have dinner in the restaurant here?" he asked.

"Guess we have no choice," I said. Our parallel universes had collided.

The surreal blind date turned into a relationship. We were two months apart in age. Kids of immigrants. One sister each, no brothers. Mothers were avid gardeners. The alternative reality thing was expanding except for one thing. His family was loud: they yelled and loved at full blast. Cam would never relate to the silence of my youth.

There were other obstacles: I didn't trust men and I didn't want to settle down. Somehow, I fell in love anyway, safe in the cocoon of Cam's intelligence and family values. The green eyes and sense of humor broke down my bulletproof barrier. And of course, those sexy broad shoulders could carry my screwed-up perspective on life.

✢

I love Lisa.

"We'll plant three for every dead tree removed," she says.

"Perfect." I've come home with two goals: get the restoration planned as soon as possible, and spend more time in the garden with Max. Lisa struggles with several rolls of drawings as we stand on the terrace in our rubber boots. Tomorrow is the summer solstice, when the sun is at its highest, and today our shadows are short one-foot versions of ourselves. The light is so clear, it's as if we're under a spotlight. Maybe we are. Maybe the sun is highlighting our every move to make sure we make the right decisions.

"The pool will be part of the terrace. Small, and no intrusion on the ravine," Lisa says.

"Fine," I say. So Max will grow up with a pool; we need to make sure he is grateful for his privilege. I suddenly realize he'll never know of my parents' humble beginnings, because they never shared them with me. How will I teach him to appreciate the hard work, beyond our own, that brought him here?

We follow Cam through the garden. The sun warms the top of my head, soothing me as I walk through the tiny dust particles that twinkle in the air. I breathe them in, happy that the minuscule pieces of the garden are becoming part of me, healing the sadness of Mom's move. At least she's safe in her new garden, breathing in the same dust and enjoying the same sun.

"I'd like a cutting garden for flowers. Especially roses," Cam says. "A small corner somewhere."

"We can carve out a small area near the pond. You'll have sun, but I'm not sure about the soil," says Lisa. "The rest of the garden will be shady once we plant the trees."

It's hard to imagine because the tree shadows are small stumps in the high sun, the brilliant white star, whose rays push through the chartreuse oak leaves and highlight the path ahead of us.

"We need to fortify the dry soil in some areas," Ben says. "The slope has washed the nutrition away."

Bare patches of cracked dry soil and glinting rocks cover the downward pitch. This is part of an escarpment, a transition from one type of sedimentary rock to another. Our garden is at the bottom of a bowl left by a melting glacier. Can we really control the erosion?

"I have an idea, and it will control the knotweed, too," says Ben.

"Okay," I say. "Netting?"

"Mulch. We'll probably need a few hundred cubic yards." Does he really think a layer of fresh bark can compete with age-old glacial moraine?

"And who will carry tons of mulch down the steps?" I ask.

"I'll get a pumper truck," Ben says, as if people do this every day. "We'll blow it down from the top."

A mulch storm over our house.

"Sounds expensive," says Cam.

"It'll be less than the labor to carry it," says Ben, making a note on his pad.

Cam looks at me, eyebrows raised. I shrug, ignoring the vision of bills on my desk, reminding myself of my new resolve. We wanted the experts and now we have them. Besides, Max will love the mulch truck.

"So we'll start first thing in the spring," Lisa says, "assuming the approvals come through."

"Spring?"

"The City Authority has to go through it. This won't happen overnight," she says.

Spring, really? This process is slower than watching a seed germinate.

"We'll keep cleaning, then," Cam says. "And you can finish with the painting and the guest room."

Inside again? My heart wilts.

"It's old bark and branches. It will protect the soil from weeds and keep it moist," I explain, telling Max how we will mulch next

spring, as we trudge through the garden. I'm secretly looking for a
project because I want to spend the rest of the season foraging with
Max. Or should I say, gently forcing Max to forage.

"I hope it's a huge truck," he says. "Let's climb up here."

Max heads up the slope behind the pond where the erosion has
created the steepest area on the property. Grayish-red tree roots
poke through the soil, some spindly, some like thick fingers that are
clinging on for life.

"Too steep for me," I say, watching him ascend. He uses the
webbed ladder of roots for balance and steadies himself by grabbing
at the thinning bushes.

"Ouch!" he yells, letting go of a spindly branch. "Thorns!"

I look up to see him grasping his fingers beside a shrub with flat,
pale pink flowers.

My stomach flips with excitement. I'd know those flowers
anywhere.

"It's a prairie rose, Max!" I yell. "Pick some for me." We need to
get that mulch as soon as possible.

Max pulls off the flowers, squeezing the petals into a mess as he
makes his way back down to me.

"These grow wild where I grew up," I tell Max, holding the
bruised petals to my nose. "In the ravine behind our house." I shut
my eyes as the fragrance opens my memory.

"They're not that nice," he says.

"Our neighbor used to decorate cupcakes with them," I tell him.

I relive the wonder I felt as Mrs. Brendan made the candied petals; we were going to *eat* flowers. She let me pinch off the white
section at each petal's base and guided me as I beat together the egg
whites and water with an old blackened fork.

"Lay them to dry, open side down," she'd say after gently dipping them in the egg. "Then we'll coat them in sugar and let them
dry overnight."

"Should we do that?" I ask Max. I want him to smell a rose when he's older and think of me. I want him to tell a story about me to *his* son.

"I'm good," he says. That means *no*.

We bring the roses to Cam, who looks at the pinkish blooms with distaste.

"No form," he says. *Snob*.

"Create Your Own Home Still," states the Internet article.

I place a large flagstone in our soup pot, a metal bowl on top of the stone, and fill the pot with water and rose petals. I envision the myriad uses of rosewater—cooking, bathing, room spray—while I wait for the water to boil. This is one of my *best* ideas. I place the lid, upside down, over the boiling concoction, and fill it with ice cubes.

It works! As the petal-filled water boils, its steam hits the cold lid, immediately condenses, and drops into the bowl. Every twenty minutes, I lift the lid, add more ice, and spoon out the few table-spoons of rose water that have accumulated in the bowl. Okay, per-haps this is a lot of work for a few tablespoons. The dream of a scented bath keeps me going. Perhaps a few floating petals, too, and a flickering candle.

"What are you doing now?" asks Cam when he sees the pile of stripped stems.

"I'm making attar. That's rosewater to the uninformed," I say. "I'm hoping Max likes my homemade still. Imagine the flowers we can boil."

He eyes the ice-filled pot lid. "Honestly, Alex, do you have noth-ing better to do?" My happiness withers like a spent petal.

Max walks in before I can respond. "Smells like chicken and peas," he says.

"Chicken and peas? Try again." I shove the bowl under his nose.

"Yup. Chicken and peas." I wonder if I can change families.

"How about you?" I hold the bowl to Cam's face.

"Cheap perfume."

That's the problem with rose fragrance—it's every grandma's perfume. It isn't wearable anymore, unless it's a tattoo.

"I'm taking a bath," I tell them, heading for the tub with my four ounces of rosewater.

Cam knocks on the bathroom door twenty minutes later. "What are you reading?" he asks. He's trying to apologize. He steps into the room, closing the door behind him. "Doesn't smell like roses in here."

The rosewater didn't have much impact so I gave up and topped it off with lavender bubble bath. *A History of Ukraine*, all 572 unread pages of it, sits on the counter by the sink.

"Nothing."

"Want to talk about it?" he asks.

"I brought a bunch of old papers from Mom's. Stuff I've never seen before, written in German and Russian. War documents, I guess."

"And?" Cam's eyes are veiled. He's shocked that I didn't tell him sooner.

"I don't know what to do with them. I hate war shit." I blow at the bubbles and watch the shiny balls float upward and burst. "Maybe I'm fine not knowing," I add. "They didn't share their history with me then—why should I care about it now?"

He runs his hand through his hair as if he's making an important decision.

"Maybe you're comfortable hating them for that," he says. "Maybe you've been covering up what's missing in your life with your careers, us, the *garden*."

I look up at his face and his eyes stare back into mine, direct and steady.

"Maybe it was time to find this stuff," he says. "What are you afraid of?"

I look down at my hands. My wedding band is dulled by the soap.

My face burns in anger while my mind races with confusion. Maybe I'm afraid of what I'll learn.

"Who do you think you are, coming from your loving, *perfect* family?" I ask. "You have no idea how I grew up."

Cam doesn't respond as he turns to leave; I sink, with shame, back into my transparent bubbles.

SUGARED ROSE PETALS

These are beautiful as garnish on cakes and cupcakes, especially at a garden tea party. Use other edible flower petals for variety of color and flavor.

Ingredients:

1 cup washed and dried organic rose petals, bottom tips removed
1 egg white (or equivalent using meringue powder and water)
1 cup superfine sugar

- Beat egg white slightly in a small bowl. Cover work area with waxed paper or parchment.
- Holding petals with tweezers, brush both sides with egg white, using a small watercolor brush.
- Still using tweezers, gently dip petals into sugar, or sprinkle both sides with sugar.
- Place on waxed paper or a wire rack. Dry overnight in a cool dry place. (A cold oven works well.)

See page 267 for information on safety and sourcing of plants.

〜

CHAPTER 12

Bleeding Hearts

IT'S SPRING. LISA AND BEN have approvals in hand and are ready to start. After an autumn of visiting Mom at the nursing home, I'm relieved she has settled into a routine and befriended a Ukrainian-speaking volunteer, despite her increasing dementia and drug doses. I spent the rest of the winter avoiding *A History of Ukraine* and arguing with Cam incessantly about the myriad details of the restoration plans. We're ready.

Max and I walk toward the garden steps after Saturday morning tae kwon do; he's grudgingly agreed to help me find trees for our future hammock. Thoreau is right — an early morning walk *is* a blessing for the whole day. The air buzzes with activity: birds, crickets, and acrobatic squirrels dropping from one branch to another.

"Are you and Dad having a fight?" he asks. The air becomes still.

"No."

"Is it about me? It's my homework again, isn't it?" His shoulders sag under the weight of grade-school pressures.

"Okay, we argued about . . . um, getting a new dog," I improvise.

"What? We're getting a dog? I thought Dad said no. Really?"

Shit, that was a dumb lie. We argued about the restoration budget. But now that I've said it —

"What's that?" I ask to distract him, pointing toward the service-berry. "Under Benji's tree."

A pink horizontal line rises two feet above the ground. Really, *what is that?*

"Pink flowers," he says, bored.

I scramble closer to see a bleeding heart, its leaves touching the bark as though it sprang from the same root. My chest constricts.

"Benji," I whisper.

I pick an intricate flower. "There's a fairytale princess story here," I say, pulling apart the pieces. "Want to hear it?"

"Too lame, Mom." Max runs ahead down the steps as I sit down to patiently dismantle the flower, placing the parts that resemble a dagger and a heart on the step beside me. But instead of the prince offering the petals that resemble bunny rabbits and oriental slippers to his beloved princess, I rewrite the story: Cam gives me a garden of hares and some rubber boots, and I ignore his attempts to make me fiscally responsible, so he stabs himself.

It's probably time to kiss and make up.

"Maybe the seeds floated there by chance," Cam suggests, when I show him the miracle. He's being more open-minded than usual because we've both quietly decided to move on from our disagreement.

"What's the chance of that? From where?"

"So you think Benji sent them?"

"Maybe." I pause. "We're getting a new dog."

Cam has hesitated up to now, not wanting to relive the pain of losing Benji, but he knows the argument is over. We adopt Hunter from a foster home the next weekend.

"Ohio?" Megan asks. She's visiting for a few days as part of a business trip.

"A temporary foster home near here takes in the overflow," I explain, sipping my tea. Hunter, poised on the balcony, unmoving, is focused on the raccoon condo. Not even his white fur, punctuated by three perfectly round black spots like a giant ellipsis, moves in the breeze.

He is *stalking*.

"He looks like a cow," she says. True. A rotund Holstein on long thin legs.

"He's Jack Russell and treeing Walker coonhound, apparently," I say. We'd never heard of the foxhound breed, named for its ability to chase prey up a tree.

"May not have been a wise choice," Cam says from his nearby lawn chair, as Hunter emits a low growl. "We should have asked what his breed is before we signed the papers," he adds. This from the man whose strategy was to pick the dog that least resembled Benji.

"A coonhound," muses Megan. "Kind of funny, given your condo down there."

"Hilarious," I say.

Hunter barks again. And again. And then he growls. He hasn't stopped since we brought him home. I'm worried that he'll never settle in to city life. If he's miserable, we'll have to return him.

"He has a fully stocked yard," Cam says proudly. The dog isn't dewormed and Cam's already in love.

"He was abandoned because he's a bad hunter," I say. "The raccoons are probably laughing at him."

Hunter gets bored with the condo and tries to bury his new bone in a nearby plant pot, creating a considerable mess.

"Not too bright," I say, watching the dirt fall onto the balcony floor.

"He sure is cute, though," Megan says.

"He's a super model," says Cam. Hunter has found his home, another bleeding heart flower on the stem.

Hunter sneezes into the soil, simultaneously falling into a squat. No wonder our *Guide to Dogs* says these hounds lack spatial direction.

If Hunter's a bleeding heart, he's the whimsical plant species commonly called Dutchman's breeches. The white flowers, with two large upper petals in a V-form and two small lower petals, look like Hunter's triangular head and two floppy ears. The flowers are poisonous and make grazing animals wobble. It appears that Hunter is our own silly, staggering cow.

"Want me to take him into the garden?" Max walks onto the balcony with the leash in his hand.

What? I've been waiting years for Max to ask me to go for a walk in the garden, and Hunter gets an offer in days.

The dog stays.

My dog is my best friend, but so is Megan.

We start down the garden steps. She's wearing my new green Wellingtons, courtesy of Sonia, who sent Cam, Max, and me each a pair in honor of the garden restoration. I want to share the ravine with Megan. She was my fellow escapee on the forest trails of our youth, and her house today backs onto a natural walking path. She gets it, and she needs it as much as I do. We both breathe deeply, inhaling the fragrance of tranquility.

"There's your bleeding hearts," she says, pointing at the drooping flowers. "Mom grew those in her garden."

"Yeah, mine too," I say.

"Watching her decline leaves you helpless, huh?" she asks as she examines a teacup-sized magnolia petal.

"I'm having trouble with it. I'm either angry with her or sad for her. I feel guilty being far away, but not guilty enough to move back. She wouldn't have wanted to live this way. First she lost her youth, then her body, and now her mind."

Megan nods. Her parents died several years ago. I wasn't at either funeral, although I should have been. I am her best friend. Living across the country was no excuse. I want to apologize, but my cowardice blocks the words. Our tranquil walk is suddenly making me feel inadequate.

"I want to raise Max differently," I tell her. "I think I am."

"Same with Nathan," she says, referring to her son. She pauses.

"You know our parents did the best they could."

The blood rushes from my face.

"I'm not sure I feel that way," I tell her. Inadequate *and* immature.

"Maybe it'll come," she says, leaning over to pick up a sparkling gray rock, "when you finally look through that envelope. Want this for your collection?"

I tuck the rock into my pocket. They say a friendship's shelf life is about seven years. In our case, it will be *seventy*, and we're more than halfway there.

"I've been thinking," Megan says, "about what you are to me."

"Okay." I'm afraid she's going to say something sentimental. I take a deep breath, hold it in, and focus on the branches protruding from the pond.

"You're my lifeline. No matter what happens, I know you'll be there."

The branches become a brown blur. "Same here."

I have a lifeline.

"That pond is a disaster," Megan says, following my gaze to the murky water. "It's a swamp. You better clean up what's in there or you're going to have mosquitoes."

Megan's departure has left me hollow. Our conversations run through my mind as I tackle my messy den. The tidy bills and books leave a rare clear space on my desk. I've avoided it for a year, but my best friend sent me a message, and it's time I listened.

Here goes.

I open the mysterious envelope from Mom's apartment and lay the documents in front of me, my heart pounding. Once I enter the past, I can't exit. I shut my eyes, breathe in the odor of old paper, and open them. I may as well start at the beginning. I select two yellowed pieces of paper that contain the Latin word *baptismi* and put the rest away.

Father's birth certificate is about six by eight inches, a stained piece of paper with brittle, tattered edges. The old-fashioned scrawl of a fountain pen makes it difficult to tell the difference between capitals I, T, and F. It was folded into eight at one time and the fold lines have become tears secured with yellowed tape in the back. The paper is splattered with tiny reddish-brown stains. I lift it to my nostrils, inhaling must and menthol. I try to fold it, to figure out the order of the folds as if I'm refolding a map. It takes a few tries before I succeed; the finished paper is the size of a credit card. Father must have carried it in a wallet. I feel like an intruder as I hold the paper that might have traveled in a breast pocket so close to his heart.

He was born in 1921 and Mom three years later. The certificates mention Poland and the region of Galicia. I pause to research Galicia and find it is the historical region that included current western Ukraine. In 1921 the region came under Polish rule, following a long period of Austro-Hungarian rule that collapsed after World War I. My parents were born into a nation that desired to be an independent country, something Ukrainians had been seeking for centuries. My head spins as I read about each complicated invasion and war, resulting in another moving border. During the past few centuries, political *and* ethnographic Ukrainian territories changed and morphed in the context of surrounding countries, and not without strife.

It's too much to absorb. I'm overwhelmed, and I've barely begun. I can't learn the history of a country in a few hours or days. The most salient thing I learn is that the Ukrainians were strongly defined by language and culture, without a clearly established territory of their own. Shouldn't this make them cling to their culture even more? I never saw it.

I can't make out the spelling of the district listed on each birth certificate. I search the web, testing different first letters, and find different versions in Ukrainian, Russian, and Polish. The Cyrillic symbols confuse me. I slump into my chair. Four hours for nothing.

"What are you doing?" Max asks, coming into my den to say goodnight.

"Hunting for stuff about my parents' history," I tell him.

"What search engine are you using?" he asks, and before I know it, I'm watching his long, graceful fingers race across my keyboard as he changes my web browser and sets up several new search engines. Those are my father's fingers, the ones I watched push wood through the table saw. Pride unexpectedly washes over me. I examine my short, stubby fingers, dirt under my broken nails.

"That'll be faster," he says, walking out of the room. "Good night, Mom." I watch him walk away, his pants too short for his legs. Did he grow again?

It's as if Max has opened up a floodgate. I'm awed as ancient maps and villages and translated names float across the screen. I print a topographical map of the Kingdom of Galicia, including a legend with lakes, rivers, peaks, and marshes. Green flatlands give way to yellow for higher elevations to dark orange for the Carpathian Mountains. Poland is to the north, Hungary to the south, and Russia is eastward. The names of regions and districts are printed across the map using normal English letters.

"There they are," I sigh with awe and relief, circling their two districts with a pencil.

They had a home. Father's district is mountainous and forested, more than one hundred miles away from Mom's. His tiny town is nestled in the soaring mountains and forests, population six hundred or so. What did they grow for food there, when most of the water flowed from deep in the earth via steaming thermal mineral springs? No wheat grew amidst the beeches, oaks, firs, and spruce. Possibly cabbage, onions, and oats in the meadowlands. No wonder father had oatmeal for every breakfast. It wasn't just comfort food; it was his *youth.* My lifelong obsession with rocks and the White Mountains comes from somewhere—I was born with mountain blood and didn't know it. I pause, peering into the large wooden bowl where I store my rock collection on a side table near my desk, where the mix of sharp and smooth granites and sandstones, veined and marbled stones, represent the history of the planet. *Or maybe I did know it.*

Mom's region is flatter, about fifty miles from the city of Lviv, the region's capital that remains a historic old city in western Ukraine. Her town was small, too, in a region dominated by agriculture—grains, beets, potatoes, and cattle farming. Alcohol production and butter. Our refrigerator shelf, loaded with thick white dairy cream in quart-sized Mason jars, floods my memory. Mom's farm friends from work brought her fresh cream to make butter, the pale unsalted lumps that she melted on her favorite toasted rye bread every morning. Now I knew where her breakfast came from, too. And her ease around our illegal alcohol distiller in the basement.

The map is now in my consciousness, and my subconscious, etched there forever. My printer blurred the lines and colors, but it doesn't matter. I insert it in a clear plastic sheet protector and carefully place it at the corner of my desk.

Pain shoots through my neck as I stretch to the left and right. I bend my neck forward, leaning my forehead into my open palms, and shut my eyes. Now what do I do? Would anyone believe this is how I figured out where my parents were born? I wasn't adopted, yet I'm searching for my long-lost parents. Anger flows through me. Why didn't they simply explain where they were born and tell us about the beauty of the mountains and the prairie steppe? I dig deep into my heart, looking for a connection. I don't feel one to my parents, but I'm struck by the map's topography. Kingdoms have come and gone, but those mountains and soil are still there, holding the secrets of war and of my parents' footsteps.

I stare at the birth certificates and notice they have one thing in common—both are dated 1941, twenty years or so after they were born. Why?

About twenty large trees and shrubs cover the truck bed like a movable forest, the burlap-covered root balls secured with wire cages. I pace quickly, back and forth, waiting for the gardeners to unload. I am the luckiest person in the world. The yellow nursery tags flip in the wind, and my fingers itch to remove the evidence that these trees have been grown on a distant farm. I want to pretend that they've always been here. It doesn't matter where they came from, I tell myself, as I watch the crew wheel them on a dolly to the top of the stairs. They start with the yews, which Cam wants to plant along the top of the retaining wall. The men take one step at a time, dropping the root ball onto the first step's tread, resting, and then onto the next step. This will take *ages*. I follow them, watching the sweat seep through the back of their T-shirts. After a few trips I realize I'm making them nervous, so I head for the few plants now accumulated on the terrace. Time to get to know each other.

My hands tingle as I run my fingers over the leaves, comparing the textures and colors. The variety reminds me of one of the main reasons this garden is special: it encompasses several hardiness plant zones, from 5 to 7, and numerous growing conditions, including shade, sun, an arid slope, and wetlands with a pond. It's a gardener's dream.

The top of the slope at the entrance to the garden is dry and sheltered from the wind by the high retaining wall. It's the sunniest area, with parched, eroded soil and no large trees except the old magnolia halfway down. It's as close to a zone 7 microclimate as we can get.

"Buddleia," announces one of the guys as he places five shrubs in the arid zone along the narrow flagstone path that follows the retaining wall's base.

"When will the butterflies and hummingbirds come?" I ask him. I know we're taking a risk with the fragile butterfly bushes, but if the magnolia survived, they've got a chance. And butterflies? We need as many of those free-spirited pollinators as we can get.

He looks at the few purple upright flowers. "Soon," he says, heading back to get more plants.

I decide to plant oregano and thyme between the flagstones to provide a fragrant landing pad for the butterflies.

Along the steps' descent, there's room for additional magnolias and a few eastern hemlocks. I love the feathery flat needle sprays where the woodpeckers will rest. Ben warned me about the unreliability of slow-growing hemlocks, but I'm willing to take my chances.

At the base of the steps, where the slope flattens, shade takes over because fifty-foot-tall evergreens loom behind the pagoda. Closer to the bog's base is a white—or is it black?—spruce, and beyond it, a few crooked-trunked Scotch pines, leaning sideways as if their roots are losing their grip on the soil. I collect a few broken spruce branches so I can look them up in my tree guides, and pile the pinecones into a corner for mulch. I can taste the evergreen tea already.

The land right in front of the pagoda is a zone 6 wetland, bordered by mixed forest. The guys plunk several willows onto the ground, with a few yellow-spiked elephant ears and purple Siberian irises for color. Lisa has taken Cam's request for cutting flowers seriously.

Along the city fence behind the pond, we'll plant white cedars to hide the chain link. There's already an enormous cedar there to the west of the pagoda, shaped like a giant pinecone, and a thick layer of dry needles underneath makes an inviting carpet. I break off a bough and sit down, letting the pungent woody oil open my lungs. This is the perfect place to do yoga, I decide as I move into a cat stretch, putting my nose closer to the earth. The aroma of fresh rain and moldy leaves melds with the cedar's fragrance, and my worries about the garden dissipate, replaced by my thoughts of Gordon's song, *Beautiful*.

The guys arrange twenty cedars along the fence where they will protect the primroses from the summer heat. I move into a cross-legged position and press my palms together, bowing to the emerald wall.

Namaste.

The garden's flattest area, the dry tableland on the other side of the pond, is shaded on three sides by oaks and maples. Dappled sun highlights the area where the construction debris was piled. Ben brought some redbuds and a balsam fir for here because the soil is rich, a zone 5 deciduous forest. Farther north, the Secret Path upward toward the sugar maples is steep, and tall trees create the deepest shade and the driest soil. Erosion has taken its toll, and the enormous oak roots take any moisture left in the ground, leaving only spindly shrubs underneath.

"You're going to need irrigation," says one of the guys, staring up the dry slope. "The trees need to get established."

"I'm not irrigating here," I answer. The plants will have to make it on their own.

"It's a big risk," he says, wandering off, as if running pipes through a ravine forest is normal.

Another decision. Mulching is enough intervention. I look up to the sky and ask for rain.

"That smells good," says Cam. "Are you making me a flower arrangement?"

I admire the long cedar boughs as I wrap the branches with string. "*Balais*," I answer.

"Really, Mom, you're making a broom?" Max asks, looking up from his computer. Those French classes have paid off. "Looks too short."

"The *Eclectic Guide to Trees* says French settlers used white cedar for a deodorizing broom," I say as I start to sweep the crumbs around the kitchen table. It's not effective, but I'm not going to admit it. The fragrance part is working.

Cam looks at the maple sugar near the coffee maker. "Your mother is turning our house into Pioneer Village," he says to Max.

Hunter walks into the kitchen, smells my broom, sneezes, and falls onto his butt.

"We have a good selection of evergreens down there," I tell Cam. I *love* Pioneer Village. "Come see."

I lead him to my desk, where I've laid out my cone, twig, and needle samples, each on a labeled paper towel.

"I'm guessing this is a white spruce based on the cone and the twigs," I tell him. "And I found a YouTube video on how to make natural chewing gum from the resin."

"Really?" he asks, gazing at my samples doubtfully.

"What?"

"Chewing gum? How many hits did it get?"

"Eighty-one." Did he roll his eyes?

"Well, thank goodness for the Internet. How else would you find your peeps? Now there's eighty-two of you."

"It's so sanitized it looks like black peat moss," I tell Cam as he places my water bottle on a step beside me. I'm fertilizing the soil around the new plantings. "It's fake sheep manure," I continue, "with all its manure personality removed—no lumps, no stink, no undigested pieces of grass."

He laughs, heading away with his pruners.

Not that I mind. The white plastic bag with an adorable sheep photo makes me forget I'm spreading shit. But maybe it's so sterilized it doesn't even work.

The instructions mention keeping away from children and pets, as well as careful hand washing after use. Okay, sounds like there are some remaining active ingredients. I open one heavy bag at a time wearing double gloves, and till it into the soil with my pitchfork. I walk gingerly, not wanting to spread fecal matter all over the paths, which will then enter the house, and Hunter's paws and our food and digestive systems, possibly killing us with some strange bacteria. When Mom spread chunks of wet, smelly manure, it was everywhere, including on her clothes. She cooked our pork chops and mashed potatoes in her stained gardening shirt, and no one died. But times have changed. Our lives are so sanitized that we've lost the ability to fight off half the germs I probably used to eat with Mom's garden vegetables. I did consider composting Hunter's poo, but apparently it takes at least three years to get rid of harmful parasites. My patience is expanding as I become more of a gardener, but not that much.

BLEEDING HEART VALENTINE CARDS

Please note:

Bleeding hearts can cause a skin reaction in some people. Handle with care and do not ingest.

Materials:

Fresh bleeding heart flowers, firm and well hydrated
Flower press or large heavy books
Paper towel or blotting paper (available at craft stores)
White glue
Toothpicks
Tweezers
Blank note cards

Use flower press as directed, or follow these steps:

- Place the flowers inside a folded paper towel, ensuring they don't overlap. Place the folded paper towel into the middle of a book, close it, and place at least 20 pounds of other books or heavy objects on top.
- Check on flowers every 2 or 3 days, changing paper towel every 5 days. Total drying time will be about 2 weeks. Flowers are dry when they are brittle and do not bend.
- Pour some glue into a shallow dish. Arrange flowers, without glue, onto notecard into desired pattern. Use toothpicks to dot glue onto underside of dried flowers, one at a time, and press them gently onto note card. Use as little glue as possible.

See page 267 for information on safety and sourcing of plants.

CHAPTER 13

❧

Wild Grasses

"Why are you covered in grass seed? It's even in your hair!" I yell at Max, as I notice a fine layer of seed also floating on the pond's surface. Shit, where else did he spray it?

"Dunno. I did exactly what you said. This is stupid," he says, in his I'd-rather-be-on-my-computer voice. He looks down at the handheld seed spreader in frustration.

"Just forget it," I say. The grass won't take down here anyway, where weeds and my beloved dandelions have taken control. Cam's vision of a rolling green hill by the pond will have to wait. Meanwhile, if I spray Max with water, I'll have my very own Chia Pet boy.

Max angrily throws the seed spreader into the large storage bin behind the pines and heads up the steps.

"Are you excited about the mulch truck?" I tease him from behind, examining the seed stuck to his back. Did he *roll* in it?

"Nope," he says.

"I am."

"Well, I'm not." He continues up to the house while I stop to check on Cam, who is battling his way through the bog.

"This is war," Cam says. He's protecting his prized irises by pulling out a patch of stately wild grasses. His clothes are splattered in muck, his hair is mussed, and his boots are deep in sludge—caveman meets Dockers.

"Don't pull them all out," I say. "I think they're gorgeous."

"Living swords." He grasps a five-foot-high stalk. I don't bother mentioning his lack of gloves. The ornamental grass doesn't budge. I also decide not to mention that's he's pulling out grass exactly twenty feet from where he has asked us to grow more grass.

"Shit!" he yells. Razor cut to the palms. I bite my tongue again.

I already know he's fighting a losing battle with his evil pond predator, the *Miscanthus*—I've researched it. It sprouts rhizomes under the mud like obstinate worms boring holes through spongy soil.

"The Japanese use them to celebrate the autumn harvest," I say.

He pulls harder. "It's an invasive bully. Maybe you can weave something with it," he jokes, nodding at the pile of uprooted grass. "A hammock or something."

I put down my bag of collected pinecones and pick a grass blade, balance it between my thumbs, and whistle through it. I've still got it. The sound resembles a muted foghorn.

"You're such a prairie girl," he says.

Not anymore. I'm a mountain girl, descended from ancient nomads of the Carpathians. I blow my grass horn again, to call my imaginary herd of sheep, and I head inside, leaving Cam to lick his wounds.

"They're scented fire starters," I explain to Cam when he comes in for a break. The kitchen counter is resurfaced in newspaper and glistening pinecones.

He looks confused. "Fire starters? I thought you were using them for mulch."

"I dipped them in melted paraffin," I say. Hunter jumps, lands his front paws on the counter, and sniffs.

"Smells like pie. Did you make pie?" Cam asks hopefully, as he pours his coffee.

"I put cinnamon in the wax."

"Your mother made the *best* pie," he says wistfully.

She really did. I still hate pie.

I stare at my counter of pinecones—natural mulch, the same stuff I'm about to blow across the garden with a giant pumper truck. Maybe I should have left them under the trees, like Cam should have left the grasses. The thing is, as much as we think we're working *with* nature in the garden, we're also working *against* it. We celebrate it, and then we manipulate the hell out of it. I hope Mother Nature forgives us.

Sonia calls with an update on Mom's health, interrupting an after-dinner glass of wine on the balcony. Mom's not eating well, she explains matter-of-factly. I sense the resignation in her voice.

A wave of panic courses through me. "She needs a change of scenery," I say. "Can we fly her here for a visit? I'll come get her, and we'll hire a nurse to come, too."

"She can't fly, Alex," Sonia says. "With her heart, it's impossible."

My anger comes from deep within, rising quickly like a new spring, surprising both of us. "How do you know it's impossible? Have you asked her doctor? *You're* not the one who decides."

"She'll have a stroke. Her arteries are blocked. She *can't* fly," Sonia says firmly.

"I want you to ask," I tell her angrily. "Let her doctor decide."

She agrees, offended that I don't trust her. I'm offended that she has become the gateway to my own mother. We hang up, both wanting to say more. My sister has lost hope.

"Sonia's not giving up," Cam explains, when I tell him. "She's preparing for the inevitable."

"That's ridiculous," I say. "Air ambulances fly people all the time."

Mom *has* to visit. We planted a cherry tree.

Mom's decline sends me back to my pile of war documents.

"Why is this so difficult for you?" Cam asks, as I put down my teacup with a sigh. "You're lucky to have found something to connect you to your parents' youth."

He's in his usual spot on the sofa, with his feet on the table that holds my rock bowl.

"It's the frightening reality of wartime. It's the same reason I don't watch war movies. They bring me down. Human nature brings me down."

"We learn from studying history," he says.

"*You* learn. I can't cope with what we're capable of. It's the same reason I was terrified to have a child."

Cam nods, but he doesn't remember how I used to stare at my denim-clad growing belly in a cold sweat, fearing every time I watched the evening news that we'd made a mistake.

"Yet you have one," he says quietly. "And he makes the world a better place."

He's right, of course, but that's no help.

🌿

The 1917 Russian Revolution divided the then Ukrainian homeland between the Soviet Union and Poland, and in 1922, the Soviet Union created the Ukrainian Soviet Socialist Republic. Born in the 1920s, my parents, like many western Ukrainians, grew up hearing about the great 1932 famine in eastern Ukraine, the Holodomor, in which it is now widely believed that about 4.4 million Ukrainians starved to death. Is it any wonder, later in Canada, that as long as we had food and a house, it was a considerable step up from their youth? I remember Father's silence as he worked through his meals, eating simply because it was time to eat. Mom would be quiet, too, itching to get back to her plants, and I escaped into my most recent book at the table while I ate.

I never thanked Mom for dinner, I realize, something we strictly enforce with Max. I took the food on the table for granted and ate quickly in order to escape the oppressive quiet that pervaded the kitchen. I realize now that my parents were grateful for their food, the land they grew it on, and the safety in which they ate it. The past was a burden better left behind.

In 1939, Mom was fifteen and Father was eighteen. The Soviets annexed western Ukraine from Poland. During this period, many Ukrainians, though finally united, lived in terror of being declared enemies of the state. Thousands of people were shipped to Siberia for hard labor, and many died. Fear and paranoia were pervasive. Two years later, in 1941, Ukrainian lands were occupied by Germany.

There's my answer: 1941. Under occupation, a scramble for documentation ensued; my parents were among the many who lined up at their local parishes seeking birth certificates that would confirm their identity, race, and religion. Ukrainians fell into the "inferior" whites category of Nazi race classification and mostly were used as forced labor to fulfill Germany's war needs. They were experienced farmers, and Germany wanted to exploit the unique region of fertile land—meter-thick *chornozem*, or black soil, rich in humus, phosphorus, and calcium, that existed in only two regions of the world.

Suddenly, the two tattered birth certificates on my desk take on a whole new meaning. In wartime, they meant survival.

My parents' fate for the next five years, until the end of the war, is not completely clear. Sonia recalls that Mom told her she worked on a German farm until the war ended, where she was mostly hungry and resorted to stealing food. Nothing more. There are no pictures or documents of her during this period. No stories, no shared memories.

I find a sad, melancholic sepia picture of my father and a young man, who I assume must be his brother due to the striking resemblance. The date 1942 is penciled on the back. My uncle. I don't even know his name, I realize, transfixed by their worn, tired eyes. They are dressed up, surprisingly, in nice shirts and ties, posing side by side with their arms touching but not around each other. My hands tense as I focus my magnifying glass on the backdrop—it's a faded painted wall, a fresco in a photographer's studio, the cloth bottom of the canvas visible behind their worn shoes. Branches droop, with

radiating leaves that look like those of horse chestnut, over a concrete pillar encircled in vines. There's a large pond in the distance—
a portrayal of a formal garden, and it looks vaguely familiar.

My head spins.

It's as though my father and his brother are posed in front of
our pagoda. The pillars appear identical. What would Father have
thought then, at twenty-one, about to go to work in Germany, if
someone told him to imagine this idyllic scene for real, and that in
seventy years I would photograph his grandson in the same position,
against a similar concrete pillar, for a family Christmas card?

My father went to Germany a few months later. The yellowed
card in my hand identifies Father as a Ukrainian worker in Germany,
a locksmith. A purple stamp confirms that he was allowed to receive
food rations. Why did he and his brother dress up and have a picture
taken? Where did his brother go? The expression on their faces signals that this was one of the last times they might be together, and
they both knew it. They were saying goodbye, creating a souvenir.
My body is still as the picture speaks to me.

My simple little blurry map on the corner of my desk, the one
that gave me hope, now gives me heartache. It showed me my parents' birthplace, but it appears they left it, and their families, and
their story is missing.

❧

Cam's family is in town for a few days. They're my family, too, after
all these years. They provide everything I didn't have growing up—
loud meals and overwhelming love. From the moment I met them,
they filled a void and made me complete, but also showed me, like a
shocking pail of ice water over my head, what I had missed.

"Alex?" Cam's father, eager to go, waits at the back door. He
wants to buy us a push lawn mower. A few blades of Cam's grass
have popped up from between the weeds.

"I feel guilty," says Cam. "Inept."

"Not enough to come with us," I say.

"You are the son I never was," Cam says. True, his father wanted a handyman son. A successful businessman in silk ties is a tremendous source of pride, but far too complicated.

I saved the day with my red toolkit. When Nonno and I first met, we didn't speak the same language, but we understood drill bits and screw heads. I didn't know then that years later, when he would meet my father before our wedding, the two of them would silently put together our first wedding gift, a barbecue. I worried for the four hours it took, and they managed to do it, without words, using a few hand signals and grunts. There were pieces left over, of course, and I remember our fear of an explosion when we used it for the first time. It silently ignited, an ode to those who built it.

The sound of the opening door brings me back to the present.

"Yeah, I'm the son your father never had, and the daughter my father never wanted," I reply.

"*Via!* Off you go," Cam says to his father and me, as he heads back to the kitchen to have another espresso with his mother.

The Home Depot doors slide in front of us. Warmth courses through me as I enter my oasis. Nonno, meanwhile, is bristling with excitement, practically rubbing his hands together in anticipation. An orange sign greets us warmly, as does the sharp odor of lumber and metal, or, as a good friend calls it, the smell of opportunity. It occurs to me that I recognize that exact shade of orange. *Hermès orange*, the color of Cam's beloved tie boxes. A classic brand—I love it —but not as much as the warm embrace of Home Depot.

Nonno and Nonna have been married for over fifty years. Max adores the full house when they visit, the boisterous fusion of English, Italian, and French, biodiverse like my mixed-grass seed. The prized only grandchild, he is lavished with adulation. In addition to my special bond with Cam's father, I equally adore Cam's mother, Rosa, a generous cook and prolific gardener. I hate it when the family harshly criticizes her meals—too much salt, too dense a meatball —but Cam says it's sport, and that this is how they keep each other honest. Their dinner table is an alien place to me, surrounded in a cloud of simultaneous fighting, yelling, and adoration. Even tears, because every family has tears, eventually evaporate with the steam of the pasta pot.

What do you mean you love your mother-in-law? friends ask me. How can I explain to them that she's the mother I missed, that she feeds me with unconditional love and my favorite stuffed artichokes? *No one's perfect*, my friends say. I agree, but she's perfect for *me*.

Cam's younger sister, Fio, is not a gardener. She's a passionate baker with the same crazy patience, her craft perfected after years of family critique and approval. My last birthday cake was covered with roses and dahlias, their ornate stems and leaves winding around the sides. The flowers, made of sugar fondant, right down to the yellow stamens, ridged petals, and serrated leaves, were impossibly realistic.

"Do you like it?" she asked, her green eyes wide with pride.

"Unbelievable," I said. "But I can't cut it."

"I can," she said, and she sliced enthusiastically, an artist destroying her own work. She was already on to the next edible canvas. Like her mother, she's full of life and happiness, and I drown in her generosity. Max doesn't realize what he has, between cupcakes from Fio and hand-knit sweaters from Sonia. Would he fathom that I don't even know my aunts' names?

Although my in-laws are overwhelmed by the garden, they spend most of the week outside, tidying, watering, and examining the new plants. I realize that Cam's parents, with the farms of their youth, their gardening, and their self-reliance, might have been exactly my parents without the silence and sadness. Two farming families caught up in World War II, but Cam's parents were too young to be participants. Their villages suffered as a battle zone while they sheltered in the nearby mountains, but they eventually were able to return and keep their land. What a difference being born ten years later can make.

"What are you doing in here?" Cam asks. "They're looking for you." Some days, I need to hide in the bedroom because his family's intimacy makes me inexplicably melancholy.

I stare at the ceiling, watching the dust particles dance in the stream of sunlight through the window. Loud voices float in from the kitchen, where Max is making fried doughnuts with his grandmother.

"It's too much," I say.

"What's too much?" he asks. "The noise?"

"Your family makes me realize what I never had." It's a selfish emotion that I should keep to myself. But some days, I just can't help it.

Cam sighs. "You need to get out of bed."

Worse, Sonia called. The doctor says Mom can't travel, for all the reasons Sonia outlined, and more.

The truth was obvious. I ignored it *and* was rude to Sonia. I was desperate to show Mom the trees. I'm also ignoring the fact that she probably couldn't care less. She's lying in a bed, losing the little mobility and mental faculties she has left. Trees are not what she's thinking about in her fits of hysteria, when her screaming can be quelled only by a fast-acting sedative. Her short-term memory has disappeared, and she remembers only things she knew in the past, which is why she remembers our faces but not what we said two minutes ago. Are her terrifying thoughts of the war? It seems we are on a parallel path, my mother and I, of reliving the past—her in her memory, and me in my research. Sadly, we each walk alone.

Silence weighs down the household. It's uncomfortable, as if I'm wearing someone else's clothes.

"You don't think you were a bit harsh?" Cam asks me, as we walk through the garden.

I breathe deeply. "Maybe, but it's done." Max ignored me one time too many from behind his large headphones, especially when Cam's family was visiting, so I packed all his computer games in a box and put it in the furnace room.

"Until further notice," I told him. "You have no idea how lucky you are."

Max's body stiffened in anger as he pushed his chair from the kitchen table and stomped to his room.

"He got his black belt, you know. His grades are good and he loves his family. But he's only eleven. You should cut him some slack," Cam says.

I recall the lightning-like crack when Max's heel flew into the pine board, while he floated high through the air, his hair flying. The confidence and pride etched on his face when the Master tied the stiff new belt around his waist and tightened it with a sharp pull, and then ruffled his hair, shook his hand, and bowed.

"They're unrelated events," I say. "That's how we get sucked in as parents. One good thing doesn't forgive a bad." But I feel my resolve softening.

"I think you'll need to tell him how to earn them back," Cam says.

"You do that," I tell him.

It's mulch day. Soon a layer of shredded organic love will protect the garden, like the blanket I would tuck around Max when he was a baby, fallen asleep after hours of soothing. I miss those days, when adolescent angst was a faraway concern.

I greet the crew, surprised by their orange suits with big yellow X's across their chests and backs. This is serious. The men unwind and connect heavy tube lengths together to create the 300-foot-long power hose. It's slow going. It snakes from the enormous eighteen-wheel blower truck parked on the street, along the driveway, the side of the house, and over the retaining wall.

They adjust their helmets and eye protection, and advise me to stand back.

"It'll be dusty," one warns me.

"Go," says the lead man, and the blower's wheeze is followed by the roar of thunder as mulch starts to flow through the tube at hundreds of cubic feet per minute. The tube jerks under the velocity as the man grips the wide funnel at the hose's end and begins to spread the windstorm of bark chips. Dust surrounds him and rises above the property in a granular cloud.

If only Mom could see this. It's a long way from the straw mulch she sourced from a friend's farm. She'd be embarrassed that technology is making me an observer instead of a laborer. Speaking of which, I head up to the street to check on the truck. An elderly man from down the street stands beside it, arms crossed, the veins on his neck pulsing under his papery skin. The truck's engine reverberates around him, seemingly shaking him. He's hard of hearing; I'm not sure why he's the one complaining.

"Sorry, mulch for weed control," I holler, pointing at the vibrating hose.

"Damn right it's out of control!" he yells.

"It won't be long."

"Damn right it's wrong!" he yells. "I'm calling the police."

I race down the stairs and tell the men to rush, reminding them to stay clear of the pond and the grass seed. Every time I try to ask a question, a fine film of grit covers my teeth, matching the sticky dust layer on my clothes and skin. No matter—by day's end, the garden is musky cedar-scented nirvana; I want to pitch a tent and sleep in the fragrance. I walk the men to their truck in time to see another infuriated neighbor charging down our driveway.

HOMEMADE GRASS CHIA PET

Materials:

Potting soil
Grass seed or chia seed
Knee-high nylons/pantyhose
Craft eyes, colorful felt decorations, pipe cleaners
Hot glue gun and/or straight pins

- Mix soil and grass seed together in a ratio of two parts soil to one part seed.
- Fill toe of knee-high with 1 cup of mixture and close with a tied knot, leaving the length to act as a wick for water. Set pet on top of a terracotta pot, glass, or paper cup filled with water, hiding the wick inside.
- Glue or pin eyes and felt decorations to pet as desired to make a face.
- Place in a sunny spot and add water daily, misting pet as well.
- Grass hair will sprout in a week to 10 days.

See page 267 for information on safety and sourcing of plants.

CHAPTER 14

Irises

IT TAKES ME HALF A DAY to mow the lawn. I work in a line, arms aching, up and down the slope above the pond. The fragrance changes every few feet, from candy-sweet floral to dank peat to citrus and pine. The scents refuse to be captured, and I'm soon lulled into a rhythm by the old-fashioned mechanical whir of the push mower's blades. They're not sharp enough to cut the crabgrass that defiantly pops up behind me. My strategy is simple: don't mow too low, and then throw grass seed at the problem. I catch the birds flying in for a snack as I trudge up the steps, exhausted but triumphant.

From afar, the illusion of a perfect golf course green lies below me. From this perspective, Cam's ideal lawn exists, and his dream meets reality. Maybe that's all that matters, just like I choose not to hear the city traffic over the birdsong every morning, until, in my consciousness, the traffic simply ceases to be there. There's no pure state in a garden.

I bring Max and Cam down to see the lawn.

"It's fantastic, Alex," Cam says. "Spectacular."

"Awesome, Mom," says Max. "But where are the koi?" He peers into the large pond.

Where *are* the koi? We should have seen the flashes of color whizzing around by now. I remember the two captivating red foxes I spotted from the kitchen window a while back. Or was it the raccoons?

"Did they die?" he asks sadly.

"I'll check for them when I clean out the ponds," I say, swallowing over the lump in my throat. "After the ducks are done nesting."

"You can't clean these, Alex," Cam says. "Shouldn't you focus on finishing the swimming pool?" he asks, forgetting that I don't like his fake concrete pond.

As if to make my point, the two mallards fly in and make a splash landing. I love it when they do that.

The three of us move to the bench to watch. Bright orange webbed feet flip quickly under the water's surface, while the mallards' necks turn 180 degrees as they preen their backs. Where did they fly last winter, I wonder. The Caribbean? Mexico? I'm envisioning my ducks in tiny sombreros when Cam interrupts my thoughts.

"Those irises must be five feet tall," he says, pointing to the vivid mass beyond the hammock, now temptingly hanging between the redwood and the dead tree trunk.

"Did you know they can filter sewage?" I ask.

"How do you know that?" He's upset that his favored flowers perform menial cleaning tasks. They are his *fleurs-de-lis*, the noble emblems of all things once French and Florentine, found on coats of arms and flags, and bridging his two worlds, Québec and Tuscany.

"*The Magic of Irises*. I bought it last fall." *My husband's an iris*, I told the clerk as I paid for the worn book from the sale bin. *What a deal*, she said—*decipher your husband for $7.99*.

Cam and I tiptoe across the weed-lawn to get a closer look, while Max stays with the ducks.

"They're kind of weird-looking, aren't they?" I ask, examining the three upright petals and three downward ones.

"They're elegant," Cam says. "Simple yet complex."

"They look like they can't decide. Do I face up or do I face down?"

"And the color," he adds, ignoring me.

Of course, Cam loves the rainbow offered by irises. If he were a room, he'd be his library, where the colorful book spines surround him, creating a kaleidoscopic cocoon of dispersed color.

A squawking from the pond gets our attention in time for us to see a third duck, another male, land near the first two. A fight of flapping wings begins between the males. Disappointment runs through me. It's like enjoying peaceful animals on *National Geographic* before they suddenly try to kill and eat each other. The ducks flap for another minute until one male flies away.

"You know that only the female quacks, while the male kind of grunts?" I ask.

"Sounds familiar."

"Well, I suppose all relationships get tested," I say, as we walk up the steps behind Max.

"Cookie, this garden's making you bonkers," he says.

"What the hell are those?" Cam asks. It's Saturday morning and the ducks seem to be gone.

"Waist waders. I'm going to clean the pond." I twirl around in my green rubber suit.

"You look like Gumby."

"I'm waterproof," I say, flipping my suspenders.

"That algae is slippery. Shouldn't Stan be doing this?"

"We can't afford Stan for this. I've got him working on a fountain to clear the water." I adjust my gloves. "Besides, Ayca's coming to help."

"That doesn't make me feel better. Tell her to not wear her jewelry. I'm not hiring divers to go after her fancy watch," he says.

"She *asked* to come."

"You shouldn't have told her she reminds you of a water lily."

"But she does. I think there's a gardener in there."

"Don't think so," Cam says, heading for his library.

I'm willing to find out. Lately, I need to share the new garden,

especially with the unconverted. Charles Lewis, the famous horti-
culturalist, said that the "mental" garden creates feelings in us before
we are conscious of them. He's right. I see it in friends' faces every
time they discover the spiky pink water lilies peeking from their
mass of floating leaves.

"You're wearing a white shirt?" I ask Ayca when she arrives.
There's definitely no gardener under that. Her nails, hair, and
makeup are immaculate. I sigh, handing her an extra pair of gloves
and boots.

"What?" she asks, as we head for the pond. "Is it that deep?"

I met Ayca as a fellow parent at Max's school, and our families
have become inseparable friends over the years. She's irresistibly
charming, one of those endearing people who can laugh at themselves and make their endless admirers laugh too.

"Look at those grape vines!" she yells. "My mother needs to see
those." Ayca's mother makes the best Turkish *dolma* in town. "Don't
tell anyone else about them," she whispers, looking around posses-
sively. "This is a gold mine."

"Secret's safe with me."

Half an hour later, we're exhausted.

"Wow, there's a lot of work to do here," Ayca says, pushing algae
clumps to the edge. Her gardening boots are water-filled, her shirt is
covered in bright green stains, and the tips of her long auburn hair
are lengthened with tendrils of slime. Through it all she preserves
her elegance. She is Naiad, the Greek—well, in her case, Turkish—
water nymph.

I wade deeper into the pond, feeling the pressure of the cold water suck the waist waders close to my body. Four feet deep into it,
there are uneven slippery rocks at the bottom of the pond, making
it impossible to move safely, although I use the pond rake to steady
myself. This is not the place to fall—more than dead koi might lie
at the bottom of the darkness, and I'm now sure they died. We're
responsible. We broke nature's gentle equilibrium with our garden
cleaning.

Ayca's voice brings me from my musings. "Where can I get a pair of those rubber pants? Do they come in other colors? I think you should put the lilies here," she adds. "And the fountain there," as if she's rearranging her living room.

I wonder if we can dry and eat our bounty. Dr. Oz says seaweed and algae are brain food. I decide not to tell Ayca that algae can double their numbers every few hours.

"You look like a water nymph," I say instead.

"Me?" she asks, smiling mischievously.

"Supernatural Greek femme fatale. Could be you."

"Could be," she agrees, pleased. I've seen Ayca nymph cajole her way out of parking tickets. There's no doubt in my mind.

After several hours, a mountain of old leaves, broken branches, and algae drains at the pond's edge. We've barely begun. Ayca promises to return next week.

"You're the only woman in this neighborhood with waist waders," she says proudly, as I step out of my slime-covered rubber suit and hang it on a tree branch like a scarecrow. "By the way, can I transplant some of that lily of the valley? It would look great in my yard."

"Of course." Success. The garden has gotten under her skin as well as all over her shirt.

"Perfect," Hans says, a few weeks later, as he adjusts the cedar two-seat swinging bench. The bench hovers above the slope, facing the now-tidy pond, hidden on three sides by leaf-covered branches.

"Max will adore it," I agree.

Hans is in charge of our landscape work since Lisa and Ben moved on to their next contract. I miss them, but Hans is a godsend, a lanky, capable gardener with a confident smile. He's helped with so many finishing touches that I secretly refer to him as my garden rent-a-husband.

It's difficult to climb the steep slope and hoist myself onto the bench, but the vantage point is worth the effort. I have a perfect aerial view of the pond, the rainbow of sun shining through the new fountain's spray, and the spreading water lilies whose pointed leaves are unfurling at an astonishing pace. It *is* perfect. No wonder Monet was obsessed with water lilies. The flower petals are shaped like almonds, like Ayca's eyes.

❧

Father's eyes haunt me. I'm obsessed with his small identification card from Germany. The folded paper is more worn than his birth certificate. I look for pictures of similar cards on the Internet, and, to my amazement, find them. The eyes of the strangers' photos on my screen share an aura of gloom. One woman's youthful lips turn downward. Another man looks sideways. I look back to Father's photo and suddenly realize why it feels eerily familiar—his square chin with the hint of a cleft also belongs to Max.

I hate these war documents. It was easier to be ignorant and resentful. Instead, I'm reliving moments of my youth, as scenes play through my dreams: My parents. Fighting. Silent meals. Their friends singing melancholy tunes. Their need to stay together. The way they took care of each other in their last years, alone in the house and hiding their frailty. The row of gravestones.

My research has made me wiser, and the wisdom has brought heartache. The watered-down high school war facts are gone; I've read *descriptions*. The smell of death. Of children's distended stomachs on starving skeletons. Fear. Despair. Suicide. Hope.

I'm closer to understanding Mom's youth, while she lies in her bed in the nursing home, her dementia making her forget the present while tapping into a past she can't communicate. It's a crazy stupid twist of fate, as if I have to find my own way in while she takes her own way out. This isn't how legacy is supposed to happen.

These people witnessed Hitler's ruthless exploitation policy, ghettos, and execution camps for Jews, Gypsies, and Soviet Russian prisoners of war. They saw their rich agricultural land used to supply food for the war effort while they were fed rations. And yet, compared to others, they were lucky. What did they think about as they worked? Their lost families, terrifying rumors, and probably escape. How did they feel as they survived?

As I continue to learn, each descriptive passage of human suffering makes my stomach lurch. In his book *Bloodlands*, Timothy Snyder uses that term to refer to the areas that comprised Poland, Soviet Ukraine, Soviet Belarus, the Baltic States, and the western fringe of Soviet Russia between 1933 and 1945. He claims these regions, caught in the middle of Stalin's and Hitler's regimes, saw bloodshed many times worse than any seen in Western history. He suggests that up to fourteen million noncombatants were caught in the crossfire, including those who perished in the Holocaust. He is one of many authors whom I explore, each more controversial than the next, but the word *bloodlands* penetrates my consciousness, maybe because I've read so much about the rare and fertile chornozem soil. Now I see it irreversibly soaked in misery.

I realize that Father lived and died quietly with his painful memories. Memories that, I see in retrospect, festered inside him while he hoarded junk picked from garbage cans, and the barter items in his safe, not trusting anyone, including his own children, with his paranoid thoughts.

🌿

I open my eyes to a green summer haze, get out of bed, and walk to the window to check out the morning garden, which now includes the swimming pool's deep blue water, a dramatic contrast to Cam's overgrown jade-green yew hedge.

"Uh, Cam, you may want to see this," I say, as Cam hoists his legs off the bed.

He joins me at the window to watch two ducks — *our* two ducks — casually swimming and dabbling in his new pool. They own it.

"Shit," he says.

"Probably," I agree. That chlorinator better work.

"I thought they left," he says. "Maybe they felt unsafe in the pond. They probably think your superhero waist waders look like there's a duck hunter hanging from the tree."

Blood rushes from my face. First the koi—now I've terrified the ducks?

"Look what Mom had in the basement," Max tells Cam that evening, examining the battery-operated UV-light water purifier.

"You need two," I explain, handing him the carbon microfilter. "With both, any water in the world is drinkable. Including our pond *and* the pool."

The filters are my backup in the event of a city reservoir problem. After several power outages, I decided we need emergency gear. That's why I also have a cupboard full of canned beans, tuna, flashlights, and batteries.

"Really, Alex, you're becoming your father."

I catch my breath. Holy shit. *I'm becoming my father*. I even have spare cash in the safe.

"I've been reading too much," I say. But I stashed food well before my World War II research, and we both know it.

I'm a weirdo with a doomsday kit. Why didn't Cam tell me? It's partly inherited and partly from watching my parents, I suppose. Max shakes the microfilter with curiosity. Cam is hope; I am paranoia. Please let Max be the duck that adapts to whatever the world brings him.

I should feel guilty that I'm about to prune the natural grace of the dense yews into submission, but the dream of a perfectly manicured English garden hedge beckons. I unroll the orange extension cord, untangling past three of Cam's repaZirs—bulging balls of black electrical tape like galls, the abnormal growths on a tree trunk.

"I will not cut the cord," I say out loud to the humid summer air as I position the electric hedge trimmers.

Cam is winning two-to-one on extension cord chopping. I remember the reverberating shock when I cut through it with these same trimmers, maybe because it was a damp morning. I killed some brain cells, the ones that help me remember where I put things, like my tea cup and my favorite clippers. We should probably get a new cord, but I feel guilty retiring our soldier just because he has a few scars. I pray that the electrical tape is doing its job. Cam's father taught him how to rewire the cuts, but I still worry about getting zapped. Cam doesn't have his father's years of experience built into his touch, born of repairing everything from lawnmowers to light fixtures. He's got hands like mine, nimble at typing, and newly cut and calloused from garden work.

A friend suggested that I tie strings to wooden stakes at each end of the hedge to create a precise cutting line, but I fear I'll shear through a tangle of electric cord *and* string. Maybe if I go slower.

I start with the difficult part first, the side of the hedge along the stone terrace. My work space behind the hedge is one foot wide, a narrow ledge along the five-foot drop down the retaining wall to the garden below. I'll have to walk backward and sideways. I throw the extension cord over my right shoulder, the way an elegant woman might flip her silk scarf to keep it out of the way, flex my arms, align the clippers perpendicular to the growth, and push the black "on" button.

The familiar buzz thrills me, providing immediate gratification, a generally rare concept in gardening. A straight section appears, filling me with pride as I back up carefully, trim a section, and back up some more. I'm in control of this one bit of unruly garden, although the occasional crunch of a thick branch startles me. I creep backward a bit more, managing the cord, not looking down the sheer drop beside me. *It's perfect*, I tell myself as I near the end, pausing to admire my cutting. I step back to get a better perspective.

Into thin air.

The immediate dread that I am falling with hedge trimmers in my hand stiffens my body into an upright position, and in a terrifying second I land erect on my feet. Gravity meets the power of the earth and sends searing pain straight up my spine. I tumble forward onto my knees, hitting the stone path, the trimmers flying from my hand. Pain reverberates from my legs to my back to my shoulders. I've surely broken something. I lie on the ground, overwhelmed and groggy, hearing birds and rustling leaves, garden life continuing as if nothing has happened.

After a few minutes, I take stock. I can move my arms and legs —not broken—but my back and shoulders sear in agony. At least I didn't strangle myself with the cord. I look up to see one of the black tape galls stuck in the hedge. I limp into the house, shaken and humbled, knowing full well I could have cracked my head open, seeking Advil, a cup of tea, and the sofa.

SEAWEED SALAD

Ingredients:

1 ounce dry seaweed (use store-bought only)
4 teaspoons rice vinegar
1 tablespoon toasted sesame oil
1 tablespoon soy sauce
1 tablespoon sugar
½ teaspoon salt
½ teaspoon fresh chopped ginger
1 tablespoon toasted sesame seeds
1 finely chopped scallion

- Soak the dry seaweed in cold water for 5 to 10 minutes, depending on the texture preferred.
- Whisk together the rice vinegar, sesame oil, soy sauce, sugar, salt, and ginger to make the dressing.
- Drain the seaweed and squeeze out excess water. Toss thoroughly with dressing, sesame seeds, and scallions.

See page 267 for information on safety and sourcing of plants.

❧

CHAPTER 15

Oaks

"Happy father's day," Max and I say in unison. Where did the winter go?

It seems like Christmas was just yesterday, and Max and I worked hard on this gift through the spring. He'll be devastated if Cam doesn't *love* it. I hold my breath and watch Max watching his father.

Cam looks at the wall where I have painstakingly penciled out forty-eight rectangles, eight across and six rows down, each the size of a simple black IKEA frame. I tripped off the step stool in the process of hanging them and have a bluish bruise on my elbow, more pain to add to the dull ache of my lower back, a constant since my fall off the retaining wall last summer. Max has photographed several garden plants with his new lens, and I've written the Latin species name and month on each frame's mat. Our first gift installment includes cheerful yellow daffodils, magnolia flowers, purple and yellow irises, lilacs, the ducks, the peony, the fragrant mock orange, and our snow-covered maple sap buckets. A spring garden sampler on the sky-blue wall.

"Is this our garden?" Cam asks in amazement, looking from one frame to the next.

"Pretty professional-looking, huh?" I say. It *does* look good.

"Max, did you take these?" he asks.

"Yeah, it was easy," Max says, his eyes bright. "I experimented with *bokeh*."

"It's a technique," I tell Cam. He reaches out to gently adjust a frame.

"Look, Dad, I got a close-up of an ant on the peony. Cool, huh?"

Cam steps to the frame for a closer look. "Incredible," he says. What's incredible is that Max knows the word *peony*.

The unfurled white petals appear translucent, while the ant is in clear relief on the dark pink center. It's a remarkable photo, full of life, energy, and beauty. Technology and nature meeting in harmony. Max and I have crossed an impasse and both come out stronger. Maybe he's ready for the main plant families, at least Iridaceae and Sapindaceae.

Cam is spellbound.

"I'll take more pictures this summer," Max says.

"I absolutely love it, guys." Cam ruffles Max's hair. "Best Father's Day gift ever."

"Great," says Max, heading toward his iLounge. "Gotta get back to my game."

Our fleeting perfect family moment dissolves before I can say Paeoniaceae.

"Our summer flowers need work. Everything's yellow," Cam says, wiping his dirty hands on his shorts. His bare feet are encased in the gardening boots Sonia sent. She has no idea how much work she's done in the garden vicariously through her gift. And it seems that Cam hasn't learned to wear socks, even after last week's attack. An army of fire ants crawled into one of his boots and had a feast on his calf.

"Lightning doesn't strike the same spot twice," he says, when I note his lack of socks. "So, what do you think?" He gestures to the row of hostas he surgically divided and planted beside the pond.

"Nice. And it's not all yellow." The long branches of the butterfly bushes, covered with tiny violet flowers, droop and sway in the wind, as if policemen are waving purple traffic wands to direct the flow of hummingbirds.

"Other than those, we need more color down here." He does his Monet thing, waving his arm around the garden like a paintbrush, blocking color here and there. "Summer's looking rather beige-ish," he adds. Brush stroke, brush stroke.

That's a bit harsh. He's referring to the fact that I had all our house walls painted a calming neutral off-white, an affront to his Mediterranean roots.

But he's right. Spring was dominated by the pinks, corals, and purples of the primroses, lilacs, and peonies. Now we've moved into yellows. It makes sense to me; the yellows will morph to the oranges and then the reds of autumn. The garden is a prism, refracting light differently depending on the season.

"We've got bigger issues than too much yellow," I say, looking up to the pagoda. "That thing is going to come down this winter if we don't do something."

The pagoda still looms as the final frontier, too complicated and too expensive. And I haven't been able to find the right contractor, although I've been desperately trying, since more pieces of the rotting beams broke off this spring.

"The future money pit," Cam says, eyeing the cracked columns.

"It's the heart of the garden," I say. Well, actually the two central oaks are, but the pagoda is the beacon, the hundred-year-old history. "We still need to save it."

I need to look harder. The last guy I interviewed wanted to remove the entire roof, so I sent him packing.

"I don't think you realize what a big job it is," Cam says.

Oh yes I do. The roof structural beams. The columns. The foundation and the floor. The balustrade and the steps. Interior ceiling. The whole thing is sinking *and* crumbling. I just need a little more time and the right contractor. Preferably before next winter.

"He won't stop shaking," Max says, his forehead wrinkled with concern as he pets Hunter. The storm is magnified tenfold as the rain pelts the skylight. For the first time, I worry that the glass on the roof, normally my treasured picture window of the sky and tree-tops, is a bad idea.

Hunter pants heavily, his floppy ears pinned back in fear. Sharp cracks of thunder punctuate the reverberating rain. I dare to check the garden slope, peering out the kitchen window.

Dread surges through me, faster than the last lightning strike.

A river of water, earth, and mulch rolls down the main steps, straight for the pagoda. Why didn't we terrace the slope, or create a dry creek for rainwater?

"This is a disaster," I tell Cam. "All that water's flowing straight into the pagoda. As if it wasn't bad enough."

He's silent as he runs his hand through his hair. There's nothing to do except hope that the skylight doesn't cave in from a falling branch and that the pagoda roof doesn't blow apart.

Branches break off the enormous oak tree in front of the house and crash onto the flat roof, like chunks of rock. While Cam paces near the skylight, I debate going outside to check on the plants. Maybe I can redirect the water flow somehow.

"Are you crazy?" Cam asks. "No way."

"Then we may as well get some sleep."

When we turn in, Hunter stands at the edge of the bed, panting. I've read that the static electricity built up by a storm causes dogs pain. He seemed off today. I should have paid attention to his signals —I could have done something to protect the plants.

Lightning flares outside the window, creating quick vistas of fluorescent green leaves. Max has fallen asleep despite the noise. He did inform me, before passing out, that he learned in science class that lightning is good because it adds to the nitrogen cycle. I fall asleep thinking about good nitrates raining into our soil. Maybe Cam's grass will finally grow.

I'm up within an hour. I carry Hunter into Cam's library to watch television, my lower back searing with pain from the weight, keeping all the lights off in case of a power surge. The weather channel meteorologist blames the enormous amount of water on a cluster of slow-moving storms. Power outages are rampant and he calls the storm *epic*. Rainfall records are breaking as he speaks. Great. Now I really can't sleep.

I leave Hunter on the sofa, blanketed by alternating flashes from the television screen and the storm, and head for my den. A flash of white light from the skylight lights the hallway, and immediately a sharp *crack*, like a firing cannon, makes me jump. Jesus, how close is that lightning? I didn't even have time to say one-one-thousand. My heart pounds as loudly as the torrential rain while I wait for the roof of the house to fall in, but it doesn't, so I lie on the sofa and listen to the thunder.

Did my parents hear the crack of cannons and gunfire when the final battles and surrenders ended the war? They were two of millions of workers stranded in Germany and Austria, relieved, yet unsure as to their own fate and that of their families. Where would they go now? Malnourished, depressed, and traumatized, they were lucky that they were part of those gathered into displaced persons camps with food, basic aid, and time to recover.

I reach for the memory box that holds my parents' documents. It now occupies a permanent home near my cherished bowl of rocks. Father's United Nations Relief and Rehabilitation Agency (UNRRA) referral slip, the dark yellow color of a black-eyed Susan, with a round violet stamp and an official signature from the screening board, sits on top. At twenty-five, he reported to an American sector DP camp team. This frayed slip, like the rest of Father's papers, has traveled. It's the document that most changed the course of his life. The snap of the stamp on the paper meant freedom — and that he would probably never see his brother, his family, again. Perhaps this is why my parents celebrated life and liberty with their war-survivor friends. Only they understood the trade-off of being in the right place at the right time and saying a permanent farewell to their homeland. No one else, especially us, the fortunate next generation, could.

Most Ukrainians who ended the war in the eastern Soviet sector were deported back to Russia, and many were tried for treason against the Communist motherland, killed, or sent to Siberian work camps. Western Ukrainians who were under Polish rule, like my parents, had a chance for foreign aid, although the Soviets continued repatriation efforts.

I've read about the initial DP camps set up in old army barracks and schools—they were unsanitary and chaotic. Crime and black market activities were rampant. Despondent, many people roamed from camp to camp, looking for lost relatives. As time passed, wounds healed and aid increased, and the DP camps became communities. The UNRRA encouraged cultural activities and teaching, prayer, and hobby groups to pass the time. The darkness of the labor camps gave way to hope as people created new families and friends. They *adapted*.

They fell in love, had children, and died of illnesses, all in the context of homeless strangers sharing bunk beds in tight quarters. Did they keep each other awake at night with the sounds of their hunger, tears, and lovemaking? Perhaps Darwin would say that Father's silence, introversion, and paranoia were his adaptive traits. Mom had street smarts and a forward momentum—she didn't keep *her* war documents. I wouldn't even know that my parents married in the DP camp if Father hadn't kept the marriage certificate.

I pull out their wedding picture, still amazed that it didn't get lost. *What a place to get married,* Mom probably told her friends, *wearing a borrowed dress and shoes, but look at these flowers.* In a single black-and-white photograph of their wedding, Mom carries the long stems of a white shrub rose in a bouquet the length of her torso. Her wavy dark hair is combed sideways off her forehead, under a white veil, making her slender frame look taller than five feet two inches. Father is darkly handsome, hair combed back, full lips above a square jaw. Again, I am mesmerized—Max stares back at me from

the photo, except his face is gaunt and his eyes are tired. Did my father, back then, ever laugh like Max does, the silly laughter we find
so contagious?

My parents' ceremony was performed by a *Visitator Apostolicus*, a
roving papal representative with the mission to marry DP couples.
In the photo, Mom and Father are surrounded by thirteen people.
Only one of them, a young woman in a checkered dress, appears
genuinely happy. The rest look sad, serious, and mostly resigned.

Marriage in the camps was motivated by traditional reasons —
love, loneliness, survival, and religion. Sometimes a marriage pre-
cluded couples from getting permanent work placement abroad because countries were opening up jobs only to young single people.
Yet many couples married anyway. I've read about "rescue marriages" — escapes from trauma.

I notice the rumbling thunder is more distant now.

🌿

I walked through our backyard and peeked through the open garage
door, toward where Father's wood saw rumbled. He hunched over
towering piles of thin wooden oak pieces, each about four inches
square, one-eighth inch thick, with a hole drilled off-center. Another floor lamp. It would take about five hundred pieces, maybe
more, stacked one on top of the other, on a steel rod, to complete
the height of the floor lamp's pedestal. Father stacked one thin wood
piece on the rod, glued the next one slightly off-center so the result,
when it reached six feet, would be a corkscrewlike twisted wooden
pole. The man-hours into that lamp would reach hundreds. Quiet,
boring, repetitive, meticulous hours. Father ignored me as I passed
by for my ravine walk.

An hour later, I returned to shouting, Father's harsh voice and
Mom's, floating out of the garage and into the neighborhood for all
to hear. The argument was about money. I didn't understand most
of the words, but the tone divulged all. Father didn't make eye contact. He stared at his wooden chips as he yelled, and his voice came

in short, venomous spurts. Mother's voice was softer, but equally hateful, layered with condescension. Their fury pooled like gas fumes over the sidewalk, and I waded through it, looking down and following the sidewalk cracks as if they were lifelines.

My parents didn't notice me. Instead of going into the house as I had planned, I kept walking, along the side, to the front, past the gate and back on the street to circle back to the ravine through the alleyway at the end of the block. I couldn't bear the thought of entering a house built on such anger. I wondered again why they had married and why they stayed married. When Mom moved to her assisted-living apartment after Father died, she asked me if I wanted Father's lamp stands. They were valuable pieces of handcrafted art, and she had no room for them where she was going. Neither did I.

❧

My pulse pounds in my ears as I examine the aftermath. Mother Nature declared war, leaving utter devastation across the garden's base. I can hardly breathe as I slump down on a mud-covered step. It can't be.

"What a goddamn disaster," Cam says, behind me. *It is.*

The demolished oak is lying across our path, where it fell, clipping the edge of the pagoda roof and crushing all the trees and shrubs along its way. Large broken branches litter the ground throughout, plants crushed beneath them. What's left of the oak's trunk, the bottom fifteen feet, is cracked, splintered, and stripped as if a giant axe hit from the heavens.

I squeeze my eyes shut, willing it to be a bad dream. I open them, and it's worse than I thought. The new redbud, the serviceberry, the old peonies, the mulberry tree, all the flowers near the bog, macerated. Pieces of the pagoda roof beams lie scattered in the mess.

Cam's shades-of-yellow flowers have been splattered across the garden like paint. Monet has been thrust aside by Jackson Pollock. The rockets, the tall mustard rods that protected the bog like soldiers, are in the mud, cut down at the knees. The electric-yellow day lilies are squashed, their cascading leaves flattened pancakes. The lady's mantle's furry star-shaped leaves that feel like Hunter's ears are mangled at the pond's edge.

I've never seen a lightning strike's fury. I'm unbalanced.

Cam silently examines the destruction.

I look up at the remaining oak's precariously hanging upper branches. *Shit.* The heart of the garden—my beloved white oaks, with their sweet kernels that feed every neighborhood rodent and bird—is broken. To make matters worse, mud covers the slope, and the mulch has been pushed to the property's tableland in soggy piles.

"Oh my god, Cam, all our work is undone." I wonder why the lightning, after all these years, chose *now* to destroy the oak.

In the evening Cam tells me a story about a wagon builder who always left a few exposed oak trees in the middle of cleared farmland. He claimed exposure to the elements made these trees stronger, and wagon wheels made from them were able to withstand the heaviest loads.

"I'm not building wagon wheels," I snap.

"It isn't the end of the world," he says gently.

"Do you know how much work has been destroyed? How much time and money lost? This is all I have been doing."

"I know it feels that way, but the garden will emerge stronger," he says. "And we can fix it."

"We can't regrow a hundred-and-fifty-year-old tree." Damn nitrates.

···

DRIED ACORNS

- Gather acorns, ensuring they are free of small insect holes.
- Wash in a small bowl of water, using a small cleaning brush to remove dirt. Discard any acorns with insect holes or mold. If caps have fallen off, keep them. They can be used for crafts or simply glued on later with a hot glue gun.
- Dry on newspaper or paper towels for a few hours.
- Bake on a foil-lined cookie sheet in single layer in a 175°F oven for up to 3 hours. If possible, leave oven door slightly open to allow moisture to escape. Turn every half hour.
- Cool completely before use, at least 1 hour or overnight.
- If desired, acorns can be sprayed with satin-finish clear acrylic for added shine and protection. Gold and silver metallic spray paint for seasonal decor, or any desired colors, may also be used.

Craft and Décor Suggestions

- Fill clear vases, jars, or bowls for centerpieces, adding dried flowers, oak leaves, or candles.
- Drill holes in nuts and string them to create garlands, jewelry, or Christmas tree ornaments.
- Use a hot glue gun to cover Styrofoam wreaths, balls, Christmas tree cones, picture frames, or mirror frames.
- Help children create acorn people and animals, using a hot glue gun, paint, feathers, pinecones, twigs, craft paper, and craft decorations.

See page 267 for information on safety and sourcing of plants.

···

CHAPTER 16

❧

Ginkgo

"It happens," says Adam.

"What happens?" I ask. This *cannot* happen.

I cross my arms and stare up into the dry leaves of the oak, my neck as stiff as the hardwood. It's been several weeks since the hotter-than-the-sun lightning strike felled its twin. After Adam's team took it apart a section at a time and added to our log fence around the property, Cam and I replanted, reseeded the grass, and respread the mulch. We were finally feeling a sense of accomplishment since the storm. Now this?

"When two trees have grown together for so long and one dies, sometimes the other goes soon after. Its ecosystem has changed and it's lost protection from the wind," Adam explains. "Or maybe the lightning damaged this one, too. Hard to say."

I sit down on the step and look toward the broken pagoda roof. If this tree falls on it, it will be the final blow.

"It should come down. I'm sorry."

"Can we wait until spring?" I ask. There's life in that tree and I'm not ready to part with it just yet.

"I'd do it now," he says, "but it's up to you. You're probably postponing the inevitable."

"I'll think about it. Let's work on the front of the house for now," I add. *You've been given a second chance,* I say to the oak, and then I turn and head up the steps, focused on autumn planting.

Cam suggests a tall yew hedge on either side of the long narrow driveway. He's inspired by ancient Roman tree-lined roads, although the canopy of apricot yellow created by a row of katsuras along the driveway's front is more common in Japan. We plan to put the yews between them, working around the tangled mass of smooth, shallow, gray roots that flare from their trunks. I hold the tape measure for Adam, thinking Max should photograph these strange roots for Cam's photo wall. A sweet fragrance floats around us, reminding me of a fairground.

"Do you smell candy?" I ask Adam.

"It's the katsura leaves," he says. "More like toffee. We won't be able to plant the yews in these roots."

I let the tape measure snap shut.

Toffee? As in sticky toffee pudding? I already love the cascading heart-shaped leaves of these trees — now they smell like my favorite dessert. I inhale deeply, imagining a sultry concoction of Medjool dates, warm toffee, and melting vanilla bean ice cream.

Adam interrupts my thoughts with his voice. "Damn," he says, rubbing the bottom of his boot on the rough flagstones. He's stepped on some smelly ginkgo berries; they fall onto our property from the city-owned parkette in front of our driveway.

"Max and I used to think it was dog droppings," I laugh.

For a tree-hugger, he's really scrubbing at that boot.

"Maybe it's good luck," I tell him, "like when bird shit lands on your head."

The leather sole of his boot spreads the squashed berry across the cobblestone like peanut butter on burnt toast.

The two freakish ginkgo trees look like a wiry old couple with spindly hair and gaunt limbs, but elegantly dressed in golden leaves that float down to the ground like mustard-colored butterflies. I've read that in Japan they symbolize hope because they're the only plant that survived the bombing of Hiroshima.

The odor of the ginkgo berry wafts into my nostrils and melds with the katsuras' sugary sweetness, creating a bizarre ancient–Asian-tree yin-yang fragrance. I distractedly agree to the rest of Adam's plant suggestions, no longer interested. I smell a Saturday project for Max and me.

"And they're also supposed to stave off dementia," I tell Cam, after I download the harvest instructions.

The word *dementia* hangs in the air. I think of Mom. The doctors are masking the impact of Mom's dementia with antidepressants and anti-anxiety medications when an untapped natural cure is rolling down our driveway.

"Sounds interesting. My memory's not what it used to be," Cam says. I wait for a sarcastic comment. None comes—he's holding back, he must be thinking of Mom, too. The harvest is on.

"I'm not touching those," says Max, wincing, when I suggest he help me gather the aromatic fruit.

But he does, because despite his youth, he's developed an intuition that senses when something is really important to me. I wonder why I subconsciously discount his perceptiveness—maybe I don't want to acknowledge that he can already see my imperfections. Selectively holding our breath, we gather the bruised yellow berries off the ground with gloved hands.

"They're the most primitive and adaptable plant in the world," I tell Cam and Max over dinner. The fruit will soak in a bucket on the balcony overnight so we can more easily retrieve the precious nuts inside. "Two hundred million years old. We have living dinosaurs right in front of our house."

Cam examines one of the two-lobed leaves.

"They smell bad," says Max.

"Did you know that sumo wrestlers and traditional Japanese women wear their hair up in two knots like the shape of a ginkgo leaf?" I interrupt.

Two blank faces look at me.

How can they not love a tree that launched a hairstyle?

The next morning, after their thorough soaking, I push the fruit off the nuts and roast them in an iron skillet. I'm delighted, as Max hammers them open on the old wooden cutting board, creating an assembly line of explosive cracks, as the shells shatter to reveal shiny jade-colored seeds. They look like pistachio nuts. We're about to eat living fossils. Except Max, who has drawn the line.

"They taste like a pine nut crossed with a chestnut," Cam offers, chewing thoughtfully. Both are a staple of Italian cuisine and pretty much all the analogy he can offer.

"Edamame," I say, and then an intense after-taste fills my mouth. I wait for it to pass, but it clings to my palate like, well, a bad smell. A smell, unfortunately, reminiscent of shit. I look at Cam. He relaxes back into his chair, his watering eyes daring me to admit it.

No way in hell.

"Tasty," I say.

Sonia calls that evening. I assume it's for our usual Sunday night chat. It's not. She visited Mom that afternoon and the nurse explained that it has become impossible to feed her. Even the thickened liquids choke her, and she's refusing to open her mouth when the nurses try to slip a straw between her lips. I hold my breath as Sonia explains that the doctor will probably recommend an IV to keep Mom hydrated and fed.

We are about to enter the gray zone of Mom's wishes and our strength to honor them. Sonia pauses and I stare out the kitchen window, clutching the phone. A few maple keys float down like helicopters, as squirrels on the ground munch on the interior berries. I remember when I convinced Max to eat one, telling him it tasted like a green pea. I wish that Mom had been less clear. If there is any ambiguity, it will be because we rationalized ourselves into it.

"What do you think?" I finally ask Sonia. The silence stretches between us. We are trapped in a void of indecision.

"We can't let her become dehydrated," she says.

"I agree," I say, relieved we are unified in our decision to not live up to Mom's wishes.

In a trance, I buy my plane ticket and start packing. I make arrangements for Max's activities and create long lists for Cam. I'm preparing to stay until the end, although I'm not acknowledging it out loud. Everything I do has an ethereal quality to it; I'm disoriented as I float through the mundane tasks of preparing to travel. Before I know it, I am squeezed into a middle seat at the back of the plane, requesting a tea with milk, not quite sure how I got there. Cam and Max will join me when I know more; I don't want them to miss work or school yet, and part of me knows they don't belong with us right now.

For once, the plane's turbulence matches my mood. I open my laptop to do some work, only to be greeted by a marvelous image of a ginkgo-lined street in Japan. Max! I had asked him to organize my research for my trip and to index my numerous downloaded articles. I don't know how he did it, but separate color-coded file folders are arranged in rows across my screen like a tidy vegetable patch. I drag my finger across the screen, wishing I could slow down time. I'm running against a clock to understand my mother and father's journey, although it doesn't really matter anymore. I click on the "Post-war England" folder and go backward into history, thankfully for once, if only to avoid thinking about the present.

From the DP camps, my parents were afraid to return to their beloved Ukraine, or whatever was left of it. Like most, they probably wanted to go to North America to pursue the opportunities of vast, empty land, but those doors were closed. Choices within the United Nations relocation program were limited, while demand was high. They chose England. In full rebuilding mode, the economy was growing and in need of unskilled labor. Married, with no family, friends, homeland, financial resources, education, or knowledge of the English language, they were probably terrified as they hugged their adopted DP family for the last time.

The rules of the English Ministry of Labour were strict. DPs accepted the jobs they were assigned and remained in those jobs indefinitely at the discretion of the ministry. They lived in housing provided close to the workplace.

A small certificate, the size of a four-by-six-inch photo, titled "Vocational Training Scheme," its text framed with a patterned scroll design, attests that Mom completed a course as a "ring spinner" at the Oldham Cotton Company. This was her only formal education. I'm ashamed as I recall our conversations—each time I impetuously changed my mind about my education, taking it all for granted. How ungrateful she must have found me. She probably didn't want to be a ring spinner any more than I wanted to be an accountant; the difference was choice and circumstance. I had it and, likely in her opinion, I abused it. I never framed any of my diplomas, and I never attended any graduation ceremonies. I will finally frame a diploma when I get back home, I decide—this one, from Oldham Cotton Company, in recognition of my freedom to choose.

The flight attendant interrupts my thoughts with an offer of tea. The plane engines drone on, and I wonder what Mom dreamed about as she spent her days watching endless rows of whirling threaded spindles. I imagine, over time, she made friends slowly, practicing her English phrases, while the continuous drones of the mechanical wheels created a white noise that reduced conversation into banal gossip.

Father worked as a general laborer, with no formal evidence of any training. For some reason never explained, he required hospitalization in England and part of his treatment included electroconvulsive therapy. That's all Mom told Sonia before she clammed up on the topic, making Father as much a mystery to us then as he was later in life.

Electroconvulsive therapy began as an efficient anesthesia on pigs before their slaughter, and became a popular medical treatment in the early 1950s for people experiencing severe depression or schizophrenia, of which, postwar, there were many. I almost choke at the thought of the hard rubber mouth gags that patients wore to keep from biting or swallowing their tongues while megawatts zapped through their brains, inducing full-blown seizures and, often, cracked ribs. My mind shuts down as I imagine the reasons Father might have needed this procedure. Was Mom there with him?

Sonia was born in July of 1951, amidst Mom's spinning cotton reels and Father's silent pain. Although the Liverpool docks that housed the ships that sailed to North America were less than thirty miles away, it may as well have been thousands. Mom wanted to escape the captivity of industry, yearning for her youth's farmland. The fertile black earth of her lost homeland, the chornozem, existed in only one other place in the world: the Canadian prairies. The wave of Ukrainians who went there before World War I had sent news of it. I realize now that the soil was her identity. It defined where she came from and where she wanted to go.

As the plane descends, I double-click the folder and put my research away. It's as if I'm watching my life's movie for the second time. The first time was in a foreign language. This time I understand it, but Mom is skipping to the last scene.

The nursing home walls have been refreshed from salmon pink to a dull beige color, but the walk along the hallway is the same. The competing smells of soup, urine, and bleach blend inconsistently with the smiling volunteers and the prairie sunshine that streams through the streaked, dusty windows. Sonia and I rub two copious squirts of clear gel sanitizer into our hands as we walk toward Mom's room. Call buzzers hum around us like random unanswered doorbells. We pass residents in wheelchairs, some quiet, some moaning, others conversing with imaginary friends, all neatly tucked into brightly colored hand-crocheted blankets. Bright yellow wheeling mop buckets remain on standby, waiting for the next accident. I follow the shiny floor tiles, the tightness in my chest increasing with every step.

I fear that Mom is aware she has been hooked up to an IV and that, by allowing it, we have broken our promise to her. While all she asked is that her passage from earth to the next stage be natural and unimpaired, we couldn't let go. Not yet. I search for the answer and come up short, having abandoned Mom's faith in Catholicism long ago. As we enter her room, I can barely swallow.

That evening, I ask Sonia if she recalls any other items that might shed light on our parents' history. We're both overwhelmed by the sadness of the day, sitting with Mom, watching the IV drip, one drop of guilt at a time.

"Nothing," she says, her voice weak and exhausted. "Their retirement plaques, maybe?"

"Yes," I say. "Please."

Mother's tarnished silver retirement platter reads, "On the Occasion of Her Retirement from Celanese Canada 1953–1984."

"What if I live another twenty years? What will I do all day alone with your father?" she had asked us when she retired. But the deafening spinners had impaired her hearing, and the eczema on her swollen hands made work unbearable, so she prominently displayed her platter upright in the dining room's built-in mahogany china cabinet and dove into her garden. Father's wooden retirement plaque reads, "CN Rail in Grateful Recognition of 33 Years 1953–1986." He said nothing about it. The plaque went into a drawer and he escaped to his garage.

❦

In 1953, a series of unrelated events altered my parents' destiny, as if the stars decided it was time for their westward journey to continue. The first arose when the Ministry of Labour in England removed employment restrictions for DPs who had worked in England for more than three years. My parents were free to travel. As luck would

have it, the Canadian government introduced its first new immigra-
tion policy since 1923, seeking workers for growing industries such
as mining, agriculture, and forestry. My parents must have quickly
pulled together their meager savings, and bought ship passage to
Canada before either government changed its mind. Their pictures
in their official travel documents are the first in which the corners
of their lips are turned upward. Not in complete smiles, but hope
shines in their eyes, even Father's. My parents were escaping the
industrial grit of Manchester for the farmland of their childhood.
How proud they must have been to see their names in the fancy *Canadian Pacific Ship Passenger List*. Their destination of choice was Edmonton, in the Alberta prairies.

There, in the same year, the Canadian Chemical Company
opened a factory to exploit the discovery of oil. The company,
eventually purchased by a German conglomerate, would become
one of the world's largest producers of petrochemical filament used
in making cigarette filters and synthetic yarns for the new fabrics
that were about to become fashionable. With her years as a spinner
in England, Mom was a perfect hire, and in the middle of the prairies, she again became a factory worker, destined to watch threads
spin for another thirty-one years.

Father wasn't fated to work the farmland, either. The Canadian
National Railway had begun replacing old steam engines with more
efficient diesel cars, and he was hired as a skilled laborer at the train
yards, where he would quietly maintain and repair, for the next
thirty-three years, the pipe systems that made trains run. Where was
the vast land Mom so desperately sought? In her tiny backyard lot,
next to Father's garage, once they had saved enough to move out of
their initial rooming house.

✦

"Can I keep these?" I ask Sonia the next morning.

"Of course," she says. "Maybe Max will appreciate them someday."

I wrap my soft wool sweater around the plaques, the sleeves creating a protective hug, and put them in my suitcase.

"You should take this, too," Sonia says, walking into the room with Mom's fur coat. "Maybe you can have it remade."

My stomach sinks at the sight of the mass of dry gray fur, the reminder that I'm not a boy. Well, at least I *had* a boy.

"I guess," I say. I turn the coat inside out and notice Mom's initials on tiny appliquéd squares on the lining. This coat was Mom's secret postwar dream: glamor, success, and, most of all, independence. I add it to my suitcase with a deep breath; I'm ready to go back to the nursing home.

"That looks better," Sonia says.

"I think so." I straighten the towel again, slightly to the left of Mom's chin.

"He says it's about seven days. Her organs are weakening." Sonia stares at the winter floral bouquet of leaves and berries on the calendar above Mom's bed.

"Yes. I heard."

"How can he know?" she asks.

"He can't."

"We have to trust him. She would have." Sonia reaches across the IV line to brush Mom's silver hair off her forehead.

"I'm not sure." I look outside at the snow-covered gazebo and the lawn furniture stacked neatly under it. "Are you hungry?"

"Yes. One of us should go get food. You go. I'll stay in case something happens. I'll speak to the doctor if he comes by." Sonia applies some balm to Mom's cracked lips, and then gets up to walk with me past the burgundy-colored curtain into the hall.

"She was crystal clear, you know," Sonia says, the tears starting to form.

"I know."

"But Dennis says where there's life, there's hope."

"I'm not asking Cam. We all have a different definition of life. She believes hers will continue, just not here."

"I know," Sonia says. One of Mom's last comments, when she could still force out blurred words, was that she was happy her two daughters were together, united. My old worry resurfaces, the one that Max doesn't have a sibling, and that he will bear the loss of his parents alone.

"What did she mean by *tube*, anyway? A thick tube, a thin one? A needle?" I ask.

"We both know what she meant," Sonia says.

"I don't see how he can say seven days. Maybe it's eight. Maybe he needs the bed."

"We'll never know."

"Will you tell him while I'm gone?"

"Yes," Sonia says, and as I walk down the hall, the doctor passes me, holding a pen and a clipboard. He doesn't recognize me. I should go back, but I don't have the courage. I walk outside to let my tears condense in the cold wind. Thank God for older sisters.

Cam and Max fly in the next day. We spend a few days around Mom's bedside, visiting, together like the family we never really were. Max's eyes wear his shock, but he acts like a young man beyond his twelve years. He can sense my suffering and performs small helpful tasks, like carrying my coat, getting me water, and holding my hand. His actions make my heart constrict, tighter and tighter, until I'm sure I will explode into my mixed emotions of dejection, wonder, and fear.

We talk to Mom, telling her stories. We know she's listening. She appears serene now that the IV is gone. Unburdened. Cam has decided that Max's last memory should be of Mom still alive, and I agree. I send them home, knowing that the next time we meet, Mom will be gone. I will be different. An orphan.

Mom is unresponsive. Like an indestructible ginkgo, until it isn't. She used to be able to wiggle her toes if we asked her to, but now even those small efforts aren't worth making. It's too stark a contrast to bear, a physical life so close to the earth that she *was* earth, now unable to move her fingers a millimeter. My arms are weak as I adjust the pillow under her head, as if I'm lifting a sack of salt. I sit in the chair, chilled, curl myself up into a ball, and close my eyes. I dream of Mom. She is smiling. She descends a hilly dirt path to a still, indigo-colored lake topped by a cloudless violet sky. I watch the back of her favorite flowered dress flutter in the wind as she gets smaller and smaller. She is *chi*, soon to be *sui* of flowing water and plants.

···

GINGO BILOBA

Johan Wolfgang von Goethe (1814–1836)
Goethe was a philosopher, writer, and botanist interested in the
metamorphosis of plants, and was one of the first to discuss the
notion of interdependence within nature.

> *In my garden's care and favour*
> *From the East this tree's leaf shows*
> *Secret sense for us to savour*
> *And uplifts the one who knows.*
> *Is it but one being single*
> *Which as same itself divides?*
> *Are there two which choose to mingle*
> *So that each as one now hides?*
> *As the answer to such question*
> *I have found a sense that's true:*
> *Is it not my song's suggestion*
> *That I'm one and also two?*

···

CHAPTER 17

Willow Trees

THE FUNERAL DIRECTOR'S barren office hasn't changed much in the years since Father's death: same laminated wood desk and industrial carpet. It's not designed for lingering but for people passing through, like a transitional purgatory for those left behind. I suppose the tissue box is new. How many thousands of those have been emptied here? A microscopic haze of gallons of old tears swirls around my head. I *hate* this place.

The speckled white ceiling tiles create a soundproof vacuum until I can't ignore my other senses. A pervasive odor stings my nostrils as though an invisible mist of disinfectant keeps floating by. Ammonia? I put a tissue to my nose and breathe in the minuscule bleached white particles instead.

"I think I'm unwell," I whisper.

"What?" my sister asks, looking up from her crossed hands. She's in a transcendental shock, the kind in which the world moves in muted slow motion. I can see it in her eyes.

Nothing left to add, we resume our silence. I trace the table's repeating wood-grain pattern. Maybe the stink is emanating upward from the plastic laminate. They should use real wood furniture in funeral homes. Maybe my stomach's hollowness is hunger; we forgot to eat today. I watch a tear negotiate the puffiness of Sonia's face. Oh my god, it's not ammonia, it's embalming fluid. The hollowness officially moves to nausea.

A tall, lanky man walks in and places his card in front of us, formal white linen paper stock, onto the round meeting table. Planning Director and Chief Embalmer. His face is inscrutable; his only distinctive feature is the gold nametag on his dark suit. Tom, it says, in serious black font. He catches me staring at his chest and clears his throat. The badge makes him look as if he might work at the front desk of a motel on a deserted road.

Tom clears his throat again, his eyes desensitized to bereaved families and dead bodies. If I weren't so tired, I'd wonder how he got into this job, but I suppose I have to be grateful as long as there are people like Mom who insist upon the ritual of an open-casket funeral. He offers his hand. I imagine the vet's office and the high school biology lab with a top note of plastic. Nausea overwhelms me anew.

"Please accept my sincere condolences. I remember when your father passed. We are grateful to assist you again," he says with genuine kindness.

I have no recollection of Tom. His hand is soft and moist. I imagine it covered in a sterile glove.

"Actually, we don't have much to do. It seems your mother took good control of her affairs. You are *lucky* girls." His look implies that we are weaker mortals than our diligent advance-planning mother. He looks down at his burgundy pseudo-leather file folder, open to a checklist with adjacent boxes.

The first few decisions are easy. Solid oak wood casket with wheat motif, like Father's? Check—a subtle ode to their heritage. Crustless sandwiches? Check—don't want the guests to think we skimped. Don't forget the fruit tray. Cheese cubes, check.

"When I die, cremate me. Sprinkle my ashes in Vegas," Sonia whispers to me.

"Sprinkle mine in New Hampshire," I whisper back. *Fresh air, fresh air,* I repeat in my head to stop myself from crying. It's a technique an old friend taught me. Apparently a mantra can distract your emotions. *Fresh air, fresh air, fresh air.*

"Flowers?" asks Tom. I sink lower into my chair. Sonia hides her face in her hands and her long, thick hair provides extra cover.

"Is there a problem?" Tom reaches for a tissue.

"Not really." The garden's not finished.

"You've both been incredible," he encourages. "You should see some people. They can't make up their minds."

Sonia flips through plasticized sheets of flower arrangements. They have names: Colourful Memories, A Life Well Lived, Timeless Topiary. I decide to let my hair grow so I can have a built-in hiding place like Sonia.

"Too green," she says as she points at "Upright Spray." Not showy enough. Nothing is good enough for Mom's flowers.

"She loved roses," I say. *Long hair fresh air, long hair fresh air.*

"Okay! Roses it is," says Tom, moving to a close. "A sensible choice."

"She loved glads. Remember she grew them on the south wall?" Sonia asks.

"Roses and glads, then." Tom shuffles his papers. I long for my garden's perfume.

"But she also liked carnations. Too commonplace?" I ask.

"I'll get some more tea," Tom says.

This is going to take a while. Mom's expectations are high.

"How about yellow?" Sonia asks.

Mom chose a purple dress for her burial. "Too Easter," I respond.

My sister looks at the back of the door, where we hung a dusty suit bag with Mom's dress, shoes, and her white prepurchased underwear of years ago.

"He's going to wonder why the underwear's so big," I say.

"I don't care," Sonia says defensively.

"White," I say to Tom as he enters with the teapot.

"Winter white, then. Lilies and some willow branches," he agrees.

"Mom loved pussy willows," Sonia says. "Perfect."

"Have you heard of willow coffins?" I ask. "Willow decomposes

quickly. From nature to nature, you know. They're gaining pop-
ularity. Some people weave their own casket." Now *that's* taking
control.

Sonia clatters her teacup.

"Have you picked your pallbearers?" he asks. "You need six."

"All the men are gone," Sonia says. I know she is listing them in
her mind, one strong, hard-working man after another. She drove
Mom to all their funerals, and chauffeured many of their grieving
widows, too. Mom outlasted them all.

"Anyone left is too old, too sick, or injured," I add. "Don't you
have staff?" Dennis's damaged back and Cam holding up the rear are
a disaster waiting to happen.

"Only one or two," says Tom. "We have a problem, then. What
with all the snow, those steps are steep and icy and the temperature's
going to stay below thirty. Why don't you call around? I'm sure you
girls will find someone."

I resent that Tom can't help us. This is more crucial than tea
sandwiches.

Sonia's shoulders sag lower. As Tom completes the paperwork, I
peruse the funeral home's brochure, reading that more than 150 decisions must be made in the first twenty-four to forty-eight hours of
an individual's passing. Preplanning, it claims, brings these decisions
down to a few. Mom was right: the flower selection is all we could
handle.

We can't even find anyone to carry her up the steps.

So much for Mom's perfect funeral. It's colder than usual, a snowy,
windy, overcast November day, with the temperature well below
zero. How did we become gardeners in this godforsaken place, when
1,500 miles due south in Arizona lies plant zone 11? In a brief three-
hour flight, I could be walking amidst the fragrance of desert sage
instead of wondering what the point of a garden is when it's frozen
for half the year. Wind pierces through my black wool coat, stiffen-
ing my already tense back, and our breathing creates a fog of grief.

Four pallbearers, all staff members Tom co-opted up from the funeral home, slowly struggle up the steep steps. Two wear elegant long black coats, a man and a woman; two other men wear colored ski jackets and hats more appropriate for snow shoveling or Arctic hiking. The grandiose outdoor staircase crosses the entire front and turns to wrap the sides of the church's facade, rising to our destination, the second story that houses the nave and altar. I don't understand why they haven't installed an elevator over the years.

"God," I gasp to Sonia in the wind, "They're not going to make it."

I clench my hands into fists inside my pockets as they struggle up the icy steps. The weight of the coffin is overwhelming. *Another reason willow trumps oak,* I want to tell Sonia, but I'm too stiff and cold and worried the staff are about to slide to their deaths while Mom's coffin rolls down the staircase into 97th Street traffic. It should be six pall bearers, Tom had said this morning when he called with the final details. So the four were carrying an extra third. Panic washes over me, with the unnerving sensation of sweating and freezing. I close my eyes and will the seconds to pass.

They finally get the casket to the top and place the magnificent lilies on the blonde oak. They'll have to do this again going out, with the additional downward pull of gravity. My panic returns.

"Do you think she'll be lighter on the way down, after her earthly baggage is relinquished at the altar?" I whisper to Cam, who hovers beside me, preparing for a potential breakdown.

He grabs my elbow. "Hold it together. Just another hour," he says.

Sonia and I will not speak at the service. I made a short speech at the funeral home last night to the few but dedicated widows who hobbled in from the storm, words that Cam helped write. And Sonia—well, she's not going to say *brethren* again.

I escape into my youth and stare up at the frescoes, as I did back then. Angels with gold-tipped wings and wavy tendrils of hair surround God's stern face. The outlandish figures were the source of childhood nightmares, but today I notice the sunflowers, periwinkle, and braided Celtic knots embedded into the murals. Sweet white incense rises above the ceremonial gifts of bread and wine. Through the smoke plumes, Mom's stark white flowers look like a moon garden, planted to shine in the darkness. She would have loved the drama — we got that one right.

The casket is opened, and we proceed in single file to pause and say our last goodbyes. I approach with fear. Mom looks peaceful, serene even, but unrecognizable. Tom made her thirty years younger; he erased the creases that used to be on her face. And no wrinkled underwear in sight, either. I should be grateful, but I can't let the way she looks be part of my memory. I squeeze my eyes shut, pause, and imagine a dandelion crown on Mom's smooth gray hair. The ugly purple dress becomes the favorite loose cotton gardening shift she wore with her red-trimmed black rubber boots. I open my eyes and touch her cheek to rub off the smudge of soil that is there.

"I'm so sorry I didn't finish in time," I whisper. "You're going home now, back to your earth."

I peer into the hole, a black stain marring the snowy white cemetery's landscape. It's so cold that no one has joined us except two friends of Sonia and Dennis. I have no idea how they dug through the frozen earth or where they hid the dirt. I look for it, but it's nowhere to be seen. Nothing here except our tiny group; no one left to sing like they did when we buried Father. I let the voices from a decade ago haunt our silence.

Our limp white lilies and willow branches make a harsh landing on the casket. "It's so cold down there," Sonia says. Up here, too, but I know what she means. It's as cold as Dante's ninth circle of hell. *No matter,* I tell myself. Mom's soul is already gone, basking in the warmth of her next journey.

"You still in bed?" Cam asks. It's nearly eleven on Saturday, a time I normally would have already walked the dog through the garden, had several cups of Earl Grey, and had at least four heated discussions with Max about the weekend's homework. But my back's excruciatingly sore, as it seems to be most mornings now, and there isn't a compelling reason to get out of bed.

"I'm sorry, I can't get up," I tell him.

It's winter solstice; I'm standing still with the sun. It's been several weeks since the funeral and I'm worse than ever. Aimless. I look down at the tent made by my toes under the covers, remembering Mom's unmoving toes of her last days.

"If your feet are warm, your whole body's warm," I tell Cam. "That's what she used to say."

"It's called the orphan syndrome," he says, moving the hair off my forehead as if I'm a sick child. "I read about it. It happens when your second parent dies, no matter how old you are."

"What happens next?" I ask him.

"Actually, I happen next. My parents aren't that far away. I'll get you some tea," he says, and opens the balcony door to a rush of cold air. A broken sugar maple branch hangs precariously and, with a sudden gust, falls to become winter kindling.

I don't want to get out of bed. Because Max will grow up and move away. We'll get old and become kindling. And with that thought, I fall asleep before I get my tea.

I wake up to more flowers, an amaryllis instead of the usual white lilies, accompanied by a lovely handwritten note from a well-meaning friend. Close to Christmas, I guess. Two opposing funnel-shaped blooms emerge from a single tubular stem as if they fought and are no longer speaking to each other. Facing away with arms crossed. *You're in mourning*, says one flower. *I'm not,* says the other.

Cam's Mom will love this plant when they visit at Christmas; she can take the bulb home with her and replant it for next year. She, like Mom did, loves her tropical plants, and has plants in front of every window—tall plants ranked to the back, shorter ones perched on stands in layers, as if in a school class photo. I hated the strange rubbery leaves when I was young because they got to all the light first. Mom watered and fertilized them, and Father built wrought iron and wooden stands, although he regularly yelled at Mom about the plants. I didn't understand why he enabled them to permeate the house. It wasn't until I learned, in middle school biology class, that plants release oxygen and take in our carbon dioxide, that I made peace with those hairy tentacles and sap-shooting tendrils. Under the surface, despite their weird facade, they were giving us something essential to life.

It's Sunday morning and I'm stuck in bed again with Hunter snuggled by my side. The first snow fell last night.

"Mom never said 'I love you,'" I tell Cam. "I was shocked when I met families who said 'I love you' to each other."

"But there were times when you felt love," he says.

I felt Mom's contentment, her form of love, in the garden. "She would give me freshly shelled green peas," I say, remembering the sweet crunch of them against my teeth. I stare out the window at the snow-covered branches. "And she let me play with the frozen clothes."

"Okay," he says, settling into his chair. "Is that a western thing?"

"Mom hung our clothes outside on the line, even in winter, because she said the sun acted like bleach. Father's long underwear and undershirts would freeze solid and I played with them inside."

"Weird," says Cam.

Come to think of it, it was. I had a frozen Father as a surrogate because mine wasn't available. "Don't bend them or they'll crack," Mom would say. How close that was to the truth. She didn't smile or laugh, but she let me jump around with the frozen clothes until they thawed and flexed. Then she would hang them in the basement on a makeshift line near the furnace.

"Well, that's kind of like love. She was sharing, no?" Cam is unsure.

"It was freedom. She gave me the freedom to play."

"Then what?"

"We got a clothes dryer."

Cam's eyes widen.

"*Kidding*," I say.

The memory of waffle-cotton frozen long johns that smell like winter has cheered me up.

"Time for your walk?" Cam asks, pointing out the bedroom window. I imagine dull white underwear hanging from the branches, grayed by city smog.

"Okay." I ruffle Hunter's head and call Max. We need to get outside and *play*.

"I need your help," I say to Max, dangling my handsaw between him and the computer screen.

His hands pause on the keyboard. "Okay," he says, eyeing the saw with pleasure. "Do we need the giant tree pruners?"

We don't. *Play*, I tell myself.

"We sure do," I answer. "Do you remember how to use them? They're dangerous."

"No problem," he says, eyes sparkling. "What are we cutting down?"

"Willows," I say. "We'll need the drill, too, and some small tools."

He stands up quickly. "Sounds like a big job," he says. "You better wear your gloves, Mom." He's taking care of me.

My *Eclectic Guide to Trees* call willows "baffling." The numerous species in the genus *Salix* have so many similarities that botanists can't agree how to classify them. Seeds spread by wind and flowing water and plants hybridize promiscuously. Sort of like religion, I decide, as Max and I stare at the trees in the bog—from pagan worship to supernatural gods that morphed and merged into all the absurd faiths that constantly re-root themselves today, fighting for space in the spiritual universe. Mom's religion was a hybrid of Catholicism and Orthodoxy with roots from ninth-century Byzantine missionaries. It's probably a good thing that our garden has three species of willow — white and black, both sides of the doctrine represented, and the pussy willow for the entire spiritual gray zone in between.

Max struggles with the enormous tree pruners, cutting my selected branches. Smaller cutters would be faster, but we laugh when the rope gets tangled, and when I slip in the snow that covers the bog muck. I brush myself off as a snowball smacks my head. Branches abandoned, the fight is on, and Max proves that tae kwon do has indeed given him incredible hand-to-eye coordination, while I throw like a *girl*. Max's laughter rides a gust of wind around the garden, through the trees and pagoda, and encircles me in pure bliss.

Before we drag our branches up the garden steps, I find a long slender willow branch growing close to the sinking pagoda and tie it into a knot. I hold it and prepare to make my wish. I should have done this sooner, to wish that Mom would live to see the garden. But I didn't, and that wish is dead, and Mom is dead. Father's chimes ring in the cold breeze as I notice my boots sinking into the bog's unfrozen mud.

My dirty boots become Mom's dirty boots in the mud of her garden.

My wish.

I hold the knot and wish to finish the garden restoration by this time next year. I will dedicate it, the legacy of water and earth and the plants in between, to my mother. I let go of the knot and watch the branch remember itself into its upright position, with my knot at its base, ready to be untied if the white willow grants me my desire.

Max and I don't get far beyond drawing a circle on a flat piece of old wood from the garage. We need to drill a hole every few inches to insert long screws that we will then wrap our willow branches around to create our wreath.

"We need new drill bits, Mom," Max says, staring at the yellow plastic bag of Father's old drill bits. "But we should keep these. They were your dad's, right?"

I stare at the bag in dismay. These drill bits built Father's escape walls around him in his adopted country.

Max senses my hesitation. "I can use them for lightweight stuff," he says. "Like when I help you hang pictures."

I move closer and hide my emotions in a hug. "Sometimes things don't work like we want them to, but we appreciate them anyway," I say into his shoulder. And to my father.

"I'll go to Home Depot tomorrow," I add.

Colleen's name is written on her orange apron in cursive felt pen. "Can I help you?" she asks.

I hesitate. She doesn't look like a carpenter. She looks like a mother with tired eyes and a few wrinkles from the tribulations of nasty teenagers and the losses that life brings you. In fact, she looks just like I feel.

"These are my old drill bits." She peeks inside the bag. "They're burning the wood," I add.

"Those look like my father's drill bits," she says. Her eyes are sympathetic. "I finally put mine out on the lawn with a sign that said 'scrap metal.' Someone picked them up in no time."

I bring the bag back to my chest.

"You need to buy some new ones," she says gently, and walks over to a fifty-foot-wide display wall. I look at the thousands of drill bits, holding back my tears.

"Here's a value pack," she offers.

My father would have loved it. Max will, too.

And that, I realize, is the point.

"I'm ready," I say to Colleen, picking up the pack.

EASY WILLOW WREATH

Materials:

Willow branches
String
Ribbon and natural decorations

- Cut about 15 long, slender willow branches, each twice as long as you want the wreath to measure around. The best time is once the leaves have fallen.
- Bend one branch to make a circle of the right size. Wrap the long end of the branch around itself, spiraling around the circle. Add more branches and continue the spiral.
- Lay each new spiral alongside the previous one. Keep going until your wreath is the desired thickness. Tie string around the wreath in several places to hold the branches in place, and put the wreath aside to dry for a few weeks.
- When dry, cut off the string and wrap the wreath in ribbon, spacing each turn of the ribbon a few inches apart. End with a large bow. If desired, decorate the wreath with natural decorations such as pinecones, acorns, or dried flowers.

Note: Pussy willows make a beautiful spring wreath.

See page 267 for information on safety and sourcing of plants.

CHAPTER 18

Mulberries

"Stories always come down to love," I tell Max, as we discuss his essay. He's studying mythology in English this year, including the flower myths of Narcissus, Hyacinth, and Adonis, making the signs of spring outside our kitchen window even more engaging, at least to me. Yet a wintery pine fragrance fills the room; Max actually lit the candle on my desk himself. "I like it," he explained defensively to my curious stare. "It smells like outside."

The first green tulip shoots poking through the earth represent my sixth stage of grief—the upward turn. The first five stages happened all at once over winter, when shock mingled with anger and depression simultaneously. I didn't much care about Christmas, except to give Nonna the amaryllis and one of Mom's favorite necklaces, two gestures officially anointing her as my surrogate mother.

She loved the amaryllis. "Just like the Roman god Giano, the one with two faces," she had said. *"Il dio che guarda al futuro et al passato."* Janus, one face looking to the past, the other to the future.

Sonia and Dennis didn't join us for the holidays. Sonia has been solitary in her sorrow, not communicating, and at loose ends after all the years of taking care of Mom. With more time than ever to think, she pulled away, creating a distance wider than the two-hour time difference and four plant zones that separate us. Luckily I have Max to keep me busy.

"So, Apollo accidentally killed his friend Hyacinth, and his love for him created a beautiful, fragrant flower," I explain to the back of his head, which rests on his arms at the table. "You know, we have pink and purple hyacinths on the slope, near the daffodils. And did you know that daffodil is the common name for Narcissus, from the myth about the guy who was obsessed with his reflection in a pond, fell in love with himself, and drowned?"

I drone on: "And Aphrodite created a red anemone out of her love for Adonis when he died. Spring flowers are born out of death and blood, and ultimately love, you see, Max? Death is followed by renewal. Everything is a love story in the end!"

I'm talking to myself. Max has lost interest.

"Okay, but I have math homework. How much more time do we need to spend on this flower stuff?"

"Let's take a break," I tell him, and he leaps from the table, eager to abandon his books. "I'm going outside to pick some *real* flowers."

Lemon-yellow daffodil clumps scatter down the slope like blotches of sunshine on a gray moonscape—amazing that they belong to the dreadful amaryllis family.

The honeyed scent of hyacinth wafts around me. Carl Jung was right: enchantment is the oldest form of medicine. An occasional clump of pure white daffodils with orange centers, the color of the ducks' feet, triggers my anticipation of our mallards' arrival this year. I'm certain the mates will return.

Is it Mom who held Sonia and me together? Maybe we're too far apart—in age, in history, in character—to be close sisters without her.

I turn my head to the sun like an eager flower and head down the Secret Path toward the pond. I want to avoid the pagoda and the extra wood that fell from its roof during the winter. At least it's still standing, but I don't want to see the debris. I pass by the maples and notice I haven't yet removed the stiles. Our sap run was thin this year. Sonia, my maple tree, had nothing to give.

I check the mulberry tree, the garden's most reliable frost predictor. No buds yet, which means we may still get a late freeze. By the pond's edge I notice a few daffodils that we didn't plant; a squirrel probably transported some bulbs. I head over to pick them. Loud rustling from beside the chainlink fence, near the hidden brook, startles me. In the midst of bare branches and dry knotweed, standing quietly, facing south, is the unmistakable outline of a graceful body, ears held proudly back, tail up with its fur tufts creating a white feather in the dullness.

Deer!

My heart races. I catch my breath and hold it. Deer, deer, deer! It's back.

I don't panic this time, though it's been a while. I accept my visitor with an open heart. *Hello,* I whisper. It walks calmly to an area beyond the fence where a tree has fallen near some low-lying cedars, as if to say, *I live here, this is my home — where's yours?* It's a perfect hiding place to wait for the mulberry to bud.

I race up the stairs to call someone. Anyone.

Cam and Max are equally excited. Every morning for the next several days, I look for modest signs of spring as I try to spot the deer, and I do, only twice, and then no longer. I send Sonia a picture. She tells me she's seen a deer this year, too. It wandered onto her street from a nearby golf course that borders her ravine. The nubby mulberry branches sprout miniature grapelike flower buds. There will be no more frost.

"I dunno, I dunno, *non lo so.*" Gianni lifts his faded red baseball cap, wipes his brow, puts the cap back on and straightens it, looks over to his son, then back to me. "I need to explore, you know what I mean?"

I definitely know what he means. The pagoda is a disaster.

He looks up at the decaying beams and crumbling columns and then down to the chipped floor. He kicks a broken tile. "Where to start? I dunno. We gotta start somewhere."

I hold my breath. Gianni is my last hope. I like him. My *only* hope. One of the young gardeners who helped with the spring cleanup recommended him and promised me he was ideal for the job. I glance at Gianni's son, John, who taps at the pagoda's base with a hammer and shakes his head.

"It's finished out here, Pa," he says. He lifts his cap and wipes his forehead exactly the way his father did.

"You got a tile guy?" Gianni asks me. "It's a circular floor. You need someone good. This is an old building, you know. We have to be smart, do it carefully."

Yes, now we're talking. "I'll find a tile guy," I promise.

"I have to see. I need to think about the job."

"Can you give me a quote?" I ask. "A rough idea on cost?"

He laughs. John whistles in the background as he piles up the wood pieces on the ground. He's tidying. A sign of ownership. Good.

"No way I can quote on a job like this. Never. I explore and we go one step at a time. One step here, one there, you know what I mean?"

Not really.

"We gotta raise the roof," he adds, looking at his son.

They discuss scaffolding, half in English, half in Italian, as fear grips my heart. It dawns on me that this sweet father-son team is in imminent danger. The roof weighs several tons. It could kill them.

"You have your own scaffolding? Is it strong enough?" I ask. "Have you done this kind of work before?"

John laughs. "You don't know my dad."

What does that mean?

"No quote, no job," Cam says that evening over dinner.

"You can't expect him to quote when he doesn't understand the job's scope," I argue.

"How do you know he's not going to pad the hours?"

"He looks like your dad. Gianni and Gianni—I mean John."

"You're basing the restoration of the pagoda on that?" Cam looks out the kitchen window. "I know you're eager to finish the project," he adds, concern slowly rising, "but you really have to get this step right. One wrong move and the entire thing crashes down."

"Everyone else wants to replace it. Or they won't touch it at all." I pat Hunter's head calmly and slip him a morsel of bread. His pleading eyes probably look like mine. "Gianni's our last chance. I *want* to trust him."

The truth is I *need* to trust this father-and-son team. The obvious love they share is too marvelous to walk away from; they are the antithesis of my father and me, and I want to bask in the strangeness.

"Okay," I tell Gianni on the phone the next morning, "my husband and I would like you to have the job."

"Good, Alessandra," he says, pronouncing my name exactly the way Nonno does. It's music to my ears. "We gonna come by in a three weeks, after this job, and we explore, okay?"

Okay.

The day before Gianni's first day, I make amaretti. My delectable almond cookies rival those from the small bakery in my parents-in-laws' Italian town. I make them only on special occasions.

Cam spots the glass cookie jar on the counter when he comes in from work.

"Amaretti?" he says, reaching for the lid.

"Yeah." Did I sound sufficiently nonchalant?

"Gianni's starting tomorrow, isn't he?" he asks. "You already baked him cookies? Jesus, Alex."

"I want him to keep coming back."

"Isn't that why we agreed to pay him, so he agrees to come back? Without a contract or a quote, by the way."

"I trust him," I say.

"The cookies are perfect," he says, grabbing a second. "Let's hope his work is."

"You didn't really make these?" John asks on his third cookie. He and his father arrived at 7:30 a.m., armed with buckets, huge planks, metal scaffold pieces, and no additional help. I'm shocked; this doesn't look like an exploratory mission, but I'm too excited to ask.

"They're amazing." He stirs copious white sugar into the cappuccino foam. I went all out for coffee break, using the milk steamer Sonia sent me for my birthday. Little did she know that it would fuel the pagoda's restoration effort.

"Especially after those steps. You're gonna kill us," John jokes. True, they've been sweating buckets, going up and down, up and down, in order to get their equipment set up.

"What's in them?" he asks, chewing slowly.

"Can't tell you or I'll have to kill you," I say proudly. I look up at the rickety ladder and regret my words. Gianni, perched unsteadily at the top, pokes at the rotten wood with a screwdriver.

"Still exploring, but we gonna bring the roof up next week," he says, as he bumps his head. "Then we repair the columns and replace one beam at a time."

He's making it sound easy. He doesn't understand that I've asked a dozen people to look at this job.

"Oh, there's ants here, Alessandra!" he yells down. "Carpenter ants. That's why this wood is finished. Monday, I spray 'em up."

Gianni and son complete the scaffolding setup in a few days. Like a foreman, I'm rooted to the spot, phone in hand to call 911, as they crank the jacks. The old wood creaks in protest. From the inside, the roof is an octagonal cupola, with eight rafters flowing outward from a centerpiece, creating a downward-cascading star shape. The star is supported by eight hefty rotting beams, which in turn sit on the eight concrete columns.

A few more cranks. I hold my breath, and suddenly the columns are free of their weight. Magically, they stay upright. I wait in terror, holding my breath, and hope the jacks can bear the enormous weight, but the men make jokes, laughing and clambering about like the nearby squirrels. They're either incredibly good or downright reckless.

· · ·

"Aaaak!"

I race over from the pond to see Gianni shining a flashlight down the first hollow column from atop the scaffolding.

"*Madonna mia,*" he whistles, "ants! Look, thousands in here. Thousands!"

Carpenter ants galore. A carpenter ant colony. Shit. They're coming from somewhere below. I don't want to climb up to see. Gianni's ashen face says it all.

"Never seen anything like it," he says. "We cannot work until you spray, Alessandra. You gotta call the pros. Too many for me. And if you don't fix it, they'll eat my new beams."

He climbs down and begins to pack his stuff. I slump down on the step in time to see a shiny black three-sectioned body with thin angled legs walk by. Shit. That's one fat ant.

I follow the men up the steps and out. It's time for some research.

Gianni's right. They're big, they're ugly, and they bite. After they bite, they spray formic acid into the wound to increase the pain. Nasty guys.

I exhaust the eco-friendly alternatives on the Internet. Cornmeal makes their stomachs explode and borax works if we can find the nest. Not exactly friendly. Twenty pounds of exploding cornmeal is not an option, let alone the mice and other rodents it may attract. I feel sick about killing the ants, but not sick enough, I suppose. It's the ants or Gianni. No Gianni, no pagoda.

I call the exterminators.

I feel like a cold-blooded queen ant.

The slow-moving guys from Lovebugs Pest Control wear white plastic suits with breathing apparatus under their hoods as if they are leading a Mars expedition. I hope no neighbors noticed them or our property value is going to drop.

"No one can be in the area for a day after the spray," white Darth Vader gurgles from behind his mask.

I worry about the squirrels, raccoons, and birds.

"Focus inside the columns," I tell them. They nod at me from behind their gear and gesture for me to move up the steps. With trepidation, I retreat to the house to research the balusters.

Gianni tackles the ant-free columns with a vengeance. Half of the scrolled ionic concrete caps have eroded and all the smooth column shafts are cracked with years of water damage. The Renaissance-inspired balustrade's original limestone is also crumbling, and the repeating balusters are chipped or broken beyond repair. I don't want to lose their classic turned curves. They'll look fabulous threaded with a few vines of wisteria.

"I tried to find matching concrete ones online," I tell Gianni, as we examine the railing. He stiffens and crosses his arms over his chest. I've offended him. No New World replicas for him.

"You not gonna find a match," he says confidently.

"You're right. I didn't. But did you know the word *baluster* comes from Latin, *balaustium,* because they're shaped like a pomegranate flower?"

His eyes glaze over the same way Cam's do when I share something technically enlightening. What's with these men?

"That's nice, Alessandra. Listen, I'm gonna patch 'em up instead. You know, fix 'em. No problem. The new materials today fix anything."

Gianni proceeds to bore me with the technical properties of modern polymers in broken English. I love this man. Even if he doesn't like pomegranates.

My growing camaraderie with Gianni and John draws me into the garden regularly. Our mid-morning cappuccino exchanges about espresso beans, food, and politics, with the chirps of birds, crickets, and the fountain in the background, make me feel like I am in a dream in Italy. With Cam busy at work and Max at day camp, I want to be nearby in case they get hurt. Or in case they get hungry.

Gianni explains each step in passionate detail over coffee, expecting I will fully understand, and I do. Sometimes he talks about his own garden, his wife, and his previous construction jobs. It seems, for now, that his other summer commitments have fallen by the wayside and the pagoda has become his top priority and an immense personal challenge. Our mutual excitement is infectious. They're working with sincerity and love, and the hours and the money have become irrelevant to all of us. Well, most of us.

On days my back hurts too much for gardening, I've taken to watching the work from the stone bench under the mulberry tree's drooping branches. From this elevated vantage point, I have a perfect vista of the entire structure but am far enough away that the men won't feel as if I'm looking over their shoulders. The pond's water fountain soothes me as I analyze the pagoda, inch by inch, from the Roman-inspired railing to the Greek-inspired columns to the Asian-style roof. I realize it's a garden structure with a full-blown identity crisis. How odd—what were they thinking when they designed it? Maybe it's falling apart because it can't find itself. Then again, isn't cross-pollination supposed to make plants stronger? Maybe it's like the garden, a tangled mess of love and good intentions. It's just like *us*.

At coffee break John has a surprise for me. I've noticed that if I miss coffee break, Gianni is aloof the next day, like a jilted lover, and I'm disappointed that I missed the previous day's discussion. But today John brought me fresh figs, which he offers shyly.

I lean in to examine them. They're the black variety, perfectly ripe, with sun-kissed yellow streaks on the skin—Nonno's favorite. I bite into one and savor the taste of hot sun and sugar.

"Perfect," I tell John. "From the Tree of Heaven, they say."

Gianni claps his hands and laughs. "Alessandra," he says, "I love working here."

. . .

"Yes, all good, Gianni found a tile guy," I tell Sonia on the phone one day as I supervise from the stone bench. "Good news, assuming the roof holds up," I add.

Sonia has become interested in the construction project and has offered helpful ideas as I send play-by-play photos.

"Make sure they use a good primer. They should let the wood settle and dry out first," she counsels.

The summer has eased us out of our gloom. Inspired, Sonia has launched her own project: she's building garden trellises using Father's small table saw and sending me progress pictures, too.

"You know, I realize I'm more like our father than I thought," she says with a twinge of pride and acceptance.

I shake my head, not sure I heard correctly over the fountain's din.

"I totally respect that he was a perfectionist," she continues. "And I understand why he was paranoid. Half the things I buy these days don't work like they should."

I look through the faint rainbow in the fountain's mist, thinking back to my birthday gift from her, the large box securely and systematically taped a thousand times with duct tape. It took forever to open. Yes, just like our father.

"You certainly have his packing technique," I say.

"Sometimes I wonder if Mom's frustration and bitterness influenced how she spoke to me about him. You know, tainted our thoughts about him a little."

"Probably did," I agree. "I'm flighty like Mom, aren't I?" I ask.

"Don't be silly. That was her dementia," Sonia says, but we both know what I meant.

This conversation could not have happened when Mom was still alive. Her passing has liberated us from something invisible. For the first time, we can see and talk about ourselves objectively and without guilt.

· · ·

Mulberries are scattered and squashed on the stone bench and the flagstone path, and more float in the pond. It appears the squirrels and the ducks, which returned this year despite the noise of Gianni's wood saw, had a party. It's said that the unripe mulberry can be hallucinogenic; it was a *wild* party.

"I'm picking the *gelsi*," I tell Cam proudly, as I pass him frantically snipping at the serviceberry. In my arms I balance a step stool, Max's golf umbrella, a broom, and a bowl. "Like your Uncle Federico taught me in Italy."

He nods, not hearing me. "Check on Max," he says to my back.

I head for the hammock. Max sways on his back, his book open upside down on his chest.

"Reading?" I ask.

"Resting," he says.

I smile. It's a book, not an iPad. I crawl onto the hammock beside him, practically flipping us both over in the process, and stare upward through the outline of branches on the azure sky. The cord presses into my back, imprinting the memory of the moment, the electric hum of insects, and the musty smell of the pond's rotting iris leaves. I'm not sure which is better, the summer sky or that I am snuggled watching it with Max.

"I love this hammock," he says.

"Why?"

"Because it's quiet here. And I saw Daddy's toad again."

I want to talk more, but that wouldn't be quiet, so I hold his hand, bigger than mine already, and focus on the intertwining branches.

"Do you want to pick some berries?" I ask after a few minutes.

"Can I watch from here?"

"Sure. You can help with the jam later." I struggle out of the hammock and give it a strong push so Max swings high, almost tipping. His laughter follows me as I cross Cam's weed-lawn.

Well, Mom, I say to the wind, *this is how they do it in Italy.* I open the umbrella and turn it upside down under the best branch. *Via!* I hit the branch with the broom and watch a few berries fall into the open umbrella. Most of them fall onto the ground around it. A tarp would be more efficient, but that's not romantic at all. I eat a few plump black ones, staining my teeth and tongue like a child eating colored candy.

"The Romans ate mulberries at their feasts in honor of forbidden love," I tell Cam later, appealing to his heritage.

He gapes into the small bowl of mulberry jam Max and I made. Max has already diplomatically said he doesn't *prefer* it.

"In fact, in Ovid's *Pyramus and Thisbe,* the original *Romeo and Juliet,* the lovers bleed to death under the shade of a mulberry tree, turning the white berries to crimson."

"It's quite bitter tasting, don't you find?" asks Cam, licking the jam off the spoon. "Did you make a lot?"

"No, but I also used some berries to make morat, a drink made from honey and mulberry juice." I sense Max making faces behind my back.

"Any alcohol in it?" Cam asks hopefully.

"No, but it has resveratrol, an antioxidant."

"I need alcohol to *say* resveratrol," he says. "Where do you come up with these things?"

"We should leave the mulberries for the ducks," Max says, walking back to his computer. "I don't want them to run out of food."

I guess I'll tell them about how white mulberry leaves are the only source of food for silkworms another time.

They really know how to suck the romance out of a room.

MULBERRY GRANITA

Ingredients:

2 cups black mulberries
Juice of 1 lemon
4 cups water
1 cup sugar

- Combine water and sugar in a saucepan over low heat until all the sugar is dissolved. Allow the syrup to cool.
- Purée mulberries and lemon juice in a blender or fruit processor. You should have approximately 1⅓ cups of purée.
- Combine the syrup and the fruit purée. Pour into a deep pan and cover with foil. Place into a freezer.
- After 1 hour, take a fork and scrape the ice crystals from the sides and bottom of the pan. Fluff and mash them back into the liquid. Repeat 30 minutes later. You can continue to do this at 30-minute intervals, until you have dry separated ice crystals that are approximately the same size, or you can let it sit overnight.
- Before serving, let granita defrost for 5 minutes. Scrape off ice crystals using a fork and serve immediately in a tall glass.

See page 267 for information on safety and sourcing of plants.

CHAPTER 19

❧

Wisteria

THE X-RAY IS clear. My chronic back pain is the result of disc degeneration in my lower spine. Moderate exercise is acceptable for spinal osteoarthritis; heavy lifting and bending less so. The fall off the wall is responsible, as well as the countless buckets of soil, flagstones, concrete screening, rocks, and algae I've carried over the past few years. It's amazing I can still get up the steps.

"I'm not carting stuff anymore," I tell Cam.

"Me either," he agrees.

Neither of us means it. We're both going to keep at it, like my father in his apple tree, until, well, we simply can't.

Megan is sympathetic when I explain that sitting for too long hurts, and now I know why.

"You need an inversion table," she suggests. "They cost less than one physiotherapy appointment. And," she promises, "you'll probably grow an inch in six months."

Soon, Cam and I are addicted to hanging upside down, the blood rushing to our brains, making us smarter, and temporarily filling the wrinkles across our foreheads. I know this because when we are upside down, I can see my reflection in the mirrored wall in our basement. My cheeks puff out and downward, and my head looks like a bulbous onion, with my hair a perfect replica of fibrous roots rising from my forehead. For a few hours after inversion, my pain disappears.

"You know caterpillars hang upside down to start metamorpho-sis," I muse to Cam's feet one day as he dangles from the foot straps. "Gravity helps the wings unfold, or something like that."

"Really?" his puffer fish head asks me from below. "What are we morphing into?"

"I'm not sure," I answer. Which begs the question: then how will we recognize ourselves?

Maybe through our children.

Max is coming home from camp today. He's been away for a week in the Georgian Bay backcountry of pink granite and white quartz-ite ridges. I'm jealous, living vicariously through him, imagining hiking and canoeing through the region that inspired the Group of Seven artists.

I pick him up at the bus drop-off, excited to hear his stories. He settles into the car and launches into tales about the portage in the rain and the mud in the tent.

"It was brutal, Mom," he assures me happily. "You wouldn't have liked it. Oh, yeah, here."

He reaches into his jacket pocket and pulls out a rock.

"I found it on my first day and carried it for the rest of the trip," he says proudly. "Do you like it? I thought it's perfect for your collection."

I hold the cool stone up to my hot cheek. My Xbox-wielding son carried a rock for me for seven days. It's like Jesus and the pebble in the shoe, but better.

"I love it," I say. I love it more than *anything,* this beautiful piece of the earth's crust, formed under intense pressure thousands of years ago. Is it possible that Max already understands me when I am still trying to make sense of my mother?

He tells me about the Native sweat lodge they visited where they smoked the peace pipe.

"You smoked?" Oh my god, remain calm.

"And guess what was in the tobacco?" he asks.

"What?" *Please don't let it be pot.*

"Sumac," he says smugly. "Way better than your tea, by the way."

I almost hit the car in front of me.

"Black and white," says Cam that evening, moving his chair closer to the table. "I love the black-and-white tiles in Italian palazzos."

We're so damn close to finishing the pagoda, choosing the floor tiles is one of the last steps. I listen to Cam's enthusiasm with a tinge of sadness. I didn't make the deadline. Mom's gone.

"Okay," I agree. Besides, I found a striking magazine photo of a gorgeous round outdoor room with a similar cupola with white ceiling and black beams, an ideal complement to a black-and-white floor. I walk to my desk and retrieve it from my worn black leather idea binder.

"Too stark. Not sure I like it," he says, shaking his head. "Sorry."

"Trust me," I tell him. I'm determined to give him his magnificent dream floor.

I choose black slate tiles that look like they came from the ridges of the Appalachians. They won't be slippery in the rain. The accents will be small, square, white marble tiles from Italy for Cam, and our floor now represents the grounds we each worship. The manager at the tile store designs a circular pattern on her computer screen, weaving the tiles on an electronic loom that Max would appreciate. Complicated cutting, the manager tells me. More than 150 square feet, over 1,000 pounds of tile.

That'll take a while to get down the steps.

I find fabric, too, although I can hardly lift the wide thirty-yard roll of gauze. It's white, fine enough to see through, but it'll keep out the bees.

"I wanted to sew these myself," I tell the clerk sadly. Suspended, each of the eight curtain panels will be an unwieldy twelve feet high and over six feet wide.

"That roll weighs more than you," she says. She hasn't tried to lift the tile boxes.

"I'm sorry, Alessandra, but it let in all the rain. It had to go," Gianni says, looking at the mountain of broken wood that once formed the lowest level of the pagoda roof.

I rub my suddenly stiff neck. The wood used to be a decorative trellis that protruded two feet from the roof's edge. It was damaged by the old wisteria and, in fairness, was never sufficient to protect the columns.

But *still*. I examine the wood heap in dismay.

"We're gonna make a solid roof instead. No more plants on the roof."

"But it won't look the same," I argue, my arms crossed.

I don't want to tell him that I want the old wisteria to regrow up the columns. Its roots, several inches thick, still live behind the pagoda, undaunted, shooting vines onto the city fence. I had visions of cascading fragrant petals around the pagoda roof, like an airy violet silk scarf.

"We're gonna manage the water, Alessandra, no choice."

No violet crown chakra for me.

"He could have died. Closest call we've ever had," says the gardener, his face pale in the midafternoon sunshine.

I press my hands against my temples. My body is covered in cold sweat, despite the heat, as I sit on a deck chair breathing deeply to calm myself. A branch from the surviving oak came crashing down unexpectedly and barely missed one of the gardeners I hired to start the post-construction cleanup.

He could have died.

"It was that close," he says in a deep voice. His partner sits quietly on a nearby chair, holding his juice glass.

Guilt overcomes me. I want to disappear into a crack between the terrace flagstones. It's my fault. I chose to keep the stupid oak even though I was warned. After all my worries about the safety of the pagoda restoration, a freak accident like this almost killed someone. An accident I could have prevented.

"I'm so sorry," I say. "The tree will come down as soon as possible. I was trying to save it." What was I clinging to so foolishly? Mom's life, tethered by a thread, even though it was time for her to go.

"That's Mother Nature," says the fellow with an extra life, shrugging his shoulders. "You made the best decision you could."

He's chosen to forgive me. I would feel less guilty if he were angry.

Mauro, the landscape lighting expert, grins like a proud father. I clutch his ladder at the base with white knuckles, still spooked by the near miss a few days ago. He adjusts the height of the antique chandelier a few inches lower, watching my face for my reaction.

I catch my breath. *Astounding.* I shut my eyes, memorizing the moment.

"It's perfect," I say. "Like it was made for the space."

"It is," he says, descending the ladder. My beacon has energy now, like a lighthouse.

I hold back from hugging him, although I'm certain he would understand.

The brown wrought iron chandelier is shaped into a series of tree branches and leaves with eight candle-shaped lights. It drops twenty feet on a metal chain from the middle of the soaring black star formed by the wooden rafters.

"I want to see this in the dark. Will you send me a picture?"

"Of course," I promise. *I can't wait.* The beauty is greater than the sum of its parts. Mauro has also installed tiny path lights from the house to the pagoda.

"The curtains will make dramatic shadows at night," he says. Yes, they will.

At that moment a scarlet cardinal, a male, flies right through the pagoda, in one side, out the other. Mauro pauses. I know what he's thinking. If he weren't speechless, he'd probably say, *I've never seen anything like it.*

"It's almost finished, Alessandra," Gianni says sadly during coffee break, his shoulders stooped as he circles the inside of the pagoda. Around us, the hum of nature feels normal, as if nothing new or magical has happened in its midst. The birds are louder than ever, squeaking and chirping above the crickets and the splashing of the fountain.

"Beautiful, eh?" he adds, looking up at the repaired pillars and the newly painted ceiling. "It's like we're in Italy." He picks up a broom.

I review the mess directly outside. A few surviving limp hosta leaves are covered with fine dust. They look like how I feel. I should feel happy, like the stupid perky daisies several yards away.

"I know. You did it. The impossible," I say. I can't say goodbye to this man.

"You know, Alessandra, I worked a lot of jobs. But never like this. This was the best project I ever done in my life."

I swallow over the lump in my throat.

"What's your secret cookie ingredient again?" John tries to lighten the moment. His eyes are sympathetic as he watches his father sweep invisible dust.

"I'll miss you, Alessandra," Gianni says, looking down at the tiles.

"You're not done yet," I declare, looking around desperately. "You need to look at the path."

Gianni perks up as we examine the rotted railroad ties and slope runoff on the property's steepest side. Shaking his head, he mutters about proper screening rocks, metal stakes, and drainage trenches.

"I need to do a big exploration here," he says.

Music to my ears. The bigger the better.

"I think we gonna replace everything," he continues, lifting his cap and rubbing his forehead.

John doesn't look happy. He'll be lugging wood and buckets of stone for weeks.

I don't care. My family's staying, and I need to make more cookies.

"We should have a garden blessing when the pagoda is finished," I tell Cam as we walk through the garden. He snips at shrub branches as we go, unable to stop himself. He never leaves the house without small pruners now. It's an irresistible urge, like an addiction, to snip at the plants.

Myself, I clutch my cloudy piece of quartzite in my right palm. Since Max gave it to me, I carry it everywhere. Its rounded bottom fits perfectly into the curve of my hand, and a flat side supports my thumb. It's as if it were molded for me. I try it in my left palm—it doesn't fit.

"Really? Since when did you become religious?" he asks. Snip, snip.

"I'd like to acknowledge we're done," I say. I'm thinking the anniversary of Mom's death is a good day, but don't want to tell Cam.

"I like it. Let's do it," he says, as he throws his branches into a mulch pile. "Will you invite your sister?"

"Of course. And Gordon."

"Gordon who?" He cuts a rose and inhales its fragrance. I know it will end up in a glass on Max's bedside table.

"*Lightfoot.* How many Gordons do we know?"

"Alex, we don't know Gordon Lightfoot," he says, cutting another rose stem.

"Well, I do. His poetry's been with me during the entire restoration—my entire life, in fact." Like a guardian angel.

"You're kidding, right? The guy's in his nineties. What makes you think that at his age, he's going to come to some stranger's house?"

"Please get your facts right. First of all, he's in his seventies, *and* he's still touring. He's *ageless*." I say. "I'll write him a letter."

"A letter."

"I don't expect him to sing. He used to live on this ravine. It'll be like an invitation to a neighborhood thing."

I can see it now. I'll incorporate some Native rituals. Max and I can make cedar smudge sticks for the pagoda. I'll call that Nolan fellow who does earth energy balancing. Friends and family will join us. I'll say a few words. Sonia will come for sure.

"Alex," Cam says, "You can't possibly be serious. Think about what you're saying."

"I know *exactly* what I'm saying. And let me say something else. You don't have a damn clue."

I stomp up the steps to the house before he can say another word.

I type the first draft, and then write on stationery with a fountain pen. May as well go as traditional as possible.

"Why are you doing that by hand?" Cam asks, looking at my page. He's still trying to reason with me. "It's going to take you forever."

"Out of respect. Wouldn't you be more likely to say yes if you got a handwritten request?" I ask.

"No."

"Well, then, it's settled." I continue writing.

I write until my fingers hurt. Max helps me find his home address and his business office, which is, unbelievably, on a busy street only a few miles from our house. I park in a nearby lot and walk to his office with a quickening pulse. What if Gordon's there? At least his assistant will be there. I need to calm down or he'll think I'm a kooky fan.

The entrance to the tired office building is open. Where's the security? I walk up the few flights of stairs, breathing heavily. The door is locked, but an old-fashioned mailbox hangs on the wall. My anticipation flows out of me into the grungy floor. I open the post box. It's full of junk mail and a lonely post card from a fan in Kentucky. Damn. I admire my green cursive one last time, and place my letter next to the tattered postcard.

"What are you doing?" I yell, as Cam hacks wildly at the wisteria vines. The city fence leans forward as he yanks. "You're going to pull down the fence."

"They're killing the evergreens." He snips at the pine's trunk where the thick vines have wrapped around it like a candy cane stripe. A mound of at least a hundred feet of vines in a ball, which Cam must have pulled from the ground beneath the trees, lies nearby.

"Gianni got me thinking," Cam says. "We can't let the wisteria wreck our pines, either. Do you know it can bring down a fully grown oak?"

"I hoped to at least let it grow up the new columns," I say.

"Not on my watch," he says. "After all the work this pagoda needed?"

I trudge over to the tangle of vines and start to sort through them carefully. It's as if my lifeline has been callously pruned by my soul mate. I form a sturdy vine into a rough circle and start to twine the supplest ones around it to form a wreath.

"What are you doing?" Cam asks as he dumps another mass of wood into the pile.

"Rerouting my life," I reply. Everything Cam does annoys me these days, amplified by the fact that Sonia is unsure about attending the blessing. Dennis isn't feeling well enough to travel. I know I'm being selfish, but I'm devastated.

"Okay. Let me know where you land," he says, gently kissing the top of my head before he goes back to his pruning.

I wrap around and around and around into the infinite circle of life. I guess that's where I'm going, waiting for an answer from Gordon. And now Sonia. A big fat circular zero.

Nolan, recommended by a friend, came by to meet me, visit the garden, and discuss the potential blessing ceremony. He immediately adored the space, breathing deeply as we walked, his eyes glowing as he examined the crowns of the trees, declaring some healthy and some in desperate need of remineralized soil.

"Nolan?" asks Cam that evening, an eyebrow raised.

"He's a geomancer."

He puts his book down. "What the hell's a geomancer?"

"He balances the earth's magnetism and energy with minerals," I explain.

"Okay . . ." His voice says *not okay*.

"He's also a permaculturalist. He believes in natural sustainable agriculture and he replenishes depleted soil." I hold back from telling him about Nolan's dowsing abilities.

"That's pretty out there, Alex," he says. "Are you sure he's the right guy?" He's treading carefully because of Gordon.

"As opposed to whom?" I ask. "At least Nolan understands the earth."

"I don't think I need to get involved," he says, picking up his book.

I gather the herbs for the smudge sticks first thing in the morning. In keeping with Native tradition, I ask each plant for permission to use its healing power, caressing the soft silver sage leaves and inhaling the sharp oils of the cedar fronds. *It's been a long journey, this garden restoration,* I decide, as I chew a few tiny thyme leaves. Each herb has a role: sage dispels negative energy, thyme cleanses our spirit in matters of love, rosemary heals and offers remembrance, and cedar protects. I couldn't ask for anything more—it's all here, growing at my feet, filling my lungs, and soothing my heart. I leave a strand of hair on the ground, a personal offering of appreciation, and head back up the steps.

Gordon ignored me and broke my heart. We are no longer on speaking terms. Who ignores a handwritten note?

"Maybe he never got it," Cam offers. "I bet the letter is still in his mailbox."

"Maybe I *hate* him," I say.

"Alex, he was never going to respond. Waiting was a bit naive on your part," he says.

"Waiting was naive?" my voice cracks. "Naive, like waiting for my father to say good morning just one day? For him to acknowledge my existence even though I was born a girl? *That* kind of naive? Damn Gordon, his poetry, and the stupid blessing."

There's nothing more to say.

Cam stands, opens his mouth to speak, then changes his mind.

SMUDGE STICKS

Please note:
Use only non-toxic plants. Pick herbs on a dry and sunny day because moist branches may get moldy when wrapped.

Materials:
Fresh herbs, grasses, or small branches in 8- to 12-inch lengths, such as sweet grass, cedar, juniper, lavender, sage, thyme, and rosemary
Natural fiber string (red is traditional)

- Divide your herbs into bunches for each smudge stick.
- Use a sturdily branched herb as the base and wrap or braid the other branches around it. Keep branches that burn more quickly, such as cedar, in the middle, or use the longest branches in the center and shorter ones on the outside.
- Tie the string tightly from the bottom up to almost the top and back downward, wrapping several times around the bottom of the bundle to create a handle.
- Wrap the finished stick in brown paper to keep the herbs from fading, and hang upside down to dry for a week or two.
- When you are ready to use the dried smudge stick, light it with a candle. As it begins to smoke, keep it over a fireproof container at all times. Move the stick to direct the smoke toward whatever is being smudged. In traditional ceremonies, smoke is often fanned with an eagle feather. To smudge a house, carry the burning stick and move clockwise around each room.

See page 267 for information on safety and sourcing of plants.

CHAPTER 20

Clay

"Sonia and dennis are coming!" I announce to Cam as I replace the phone handset. The blessing is back *on*. All my secret worries about her hesitation dissipate. She wants to come, although I'm not sure why. Is it for me, or for our parents, or maybe to find her own closure?

"Sonia would have died to meet Gordon Lightfoot," I add wistfully. My lonely letter is somewhere in a trash bin, or shredded into bits of meaningless vowels and consonants, and my sentiments sliced into nothingness.

"You know he was in the paper yesterday? He's playing here for a couple of nights," says Cam. "You were right about the touring."

What? Playing here?

"When exactly were you going to tell me?" I ask, folding my arms across my chest.

"I don't know. Why? You were all upset about the blessing. I didn't want to make things worse."

Not bothering to answer, I race to the computer. He's playing all right. Shit. I need to change the date of the garden blessing. End of November it will be, and we'll go to the concert after the ceremony.

"Really, Alex? You're dragging us there?" Cam says when I lay out the evening plans. "Maybe Max should stay home if he wants."

My body tenses. "You didn't say that, did you?"

Cam takes a deep breath and exhales. "You're right, of course we're going," he says.

"Good," I say.

He begins to croon the words to "The Wreck of the Edmund Fitzgerald"—the wrong ones, too. At least he knows one song, but he sounds like a sick goat.

Cam carries two wineglasses and Max holds Hunter's leash as we head down the steps to the pagoda. Dusk approaches like a gentle cloud, creating secrets around us, as the nocturnal animals prepare for their night's work. I want us to be together when the outdoor lights go on; it needs to be perfect for the blessing. We make ourselves comfortable on the pagoda bench.

Cam looks up to the ceiling and down to the tiles.

"The black and white really works, doesn't it?" he says. "Chiaroscuro."

My skin tingles as recognition bubbles to the surface. Of course. Why didn't I notice it before? The pagoda is the perfect balance of light and dark. We didn't plan it, and yet here we sit, inside a cocoon of equilibrium.

"Yin and yang," I say. Two opposing yet complementary forces found in all things in the universe.

"Just like on the South Korean flag," says Max.

Of course, Max would know. The flag hangs prominently at the front of his *dojang*. He's been staring at it since he was four years old. And so have I, year after year, watching his tae kwon do progression.

Our pagoda isn't the South Korean flag. *But it is.*

The round floor could be the flag's center, the *taegeuk*, the familiar curved symbol of yin-yang. The linear symbols around it represent nature's opposites and remind me of the straight sides of the pagoda, one side for each of Max's eight patterns.

The lights, set on a timer for precisely 8:00 p.m., flicker on, and a gentle orange-yellow glow fills the pagoda. Light washes across the rough stone columns and makes the bog willows fluorescent.

"Wow," says Max.

Wow is right. We are in an illuminated octagon that represents the balance of nature. I shut my eyes for a moment, unable to believe the exquisite beauty, and its unexpected symbolism.

Cam raises his glass to me. "You've revived a beautiful space. And it seems Max was here ahead of us."

Max shrugs.

"I'm learning there are many paths to connect to nature," I say.

"Look, it's clay!" says Max, lifting a shovel of soil as we unearth the dead rosebush. There are only a few weekends left before the blessing, and I'm anxious about the endless tasks. I've enlisted Max to help make the garden *perfect*.

I peer into the hole. Thick, wet, gray clay dominates a small amount of black soil. Water puddles at the bottom. No wonder the roses struggled. Didn't Cam notice the clay when he planted these?

"Dig up all the dead ones," I tell Max, as I cut back the few bushes that seem okay.

"Look, you can shape it," he says, shovel abandoned, twisting a clay piece between his palms. "It's like Play-Doh."

He's cross-legged on a flagstone, his thick cotton sweatpants covered in mulch, his eyes intent on the clay. A quiet thrill shoots through my heart. It's been many years since we've played with the colorful dough that left dried crumbs all over the house. I never imagined I'd see my young teenager shaping real clay from our garden. A flat disk turns into a worm between his fingers. I put down my pruners, grab a piece, and find my own flagstone seat.

We've uncovered hidden treasure. Might as well enjoy it.

"We could make pottery," Max says. "Like my phone app."

Max went through an enthusiastic phase with an application on his phone that virtually shapes clay vases, decorates and fires them, and sells them in a computerized marketplace. Ridiculous, but at least the game doesn't involve mindless violence.

The idea hits me like a ton of clay bricks.

"Let's make pottery," I tell him. "Why not?"

"But we don't have a wheel."

"We'll find one," I say, emptying the twigs in my garden pail. I no longer care about the roses. "Fill it up," I tell him.

The heavy, wet clay splatters us until we are covered in the oldest building material on earth: earth itself.

I've pretty much accepted that Max's techie know-how has become a godsend to our garden projects. The YouTube video tells us exactly what to do with our pail of clay. I haven't turned Max into a gardener yet, but I have a decent hybrid: a green techie.

"You're kidding, right?" Cam asks over dinner. "Honestly, guys. And what happened to my roses?"

"Most of them didn't make it," I tell him gently. "They don't like *wet feet*."

"Neither do I," says Cam, examining his flip-flops.

"Maybe you can plant some on the terrace," I suggest. "Now, about our pottery making—"

"Pottery making." He looks up from his feet.

"We'll be using the techniques of the Neolithic period," I explain.

Max beams. He actually knows when the Neolithic period was because of geography class.

"It was 10,000 BC," he says.

"I called the Gardiner Museum of Ceramics," I say. "They're going to help us."

Cam stabs at his lettuce.

Our pottery teacher peers into the pail. "It won't work," he says, sifting the gray dust between his long fingers. "We can't trust it in our kiln."

He mixes water into our clay powder and works the goo between his fingers like a baker sensing his dough. We hold our breath, waiting for a verdict.

"It's too sticky. It won't hold up," he says.

Max's face drops. I swallow. Our garden makes good clay, dammit.

The teacher keeps kneading. "Actually, as it gets drier, it's taking some shape," he says. "You know what, this may be better clay than I thought."

We make shallow bowls and press the garden leaves onto them, leaving impressions of the summer. Beech, ginkgo, maple, and oak. Our teacher talks about how prehistoric pottery was baked in a fire and how technology has made us forget how things were once done.

"Ancient Egyptians believe the fire god was born out of clay," I tell our teacher.

He's not listening. He's given Max a piece of acceptable clay and is coaching him to use a pottery wheel. Max presses too hard on the pedal and his clay flies off the wheel, splattering a six-foot perimeter. He starts over; soon his hands are giant gray clay mittens, and he doesn't want to stop. He is coated with our garden.

"Isn't it early for the Christmas tree?" Max asks, as we drag the sumac branches up the Secret Path.

"I want the house to look nice for Auntie Sonia," I say, untangling a branch off a nearby yew.

Thanks to Gianni's handiwork, this path will last another hundred years. He laid rocks between the railroad ties, and they strangely look like train tracks. Gianni and I didn't say goodbye, again. Instead, I asked him to repair the shifted stones on the terrace next spring. *Okay, Alessandra, no problem,* he said.

"Don't let the berries fall off, please," I yell back at Max. The bare sumac branches will be our Christmas tree, with their dark red berry cones as a natural decoration. The branches, as wide as they are long, get caught on the front door as we drag them into the house. The berry tips scratch the white living room ceiling as we prop them into a wide wicker basket.

"Uh-oh," says Max when he notices the dark red marks on the ceiling. It looks like a child on a ladder scribbled with a burgundy wax crayon.

"Oh, well," I say, hoping Cam doesn't notice. "Our tree drew us a picture. Maybe it's of the forest."

"It looks like blood," he says.

"Well, it almost is. You know that the molecule for blood and for chlorophyll is exactly the same except for the center?"

"Really?" He adjusts the basket to the right. He is skeptical, but curious, because he is studying chemistry at school.

"Really," I say. I adjust it to the left. "They're both rings with different centers. That's why we're connected to plants," I tell him. "Like blood brothers."

I don't want to put lights on the tree for fear of making it look unnatural. Max and I hang feathery bird ornaments and woven vine decorations, and instead of lights, I place a spotlight on the floor below.

"Cool," says Max, admiring the tree in our dark living room. My skin tingles with excitement. The spotlight on the floor shines through the branches and creates an image across the entire ceiling, like Max's school shadow art. The subconscious memory of the entire forest is in our living room.

I'm obsessed with the tree shadow on the ceiling. For the next few evenings, I sit in the large armchair and stare at the intricate branch architecture. It reminds me of Father—his grafting and his carpentry. His silence made him a shadow of a human being, like Jung's shadow self—our dark subconscious. He wasn't ignoring me; he was hidden in his refuge. He gave me a silhouette on a ceiling because that's all he had.

· · ·

Sonia arrives with gifts: a gardener's apron she had sewn for Mom, and a cutting from a peony from her garden, which was a cutting from one of Mom's plants. I'm overcome with relief, joy, and sadness—the indescribable mess of emotion that hits at the end of a hard journey, when you're finally able to pause and realize why it was worth it.

I watch her carefully dig a small hole in the cold soil near the pagoda, put in the root, and gently cover it as if she's swaddling a baby. Legacy is a responsibility. Finally, both our hearts and minds are ready for it.

"It's so cold down there," she says.

"Up here, too, but I know what you mean."

Sonia and I set out a cold buffet, for after the blessing. I decide to use the Minton fine china Mom bought me when I was twenty; it requires a step stool to reach it on the highest kitchen shelf. I rarely use it because it needs to be carefully hand-washed, and it's, well, just too fancy. As I dust a plate, I notice the logo on the back.

"I wonder what Grasmere is?" I ask Sonia. It's a lovely word. Grass and *mère*, mother in French.

I stop setting the table and search for it on my computer. Surprisingly, Grasmere is the name of a town in the center of the Lake District in England, hence the blue flowers adorning the rim. The town was the site of the Romantic movement of poets, whose core included Wordsworth, Coleridge, and Southey. Wordsworth's two former homes and his grave are in Grasmere, and he called the town "the loveliest spot that man hath ever found."

I pause.

It's exactly how I feel about my garden.

My china has finally found its home, and, I guess, so have I. I put a teacup from the set onto the lower shelf. From now on, I'll use it for my Earl Grey.

"I think I'll take a walk," I tell Sonia. I put on my warmest jacket and head down the steps to the wooden chairs by the pond. Yel-

lowed grass covered with dried leaves unrolls at my feet. November
snowflakes float around me. I hate it when Cam tells me we've entered the autumn of our lives. It makes me feel old, but I suppose
he's right.

The wind blows against Father's chimes, and they sound like the
ringing of a railroad crossing bell, like when a train passed by when I
played on the tracks as a child, probably a train my father had toiled
on during his night shift. And suddenly, the tears flow. And flow.
Uncontrollably. The repressed tears of a lifetime of questions, sadness, and joy. Tears for my parents, who did the best they could, and
for my sister, who actually came here, still willing to love me after
all these years. Tears because I was wrong about so many things, and
because it is finally time to forgive myself, too. Tears for years of
scrapes, an injured back, and the realization that Mom didn't really
need to see the garden; I just needed to finish it.

And when the tears are dry, I look to the chimes, and say hello to
my dad for the first time.

Max leads us down the steps, nervously balancing a short green candle on one of our homemade clay plates. Fire-lit torches create a
crystal carpet in the darkness. Silver clouds glow above us; it's never
fully dark in the city. A few close friends chat in hushed, excited
voices as we walk behind Max. The light snow brought cold, but
not unbearably so, just enough to make the glowing pagoda a warm
refuge.

Nolan waits outside the pagoda's entrance with a smoldering
smudge stick, prepared to encircle each of us with purifying smoke
before we enter. The smoke surrounds me, and I say my final goodbyes to the silence and loneliness of my youth. My resentments float
into the trees, taking their rightful place with all the shadow selves
that live there.

Inside the pagoda, candles, warm blankets, and fragrant oils welcome us. Max sits next to me on a bench, holding my hand, as if
taking care of me. Everyone finds their natural place within the cir-

cle, and Nolan passes around a small bucket of powdered magnetite from the New York Adirondacks.

"Each take a handful," he says, "and think of an intention for this moment, so it can live in the garden for future generations."

The air is electric but solemn. Everyone scoops his or her handful. Nolan asks us each to throw it over the baluster behind us, into the dark garden beyond. In the billows of magnetic dust we sense his energy, and, for a moment, believers and skeptics unite with the hope that he is right.

Nolan places three large rocks, each the approximate size of a bread loaf, in a triangle on the table: basalt from an ancient volcano, representing the earth of several billion years ago as it bubbled and decided its own fate; andesite volcanic rock, representing the earth's continental crust and its anchoring energy; and piezoelectric quartz, representing the photons of light that guide us to stand erect.

"From black to middle to light," he says, and then passes around the rocks for everyone to hold. I clutch the quartz the same way I hold the quartzite Max gave me and will its electricity into my soul.

"Our ancestors are always listening," Nolan says. He turns to me, and I pull a crumpled paper out of my pocket and begin to read. I share some reminiscences from the garden restoration, and how it helped me understand my parents' legacy.

I explain that it answered a profound longing, but I didn't know what it was until now. I thought I wanted to create my mother's dream garden; I thought I wanted my parents' acceptance. As the seasons passed, and the plants lived, died, and disintegrated into the earth, their seeds taught me that it's never too late to start again.

Sonia and I stand to make our offerings. I walk through the bog, the earth still soft under my boots, and sprinkle corn at the white willow's base. I pull my wishing branch close and undo the knot I left there. Sonia sprinkles corn on Mom's peony, and we walk back to the pagoda together, feeling the spirit of our parents imbued amidst the trees.

The blessing over, we head up the steps and inside. I stop to leave the candles and smudge stick on the table near the wall mural, where the brushstrokes of the cherry blossoms shimmer in the evening light. I didn't know back then, when we bought the house, that blossoms are symbolic of life's transience, our brief journey in this world. I see it now, because I, like every living thing, am transient too. I remain in flux, like the elements of nature that I have come to love, changing, growing, and evolving. I said goodbye to my parents when they were strangers, and only got to know them after they were gone; I became a real daughter when there was no one left to call me one.

Yet I'm never alone in the energy of nature.

Max will walk into his future connected with the earth, the oceans, and the life within. I'll watch him, and all who follow, from the vantage point of my garden, grateful that my parents gave me an unspoken connection to the land, and an understanding that life is fleeting, and that life is *now*.

EIGHT PATTERNS (YOUGUPJA POOMSAE) OF KUKKIWON TAE KWON DO

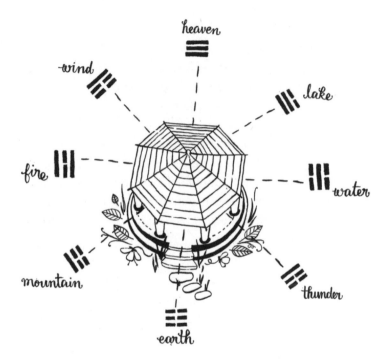

Il Jang, Heaven, bestows a solid foundation
Yi Jang, Lake, brims with inner strength and external gentleness
Sam Jang, Fire, burns with enthusiasm
Sa Jang, Thunder, roars with power and dignity
Oh Jang, Wind, blows with graceful resilience
Yook Jang, Water, flows with ultimate flexibility
Chil Jang, Mountain, stands with firmness and solidity
Pal Jang, Earth, grounds us with humility

Harvest

I'm grateful for our garden. To some it may be big, to others small, but size doesn't matter because for me a garden is a state of mind. It's a tranquil sanctuary for walks, work, play, reading, and laughter. As a family, we spend time in the pagoda, on the tree swing, or in the hammock, reading and studying. On summer weekends, the pagoda transforms into Cam's home office, stacked with books, paper files, and a coffee thermos. The garden has become a place for Max, in his teen years, to hang with friends, or escape when he needs some space.

Cam cuts flowers for the house during spring, summer, and fall. We continue to add trees, shrubs, and perennials every year, trying to rejuvenate a garden that has provided us more sustenance and nourishment than we ever imagined.

We've met earlier owners of the house, now into their senior years. Husband and wife each dropped in from out of town independently to introduce themselves and to reconnect with their past. Together we revisited the surviving plants they had planted—the same ones that we had unearthed and nurtured. Mostly, they reminisced nostalgically, and we were delighted to relive their memories with them.

Max scanned his grandparents' wartime documents, and I've shared the originals with the Ukrainian Canadian Research & Documentation Centre, a group that preserves the legacy of Ukrainian history. I've met dedicated professors and history students, and faced my new knowledge with strength and cultural pride.

Our annual traditions are firmly entrenched: Max and I tap for maple sap; Robin and I swap flower seeds; Ayca picks vine leaves for her mother; Cam prunes the trees and clears the walkways; Max cuts branches for the sumac Christmas tree and helps me forage; and Megan and I wander together on the paths during her regular visits. Yasmine is a professor, still inspiring the people around her. Cam's mother shares cuttings and seeds from her garden, where Cam's father, like his son and his grandson, prevails as master pruner. Fio's flower-inspired cupcakes sweeten our lives.

Since Mom's death, Sonia and Dennis have dedicated their time to their own garden, and a cherry tree we sent to Dennis for his birthday loyally bears fruit every year, despite being in frigid plant zone 3. Sonia tells me her love for her garden is primal, like hope.

Cam's photo wall is filled to capacity. Max continues to photograph the garden through the seasons as his camera equipment becomes more sophisticated. Seldom does he walk past a window in the house without stopping to scan the garden or comment on the season; the rhythms of nature subconsciously pulse through him.

Max has encouraged me to embrace technology, because that pulses through him too, and to blog about some of our adventures. Why not? Our worlds can coexist, the physical, the natural, and the virtual. We continue to camp, hike, and jog together because that's when nature disarms us and we share our secrets. For his sixteenth birthday I introduced him to my beloved White Mountains (and bought him a new computer). Transcending solid ground, Max has now learned to scuba-dive, taking his photography to new depths. He loves his fishes, coral, and sponges, and has eclipsed me, connecting with the natural world that covers more than two-thirds of our planet.

The raccoon condo remains at full capacity, and Hunter keeps a watchful eye on it from the balcony unless he is sleeping in the sun. He barks less, either because he is in his golden years or because he has negotiated a truce with his masked friends. The mating ducks return every spring; they haven't missed a year yet.

I still worship Gordon Lightfoot. Cam and Max don't.

The deer hasn't been back, but she's there in spirit, and the chimes are always ready to sound a quiet hello.

Every day, the garden reminds me of nature's healing powers, the ones I tapped into from childhood. As my personal refuge for introspection and reconciliation, it provides a better place to understand my parents and their sacrifices. Despite the seemingly different orbits they inhabited during my childhood, I now understand what held them together. What they jointly stood for is finally clear: independence, and a connection to the land.

I realize now that I judged them harshly. I will never be able to thank them. The best I can do is keep their memory alive through my son and the way I live my life, and I know that Max will do the same for his children. As for my parents' deep connection to nature, I will propagate their legacy through our garden. My work continues.

Foraging Guidelines

1. Avoid areas where you know pesticides are used. Be careful of major roadsides, industrial areas, or areas where heavy chemical use may occur.
2. If you are prone to allergies, be careful. Have appropriate medical supplies with you.
3. You may want to test plants by rubbing on your skin before picking. If in doubt, don't pick at all.
4. Learn to identify plants. Before handling any plants and using them in the recipes and crafts in this book, consult a reputable guide for safely identifying plants.
5. Respect endangered species in your area. It is illegal to pick them.
6. Pick only what you need, and protect the roots of plants.
7. If you are washing leaves, add a teaspoonful of white vinegar or lemon juice to a large bowl and let them soak a few minutes before rinsing. Pat dry with paper towels.
8. Some plant parts are edible, some are not. Sometimes the season affects what part of a plant is edible.
9. Some plants are poisonous. There are also some look-alike plants. It is important to be aware of these.

Acknowledgments

Thank you to:

My husband, Cam, who encouraged me to write this memoir, patiently read through countless drafts, and continues to teach me about the importance of family and legacy. A relentless cheerleader, he fueled me with his empathy and an endless supply of Earl Grey tea. I am forever grateful, and humbled by the good fortune that delivered him and my beloved son to me.

My sister, Sonia, who through weekly library visits instilled in me a passion for books and the written word that has endured for five decades. Though we are separated by time zones, she remains a loving force in my life. I am in awe of her and her husband's selflessness, as they lovingly cared for my parents in their later years.

My cherished Nonna, Nonno, and sister-in-law Fio, for accepting and loving me unconditionally. As they passionately taught me about their culture, I began to embrace my own.

My extended family, scattered across the country, including my friend Angie, who is really a sister, and Robin Thornton, Ayca Uzumeri, Michelle Gill, and Tracey McGillivray, who filled my world with humor while encouraging me to write this book.

My big-hearted and brainy agent, Sam Hiyate of The Rights Factory, my writing mentor, always present, supportive, and as authentic a person as I've ever met; and his editor-at-large Diane Terrana, a whirlwind of creative energy and inspiration and my prairie-girl soul mate. I could not have written this memoir without their assistance, or the support of the gang in Sam's Sunday workshop.

Lisa White, executive editor (and resident ornithologist) at Houghton Mifflin Harcourt in the United States, for her immediate interest and enthusiasm for this memoir, and for her innate love of writing and nature. Her many books about the natural world are gifts to all of us. I am grateful for her commitment and thoughtful guidance, and for the support of the talented HMH professionals, especially Beth Burleigh Fuller and Debbie Engel.

Diane Turbide, publishing director at Penguin Random House Canada, for her generous support, intuitive wisdom, warmth, and inherent creativity. What terrific people I've met through this process! I am also grateful to Mary Ann Blair, David Ross, and the accomplished PRH Canada team.

The University of Toronto's Creative Writing program, under the stewardship of the visionary Lee Gowan, and the nurturing teachers there, including Helen Humphreys; Sharon English, who taught Writing About Nature and sparked the beginning of this memoir; and the caring and generous Allyson Latta, invaluable mentor, memoir aficionado, and laughter-filled friend.

Dr. Lubomyr Luciuk, for his informed guidance and deep historical expertise, and Alexandra Chyczij, and Dr. Frank Sysyn for their perceptive insights, knowledge, and research.

The staff and volunteers at the Ukrainian Canadian Research & Documentation Centre.

My readers: Jules Reeves, for her unbridled love for nature; Tracey McGillivray, for her deep wisdom; and Tracy Stone, for her boundless curiosity.

My small army of supporters for their insights, partial readings, and general encouragement: Leslie Black, Kelly Gill, Morley Forsyth, Lina Gagliano, Faith Banks, Natasha Feder, Clara Angotti, Meaghan McIsaac, Anne Laurel Carter, Ryan Pather, Maisie Cheung, Simé Armoyan, Laurissa Canavan, Smita Chandaria, Carrie Jackson, Judy Stewart, and Lisa Tracey.

The many people who worked on the garden, too numerous to mention here, for tolerating my enthusiasm, tears, and occasional frustration; I am grateful for every detail you've contributed. I'm also grateful for patient neighbors, the previous homeowners who embraced the light, and the garden, and the City of Toronto Urban Forestry Department and TRCA for actively protecting and advocating for the reforesting and care of our natural resources.

Finally, David Suzuki and Gordon Lightfoot, for their unique gifts to the world, and for keeping me company throughout my life.

Bibliography

B. "Recipe: Sicilian Mulberry Granita." *The Suitcase Chef* (blog). June 6, 2010. http://www.thesuitcasechef.com/recipe-sicilian-mulberry-granita/. (Mulberry Granita, Chapter 18)

Baber, Mark. "Duchess of Richmond / Empress of Canada (II)." *Great Ships: The Postcard and Ephemera Collection of Jeff Newman*. Accessed March 15, 2014. http://www.greatships.net/empresscanada2.html.

Barrett, Rosemary, and Derek Hughes. *Maples*. Toronto: Firefly Books, 2004.

Betz, Rob. "Duchess of Richmond." *LostLiners — Honoring the Golden Age of Ocean Travel*. March 18, 2011. http://lostliners.com/content/?p=911.

Biggs Waller, Sharon. "The Old Fashioned Way: Sugared Rose Petals & Rose Sugar." *Tori Avey*. July 11, 2013. http://toriavey.com/toris-kitchen/2013/07/the-old-fashioned-way-sugared-roses/. (Sugared Rose Petals, Chapter 11)

Blouin, Glen. *An Eclectic Guide to Trees East of the Rockies*. Erin, ON: Boston Mills Press, 2001.

Brill, Steve. *The Wild Vegan Cookbook: A Forager's Culinary Guide (in the Field or in the Supermarket) to Preparing and Savoring Wild (and Not so Wild) Natural Foods*. Boston: Harvard Common Press, 2010. (Cattail Fried Rice, Chapter 4)

Bunch, Adam. "The Eaton Family Hanging Out in 1931." *The Toronto Dreams Project Historical Ephemera Blog*. October 9, 2013. http://torontodreamsproject.blogspot.ca/2013/10/the-eatons-family-hanging-out-in-1931.html.

Chalupa, Andrea. *Orwell and the Refugees: The Untold Story of Animal Farm*. Amazon Digital Services, March 11, 2012.

Chesshire, Charles. *Clematis*. American Horticultural Society Practical Guides Series. New York: DK Publishing, 1999.

Clay, Xanthe. "Cooking with Foraged Flowers." *The Telegraph*. April 10, 2012.

http://www.telegraph.co.uk/foodanddrink/9195971/Cooking-with-foraged
-flowers.html. (Primrose Meringues, Chapter 8)

Cohen, Michael J. *Reconnecting with Nature: Finding Wellness through Restoring Your Bond with the Earth*. Corvallis, OR: Ecopress, 1997.

Cullis, Tara, and David Suzuki. *The Declaration of Interdependence: A Pledge to Planet Earth*. Vancouver: Greystone Books, 2010.

Darwin, Charles, and Francis Darwin. *Selected Works of Charles Darwin*. New York: D. Appleton, 1887.

Deane, Green. "Japanese Knotweed: Dreadable Edible." *Eat the Weeds and Other Things, Too*. Accessed February 01, 2013. http://www.eattheweeds.com/japanese-knotweed-dreadable-edible/.

Devonshire, Deborah Vivien Freeman-Mitford Cavendish, and Gary Rogers. *The Garden at Chatsworth*. London: Frances Lincoln, 1999.

Doughty, Mike. "Tart Cherry Liqueur Recipe: Part 1." *Homebrew Underground*. June 02, 2007. http://www.homebrewunderground.com/40/tart-cherry-liqueur-recipe-part-1/. (Sour Cherry Liqueur, Chapter 1)

Editors of Publications International, Ltd. "Christmas Ornaments and Decoration Crafts." *How StuffWorks*. September 07, 2007. http://lifestyle.howstuffworks.com/crafts/holiday-crafts/christmas-ornaments-and-decoration-crafts12.htm. (Willow Wreath, Chapter 17)

"Fall Decor Crafts Made with Acorns: Tips and Tutorials." *Tipnut*. September 28, 2011. http://tipnut.com/acorn-crafts/. (Dried Acorns, Chapter 15)

Fayed, Saad. "Za'atar Recipe: Middle Eastern Spice Mixture." *About Food*. Accessed March 20, 2013. http://mideastfood.about.com/od/middleeasternspicesherbs/r/zaatar.htm. (Homemade Zaatar Spice Blend, Chapter 9)

Fearnley-Whittingstall, Jane. *The Garden: An English Love Affair*. London: Weidenfeld & Nicolson, 2003.

Fiennes-Clinton, Richard. "# 22 ~ The Eaton Family Legacy, Then and Now." *Toronto Then and Now* (blog). July 02, 2011. http://torontothenandnow.blogspot.ca/2011/07/22-eaton-family-legacy-then-and-now.html.

Foster, Steven, and James A. Duke. *Peterson Field Guide to Medicinal Plants and Herbs of Eastern and Central North America*. Boston: Houghton Mifflin Harcourt, 2000.

Foster, Steven, and Christopher Hobbs. *Peterson Field Guide to Western Medicinal Plants and Herbs*. Boston: Houghton Mifflin Harcourt, 2002.

Goethe, Johann Wolfgang Von, and John Whaley. *Poems of the West and East: West-Eastern Divan: West-Östlicher Divan: Bi-Lingual Edition of the Complete Poems*. Bern: Peter Lang, 1998. ("Gingo Biloba," Chapter 16)

Gordon, Amanda. "How to Dry Acorns for Fall Crafts." *Life at Cloverhill*.

September 2012. http://www.lifeatcloverhill.com/2012/09/how-to-dry
-acorns-for-fall-crafts.html. (Dried Acorns, Chapter 15)

Griffin, Margaret. "Lily of the Valley." *Margaret's Blog*. February 2013. http://
www.griffinsgardencentre.ie/Gardening/lilly-of-the-valley.html.

Grimshaw, John. *The Gardener's Atlas: The Origins, Discovery and Cultivation of
the World's Most Popular Garden Plants*. Willowdale, ON: Firefly Books, 1998.

Grounds, Roger. *Grasses: Choosing and Using These Ornamental Plants in Your
Garden*. The Royal Horticultural Society Series. London: Quadrille, 2005.

Hamilton, Edith, and Steele Savage. *Mythology*. 3rd ed. Boston: Little, Brown,
1942.

Hardison, Ross. "The Evolution of Hemoglobin." *American Scientist*, March
1999. doi:10.1511/1999.2.126.

Hare, P. J., and The Toronto Green Community. "Lost River Walks." *Lost
Rivers*. Accessed April 15, 2013. http://www.lostrivers.ca/.

Herd, Tim. *Maple Sugar: From Sap to Syrup: The History, Lore, and How-to behind
This Sweet Treat*. North Adams, MA: Storey, 2010.

Heretz, Leonid. "The Formation of Modern National Identity and Interethnic
Relations in the Galician Ukrainian Highlands: Some Findings of a Local/
Oral History Project." *Journal of Ukrainian Studies* 33–4 (2008–2009): 199–
218.

"Japanese Knotweed Oatmeal Crumble Recipe from Britain." *Celtnet Recipes*. Accessed February 01, 2013. http://www.celtnet.org.uk/recipes/miscellaneous
/fetch-recipe.php?rid=misc-japanese-knotweed-oatmeal-crumble. (Japanese
Knotweed Crumble, Chapter 2)

Johnston, Karlynn. "Old Fashioned, Traditional Saskatoon Pie." *The Kitchen
Magpie*. July 20, 2012. http://www.thekitchenmagpie.com/old-fashioned
-traditional-saskatoon-pie. (Serviceberry Pie, Chapter 10)

Jung, C. G., and Meredith Sabini. *The Earth Has a Soul: C.G. Jung on Nature,
Technology & Modern Life*. Berkeley, CA: North Atlantic Books, 2008.

Kershaw, Linda. *Trees of Ontario*. Edmonton, AB: Lone Pine, 2001.

Kesseler, Rob, Alexandra Papadakis, and Wolfgang Stuppy. *Seeds: Time Cap-
sules of Life*. Richmond Hill, ON: Firefly Books, 2006.

Kim, Sang H., and Kyu-hyŏng Yi. *Taekwondo Taegeuk Forms: The Official Forms
of Taekwondo*. Santa Fe, NM: Turtle Press, 2011.

Kroodsma, Donald E. *The Backyard Birdsong Guide: Eastern and Central North
America: A Guide to Listening*. San Francisco: Chronicle Books, 2008.

Lambert, Kim. "Make Your Own Homemade Chia Pet." *Crafts Unleashed*.
April 12, 2012. http://www.craftsunleashed.com/kids-stuff/how-to-make
-your-own-chia-pet-2/. (Homemade Grass Chia Pet, Chapter 13)

Land, Leslie. *The New York Times 1000 Gardening Questions & Answers*. New York: Workman, 2003.

Laws, Bill. *Fifty Plants That Changed the Course of History*. Richmond Hill, ON: Firefly Books, 2010.

Lawton, Barbara Perry. *Magic of Irises*. Golden, CO: Fulcrum, 1998.

Lehner, Ernst, and Johanna Lehner. *Folklore and Symbolism of Flowers, Plants, and Trees*. Mineola, NY: Dover Publications, 2003.

Lewis, Charles A. *Green Nature/Human Nature: The Meaning of Plants in Our Lives*. Urbana: University of Illinois Press, 1996.

Lincoff, Gary. *The Joy of Foraging: Gary Lincoff's Illustrated Guide to Finding, Harvesting, and Enjoying a World of Wild Food*. Beverly, MA: Quarry Books, 2012.

Louv, Richard. *Last Child in the Woods: Saving Our Children from Nature-Deficit Disorder*. Chapel Hill, NC: Algonquin Books, 2005.

Luciuk, Lubomyr Y. *Searching for Place: Ukrainian Displaced Persons, Canada, and the Migration of Memory*. Toronto: University of Toronto Press, 2000.

MacKinnon, A. *Edible & Medicinal Plants of Canada*. Edmonton, AB: Lone Pine, 2009.

Magocsi, Paul R., and Geoffrey J. Matthews. *Ukraine: A Historical Atlas*. Toronto: University of Toronto Press, 1985.

Mann, Rink. *Backyard Sugarin'*. Woodstock, VT: Countryman Press, 1991.

"Mary Wynne's Crabapple Jelly." *Allrecipes*. Accessed March 15, 2014. http://allrecipes.com/Recipe/Mary-Wynnes-Crabapple-Jelly/. (Crabapple Jelly, Chapter 5)

Matsumoto, Marc. "Seaweed Salad." *PBS Food*. January 08, 2013. http://www.pbs.org/food/recipes/seaweed-salad/. (Seaweed Salad, Chapter 14)

McHoy, Peter. *Pruning: A Practical Guide*. New York: Abbeville Press, 1993.

Mitchell, Alan F., and David More. *The Trees of North America*. New York: Facts On File Publications, 1987.

Newmaster, Steven G., Allan G. Harris, and Linda Kershaw. *Wetland Plants of Ontario*. Edmonton, AB: Lone Pine, 1997.

"Potpourri, Sleep Pillows, Sachets, and Tussie Mussies." *Sara's Super Herbs*. Accessed October 01, 2014. http://www.superbherbs.net/remedies3.htm. (Lily of the Valley Potpourri, Chapter 3)

Richards, A. J. *Primula*. Portland, OR: Timber Press, 2003.

Risen, Alexandra. "Smudge Sticks: It's Easy to Make Your Own." *Foraged Love*. October 21, 2014. http://foragedlove.com/2014/10/22/smudge-sticks -its-easy-to-make-your-own/. (Smudge Sticks, Chapter 19)

Rittershausen, Wilma, and Brian Rittershausen. *The Practical Encyclopedia of Orchids: A Complete Guide to Orchids and Their Cultivation*. London: Lorenz, 2000.

Selhub, Eva M., and Alan C. Logan. *Your Brain on Nature: The Science of Nature's Influence on Your Health, Happiness, and Vitality*. Mississauga, ON: John Wiley & Sons Canada, 2012.

Snyder, Timothy. *Bloodlands: Europe between Hitler and Stalin*. New York: Basic Books, 2010.

Subtelny, Orest. *Ukraine: A History*. Toronto: University of Toronto Press in Association with the Canadian Institute of Ukrainian Studies, 1988.

Suzuki, David T. *David Suzuki: The Autobiography*. Vancouver: Greystone Books, 2006.

Sysyn, Frank E. "Religion within the Ukrainian Populist Credo: The Enlightened Pastor Mykhailo Zubrytsky." *Journal of Ukrainian Studies* 37 (2012): 85–96.

Van Wyhe, John, ed. "The Complete Works of Darwin Online." *Darwin Online*. 2002. http://darwin-online.org.uk/.

Wong, James. "Maple Leaf Tempura Anyone?" *James Wong's Homegrown Revolution* (blog). October 24, 2012. http://homegrown-revolution.co.uk/leaves-and-greens/maple-leaf-tempura/. (Momiji Tempura, Chapter 6)

Wong, Tama Matsuoka, and Eddy Leroux. *Foraged Flavor: Finding Fabulous Ingredients in Your Backyard or Farmer's Market*. New York: Clarkson Potter, 2012.

World Taekwondo Federation. "Poomsae Styles." *WTF*. January 12, 2015. http://www.worldtaekwondofederation.net/poomsae-styles.